NATION
OF
VICTIMS

NATION
OF
VICTIMS

Identity Politics, the Death of Merit,
and the Path Back to Excellence

VIVEK RAMASWAMY

CENTER
STREET®

NASHVILLE · NEW YORK

Center Street
Hachette Book Group
1290 Avenue of the Americas, New York, NY 10104
centerstreet.com
twitter.com/centerstreet

First Edition: September 2022

Center Street is a division of Hachette Book Group, Inc.
The Center Street name and logo are trademarks of Hachette Book Group, Inc.

The publisher is not responsible for websites (or their content) that are not owned by the publisher.

The Hachette Speakers Bureau provides a wide range of authors for speaking events. To find out more, go to www.hachettespeakersbureau.com or call (866) 376-6591.

LCCN: 2022939599

Interior book design by Timothy Shaner, NightandDayDesign.biz

ISBNs: 9781546002963 (Hardcover); 9781668610954 (Audiobook);
ISBN: 9781546002987 (E-Book)

Printed in the United States of America

LSC-C

Printing 1, 2022

To my sons, and to their generation.

CONTENTS

NATION
OF
VICTIMS

HISTORY OF THE NACIREMA

When I was a kid, we read a book in school that stuck with me. Some of you will have heard of it. It was a study of the culture of the Nacirema, a dead civilization that inhabited the plains of the American West long ago.

The Nacirema were a strange people with strange ways. Their customs were riddled with apparent contradictions, their people consumed by odd obsessions. They were preoccupied with the thought that their own bodies were inherently unclean, and their lives revolved around elaborate purification rituals. Every dwelling had at least one shrine devoted exclusively to these ceremonies; the rich would build more, treating the number of shrines in their hut as a mark of holiness. Their private temples contained urns filled with charms and potions purchased from local medicine men, who wrote and spoke in a different language. They lived in imposing public temples where they would perform the most sacred ceremonies; vestal maidens accompanied them in ritual dress.

The natives had an elaborate hierarchy of priests—just below the medicine men were the holy men charged specifically with caring for the mouth, which the Nacirema viewed as the source of all evil because sin so often came from the words it spoke. They believed that if they didn't pay the holy men to bless their mouths their teeth would fall out as the mouth's evil rotted them.

When the corruption of the mouth grew too great, the Nacirema would see a specialized caste of medicine men called listeners, who would try to heal the sufferer by hearing them speak. They would then perform a kind of exorcism involving asking stylized questions, a variation of the call-and-response religions that develop early on in many cultures. The sufferer's friends and family would often speculate that their own parents had been the ones to curse them.

They were a strange people. They died out eventually under the weight of their own insecurities. As the book concluded, it's hard to understand how the Nacirema managed to exist for as long as they did under the burdens they imposed on themselves.

Nacirema, of course, is *American* spelled backward. The children's book I had been reading was an adaptation of anthropologist Horace Miner's famous satirical article "Body Ritual among the Nacirema."[1] Throughout the paper Miner made it increasingly clear that he was actually describing Americans themselves. He was describing their culture the way a foreign observer might, viewing them through a fog and from a distance, removed in time. His point was that we often find unfamiliar cultures strange because we don't inhabit their perspective well enough to understand their actions. Their customs will seem like magical thinking to us.

I remember that book about the history of the Nacirema sometimes when I look at the America I find myself in today. I know this is the United States of America, where I was born and raised, but I don't know what that means. This place is like a distant land that obeys arbitrary laws. We don't know where we are anymore or what the rules are, and we watch everything we do and say, always afraid we will violate some unspoken code. Many of us have known each other our whole lives, yet we fear each other like strangers. We've all become strangers in a strange land, though we haven't gone anywhere.

I wonder if my son, Karthik, born in the height of the COVID-19 pandemic, will be taught about the history of the Nacirema in school as I was. The moral of the story is insightful, and it is satire. But I worry that a "progressive" school board may decide that it inappropriately makes light of Native Americans, not understanding that the target of ridicule is actually the reader. It requires a bit of nuance to see that Miner was making fun of our assumptions about Native Americans rather than the natives themselves—he relies on our tendency to view the unfamiliar as primitive to make the point that we are the ones in error. We no longer live in a country that values nuance. I wonder if a teacher today could get away with assigning "Body Ritual among the Nacirema" without herself being sacrificed as part of a purification ritual.

When I looked at the reading lists of the schools Karthik will attend in Columbus, Ohio, I didn't see anything like that children's book about the Nacirema. Instead, I saw Ibram X. Kendi's *Antiracist Baby* and Anastasia Higginbotham's *Not My Idea*, which portrays white supremacy as a constant devil whispering from one's shoulder. I worry Karthik will be assigned children's versions of Robin DiAngelo's work instead of Horace Miner's. Miner tried to teach his readers how to think, but I'm afraid the DiAngelo adaptations will only teach my son what to think.

I wonder if Karthik will be taught calculus in high school, if he'll be placed in advanced classes in the subjects he's passionate about.[2] I wonder what he'll be good at, and if his talents will be nurtured in the strange land I find myself in today. I wonder whether my son's teachers will prioritize him or some abstract social good, whether they'll view it as their duty to mold him into an instrument to make a better world. I guess I would like them to mold him into an instrument to make the world better according to his own notions, not theirs. But the culture he's been born into may not allow that.[3]

The Americans. A strange people with strange ways. Their customs are riddled with contradictions, their people consumed by odd obsessions. They seem preoccupied with the notion that they are inherently unclean, and their lives revolve around elaborate purification rituals where they attempt to cleanse themselves and each other.

Many American rituals stem from their belief that the mouth is the root of all sin because the words it speaks have a supernatural power to cause harm. Many insist this verbally inflicted harm is an actual form of violence, perhaps even more damaging than the physical kind.[4] Americans believe in a pre-scientific metaphysical system by which the very words one speaks are the primary forces that change self and world; one's actions are considered secondary, the mere effect of words. And so the Americans are defined by their constant search for more powerful words.

This search is led by their high priests, who speak and write in a different language, one often incomprehensible to the common folk. One representative sample of this unique dialect comes from a document called "Advancing Health Equity: A Guide to Language, Narrative and Concepts." It's a sort of grimoire containing

4

descriptions of powerful blessings and curses, written by the American Medical Association and the Association of American Medical Colleges Center for Health Justice. For instance, the book suggests that American medicine men replace the word 'vulnerable' with 'oppressed,' on the apparent belief that the act of describing sufferers of bodily ailments as the victims of evil will, by naming the evil, combat it. A sort of exorcism. This language apparently reflects an effort by the priests to remind American common folk that even physical afflictions seemingly caused by nature and misfortune are ultimately to be understood as the products of human sin. Americans believe that the best treatment for any disease is simply to call it by its true name, and thus gain power over it.

Likewise, the Americans constantly name and rename themselves and each other, always seeking to gain power over one another through learning and invoking true names, a common element among magical belief systems in developing cultures.[5] One warring tribe, for instance, might name itself "liberal," intending the name to connote a sort of blessing, and their rivals will attempt to turn the name into a curse by uttering it in a spirit of hate.[6] Then the first may insist that its true name is actually "politically correct," "woke," or "progressive," and their enemies will then seek to take power over those true names in turn by uttering them. This battle over control of true names is perpetually evolving. If one refers to an American by an old name like "woke" that they have recently abandoned, the American will insist it was never their name to begin with, and that it was violence to call them by it.[7]

Some African cultures famously believe that by eating certain animal parts one gains that animal's desirable qualities. For instance, eating a lion's heart to gain courage.[8] The American version of this belief involves their implicit faith that naming themselves something in fact makes them that thing. It is common for Americans to do things like name themselves "antiracist" and insist that their critics must by definition be racist, or call themselves "anti-fascist" to maintain that their opponents are necessarily fascist.[9] Some Americans have even been known to adopt a crude kind of numerology, claiming that the incidental invocation of numbers associated with historical oppression is a grave sin. For instance, the Women's March organization issued the following groveling apology: "We apologize deeply for the email that was sent today. $14.92 was our average donation amount this week. It was an oversight on our part to not make the connection to a year of colonization, conquest, and genocide for Indigenous people, especially before Thanksgiving."[10] Their mouths were blessed; their teeth did not rot.

The Americans are distinctive among cultures in the degree to which they use their descriptions of the world to dictate their beliefs about it. All these seemingly unusual customs involve applying a weak version of something called the Sapir-Whorf hypothesis to use language to direct culture and thought. The Sapir-Whorf hypothesis is a well-known anthropological theory that says that the words a civilization uses determine the thoughts its people can have. One example of this is author Jared Diamond's story about an Amazonian tribe who had words only for the numbers one and two, and could only describe larger numbers by conjoining them. Diamond claimed that the practical limit that the language imposed prevented its users from being able to describe or imagine scenarios involving large numbers, which limited the civilization's development, chiefly through its ability to conduct trade at scale effectively.[11]

The Sapir-Whorf hypothesis comes in strong and weak forms. The former holds that an individual can never imagine a thought their language precludes, while the latter makes the much more modest claim that the language we use has a strong influence over the thoughts it's easy for us to have. In other words, language carves the mental channels that thought flows through. I believe that rare original thinkers can escape the confines of their language and determine the directions of their own thoughts, using their crude language as a scaffold to discover more complex ideas. But language certainly has a strong capacity to direct thought. That's what George Orwell had in mind when he said that the best way to control minds in a society was to control its language first

American culture seems to have been overtaken by a battle using language to exert social control. The Orwellian use of language surfaces in concepts such as doublespeak, where a regime describes an idea as its opposite to legitimize it in the eyes of the populace: war is peace, conformity is diversity, equity is equality, exclusion is inclusion. By calling a negative concept the name of its opposite, this doublespeak uses the positive connotations of the one to gradually legitimize the other.

Unlike the numerical limitations of the tribe Diamond discussed, it's the American moral vocabulary that has become most limited. This stunts our nation's intellectual growth. We describe ourselves and each other as impure, as victims of one social disease or another, whether privilege or oppression or both. This language in turn determines our actions: we act like victims, we see oppressors, and we create the world our language of victimhood describes. In my last book, *Woke Inc.*, I compared this phenomenon to Heisenberg's uncertainty principle, which holds that by observing the world at the quantum level we change it.[12] By describing the social world we observe it, and by publicly observing it, we create it.

Change in language can pave the way for change in normative thought, allowing words themselves, rather than their content, to win battles over values and ideas. This becomes a more desirable tactic the worse one's ideas are. Consequently, some radical ideologies replicate themselves primarily through controlling language. Someday soon, Americans may think "equity" and "equality" mean the same thing, just two pleasant words for social justice, with only the vaguest memory that they somehow used to be different.

There is a certain ridiculousness to the elaborate purification rituals of the American ruling class when viewed from afar. But recall that Miner's point was actually that we often find unfamiliar cultures strange only because we can't inhabit their perspectives well enough to understand their thinking. Without proper context, those who think differently from us will often seem to believe in magic.

There are three parts to every magic trick. It's not enough to take the familiar and then make it strange; you have to be able to make the strange familiar again. In Miner's article about body rituals, the Nacirema's practices seemed primitive and superstitious because we didn't know the context surrounding them. Here, when observing the apparent absurdity of American linguistic purification customs, that missing context usually involves race.

Progressives claim that racism was woven into America's fabric since its inception. This newly ascendant view is exemplified and propagated by the *New York Times*' 1619 Project, which controversially began by alleging that "one of the primary reasons the colonists decided to declare their independence from Britain was because they wanted to protect the institution of slavery." Five distinguished historians wrote to request that the *Times* retract this assertion and similar ones, saying that the project was motivated more by ideology than fact; the *Times* rejected their request.[13] It did, however, quietly walk back some of its claims later.[14]

Although progressives overstate the degree to which America's past and present revolve around racism, I have no doubt that our nation's racist past is a central part of its story. But there's more to the story than the Three-Fifths Compromise or the fact that many of our founding fathers owned slaves and even mistreated them.

For instance, we should not allow history to forget Sally Hemings, who for hundreds of years was described as Jefferson's concubine and is more often these days described as the victim of rape.[15] But Hemings herself demonstrates how the language of victimhood can obscure relevant facts. To remember her primarily as a victim obscures the remarkable degree of agency that she exerted: when she was sixteen years old and a free woman in Paris, she negotiated with Jefferson to win freedom for her future children in exchange for returning to enslavement at Monticello.[16] If we remember Sally Hemings as a victim and Thomas Jefferson as her abuser, our history may forget the story of how she claimed control over her destiny and her descendants'.

Sally Hemings should be remembered and her story should be taught to American children. I hope Karthik learns about her in school. But I hope he learns not that she was the powerless victim of rape, but that she was a slave who stood up to one of the most powerful men in the world. If we describe her only as a victim, our stunted moral vocabulary may make us forget the ways she was exceptional. Language carves the channels through which thought flows, and if the American language of victimhood directs us toward condemnation of Jefferson, it may direct us away from praise of Hemings: we may remember her existence at the expense of forgetting her achievements. Whether Hemings was a victim or a hero isn't just a story about America's past. It's a story about America's future.

Progressives insist that racism is a central part of our nation's past and present. They are, of course, correct. It is impossible to be a dark-skinned conservative commentator on politics without receiving daily reminders of this fact—antiracists regularly call me an Uncle Tom, or Dinesh D'Souza, or both, as when one progressive celebrated Columbus Day by saying "Happy Uncle Tom day, Dinesh!!!" apparently attempting to compress as much racism as possible into a concise statement.[17] Usually these comments just roll off me somewhat like water off a duck, but even I was a bit taken aback when he followed up with "Why is it that Fox puts that skin lightening make-up on you? Do you like it? Does it make you feel white?"[18] It's true that I often wear makeup before going on television. To my knowledge, most white-skinned TV guests do the same. But I spent a few minutes wondering if the lighting had been different that day.

I receive comments like these from antiracists every day, yet to this day no antiracist has ever protested that such comments are wrong, though they would seem to be wrong according to their stated commitments. This is just the price of doing business as a conservative racial minority who speaks in public. Witness the way "Uncle Tim" trended on Twitter after Senator Tim Scott delivered the Republican response to the State of the Union.[19] The original Uncle Tom character this racial epithet is based on, by the way, actually dies at his master's hands when he refuses to divulge where two female slaves are hiding.[20]

Like our namesake, all of us Uncle Toms and Tims possess more agency than antiracists believe. When antiracists call conservative racial minorities Uncle Toms, they're simply invoking one of their favorite magic spells, using language to attempt to deprive us of our agency and pretend that they don't have to take our ideas seriously because we're mere vessels for white supremacy. I don't love it, but nor do I let it occupy much of my thoughts. The racism I experience doesn't define me. My actions do that.

Words are not violence. When I was in middle school and an angry kid pushed me down a flight of stairs because he didn't like the way I answered so many questions in class, that was violence because I didn't have any choice about whether my bones broke. But when an antiracist progressive calls me by a racial slur, that is not violence, because it is entirely up to me whether I get hurt or not, and I choose not to be harmed. But I know racism still exists in this country. For the part directed at me, I choose to move on.

Likewise, my own experiences teach me that racism can be entrenched in institutions, not just individuals. "Stop Asian Hate," progressives chanted in 2020 following allegations that the coronavirus may have leaked from a Chinese lab. Yet every high-achieving Asian American kid in this country remembers the day they learned that their race would be an obstacle when applying to elite colleges, remember the way they learned the American promise of equality is in some ways still only a promise. Because colleges like Harvard can't legally admit that they're rejecting high-scoring Asian applicants because of racial quota systems designed to help black and Hispanic students, they're forced to say Asians fall short on "personality scores." How progressive.

The racism I've experienced helps me understand the racism others experience. It's not as if I only recognize racism when it's directed at me, and it's not as if anti-Asian discrimination at elite universities is the only form of institutional racism that exists in America. Black people experience it, and white people do too. I'll discuss the racism that still exists today throughout this book.

But I believe that Martin Luther King Jr. was right that though the arc of the moral universe is long, it bends toward justice. America's arc bends toward justice too. It has bent toward justice. And it has been a long road, one that King helped us travel. I know that the journey is not done, but we were headed in the right direction. We were making progress.

The right way to make further progress as a country isn't to eradicate every last remnant of racism at all costs, constructing ever-more-elaborate linguistic purification rituals to do so. Rather, we should allow those final remnants to gradually atrophy to irrelevance. By contrast, the antiracist movement in America instead throws kerosene on those final burning embers of racism—inflaming the very problem that it supposedly addresses. Antiracism often speaks racism into existence by demanding that we view and treat people differently on the basis of their skin color.

Yes, there were moments in American history when racism was so rampant that it demanded a comprehensive societal response. But that moment has passed. Now trying to mount a comprehensive societal response against a problem that was already diminishing at present raises new costs of its own. Even worse, it risks exacerbating the very problem it purports to solve— much like an overactive immune system fighting a virus that has already cleared, only to kill the host in the process.

Principles of human psychology reinforce this point. According to the woke movement, racism is part of America's self, or ego.

In Freudian terms, that makes the modern "don't be racist" mantra the equivalent of America's superego. Psychologists know that treating patients' low-level anxiety by saying "don't be anxious" often makes these patients' anxiety even worse. Similarly, saying "don't be racist" to someone who may harbor some microscopic racist attitudes are likely to inflame the underlying problem or create a problem where none existed at all.

We're a nation of victims now. It's one of the few things we've all got left in common. Black victims, white victims, liberal victims, conservative victims, Indian victims . . .Victims, ultimately, of each other, and sometimes ourselves. In this book I'll tell you how it happened and how we can move forward.

Ours is a culture riddled with contradictions, always trying to purify itself, so obsessed with its flaws that it can no longer recognize its own virtues. A dying civilization inhabiting the plains of North America, collapsing under the weight of its insecurities. A strange people, a familiar one. The Nacirema; the Americans.

Chapter One

NATION OF UNDERDOGS

Everyone loves a good underdog story.

I was reminded of how true that cliché is when I watched *King Richard* last year, a movie about how Richard Williams took his daughters Venus and Serena from the streets of Compton to the top of the tennis world.

I used to play competitive tennis myself and watched the sisters play in person countless times, so I was fascinated by the tale the movie told. Venus and Serena overcame long odds, but their dad is the original underdog of the story. He starts off the movie penniless, coming up with a seventy-eight-page plan to turn his yet-to-be-born children into tennis stars to carry the entire family out of poverty. Then he starts training them each once they turn four, having them practice long hours, rain or shine, sometimes rallying back and forth to the sound of gunshots.

The Williams sisters served as executive producers for the film, so the movie understandably takes care to leave out some complicating details. For instance, although Richard frequently tells his kids that he'll "always be there" for them, the movie doesn't mention that he abandoned five children from his first family when the oldest was only eight.[1] The fairy-tale underdog can have minor character flaws, but only ones that arise from the very virtues that make him succeed. The only faults the Will Smith version of Richard has are that he's *too* driven, *too* demanding.

The movie presents a heartwarming tale of a father determined to keep his daughters off the streets so they can get out of the ghetto. But what it doesn't say is that the family *already had the money to live in a better neighborhood*. "The ghetto will make you rough, it'll make you tough, it'll make you strong," Richard told CNN. "And so that's why I went to Compton with them."[2] His plan worked out perfectly for Venus and Serena, but their half-sister Yetunde Price was killed in a drive-by shooting in 2003.

I found the true story even more intriguing than the sanitized one. Just as the movie itself cleaned up Richard's life to distill it into a story for the big screen, he consciously designed his own daughter's lives to raise them to see themselves as underdogs. He engineered them that way, right down to hiding his wife's birth-control pills after she was reluctant to agree to his plan to turn their future children into tennis stars.[3] Richard Williams knew that everyone loves a good underdog story, so he made one out of his girls' lives. Then they made one out of his.

Narratives about one's identity hold great power—not just the power to understand a life in hindsight, but the power to create it, the power to give it meaning and direction. At its core, the appeal of the underdog story comes from its promise that we can create something from nothing, imposing our will on an unforgiving universe. The narrative promises that we can choose our own destinies, no matter how humble our starting points. It offers the hope that if we work hard and attempt great things, we can succeed. It may be easier for a favorite to win, but that only makes the dark horse's victory sweeter. In the process of working hard to overcome our disadvantages, we gain not only glory, but character. The underdog who has to claw their way to the top understands things the favorite will never know.

The United States of America began as a nation of underdogs. Our founding fathers stood up to the most powerful empire in the world, declared their independence, and then somehow turned assertion into reality. Then, a little over 150 years later, we ourselves became the most powerful country in the world. We went from a loosely affiliated collection of backwater farmers to an empire in the blink of an eye, in the eyes of history.

Ever since claiming our independence, Americans have had a special fondness for underdog stories. It's our national DNA. Every politician knows this. It's why they all have their own version of the "born in a log cabin" story. We even have a name for the American take on the trope: Horatio Alger stories. Horatio Alger made a name for himself in the 1800s writing rags-to-riches young adult novels, publishing a hundred before his death. His books were almost always about impoverished boys who made comfortable lives for themselves through hard work, honesty, charity, and a healthy dose of luck. After Alger's publisher gently suggested he tour the Western United States to inspire him to write something new, he kept writing the same stories but set them in California. His books remained the bestsellers of the era.

The presence of good fortune in the narrative may confuse some people—isn't virtue alone supposed to be enough? But as the Roman philosopher Seneca famously put it, luck is simply what happens when preparation meets opportunity. If the American system does a good enough job of ensuring everyone gets a fair chance, and they prepare themselves by exemplifying the appropriate values, the American Dream promises that every underdog eventually has their day. Democracy was supposed to give them equal rights, capitalism was supposed to ensure equal opportunity for upward economic mobility, institutions like Christianity were supposed to instill them with the right values, and then their own virtue was supposed to do the rest.

Coming in the economic boom of the Gilded Age, Horatio Alger stories spread like wildfire, capturing the popular imagination and giving many a dream that the American way of life allowed them to turn into reality. As its citizens prospered, the nation did too. That's the America I knew. It's the America my parents came halfway around the world to join.

But what happens when the longshot becomes the favorite? Does an underdog story ever end? If it does, what takes its place?

I was reminded of these questions last year when I saw a commercial for, of all things, Dodge pickup trucks. "When does an underdog stop being an underdog?" it asked. "After the first big win? The second? Try never. Because being an underdog isn't about how much you win. It's about how hard you're willing to work for it. And making sure your opponents never know your next move. Which is why some of us make a point of staying the underdogs, even when we're on top."[4]

I didn't end up buying the truck, but the ad stuck with me because it's the same message I preach to every company I'm involved in founding. We must be "insurgents, not incumbents," I say. Startups are by definition not incumbents, but the key to lasting success is that you can't ever allow your company to think of itself that way.

If it's true for companies, it's even more true for individuals. Michael Jordan really was an underdog at the start of his basketball career—as a sophomore, he didn't make the varsity team, a grudge he's held to this day. But when he was a six-time NBA champion and five-time MVP, he still saw himself as an underdog, motivating himself with imagined slights. In Jordan's mind, for instance, he was cut from the varsity team when in fact he simply wasn't placed on it. He flew out the one sophomore that did make the team to his Hall of Fame induction speech, where, after giving a few perfunctory thank-yous, he spent twenty-three minutes settling old scores, as if he thought no one had ever believed in him.[5]

Some people thought it was tasteless, but they missed that Jordan was actually revealing his secret to becoming the greatest basketball player of all time. True underdogs never stop seeing themselves that way. It's the narrative of their entire lives, not just a chapter in it. It's who they are, not a thing that once happened to them. As they achieve their goals, they constantly create new ones, always broadening their aspirations until the deck is still stacked against them. Like Jordan, they always convince themselves that they still have something left to prove.

Underdogs are always outsiders, struggling to prove themselves to a world that doesn't believe in them—not necessarily because the world actively doubts them, but because they know there's still more in them than they've been able to show. When underdogs are praised for accomplishments that seem to them small in light of their ambitions, they take it as a sign that the one giving the praise doubts they can accomplish more.

For a few people like Jordan, and apparently for organizations like Dodge, their underdog story never ends. They're always telling it to themselves to help them reach new heights. Sadly, that's not the way things usually go. More often, underdogs who succeed do eventually stop seeing themselves that way. The dark horse becomes the favorite; the insurgent becomes the incumbent. They stop growing and start coasting. They focus on keeping what they have instead of improving themselves to get more. The athlete stops learning new skills, since the old skills were good enough to win games. The company stops making innovative new products and instead keeps updating the old ones.

Once successful underdogs start resting on their laurels, they're ripe for a new narrative of their lives to emerge: victimhood.

Everyone Loves a Good Victim Story

If the story of the Williams sisters and their dad is the story of the American underdog, then Jussie Smollett's is the paradigmatic story of the American victim.

In January 2019, Smollett, a well-known actor who's gay and black, filed a report with the Chicago Police Department claiming he'd been the victim of a vicious hate crime. He said that he was attacked by two ski-mask-and-MAGA-cap-wearing men who savagely beat him, wrapped a noose around his neck, and poured chemicals on him, shouting racial and homophobic slurs and proclaiming their allegiance to Donald Trump the whole time. He was hospitalized for a day while receiving treatment for his injuries.

Conservatives instantly spotted the implausibility of the story. But left-leaning media, politicians, and celebrities ate it up. In fact, it seemed as if every prominent left-leaning figure in America felt an obligation to immediately make a public statement supporting Smollett. As if filling out a form letter, virtually identical messages condemning Smollett's attackers and calling for justice issued forth from luminaries such as Joe Biden, Kamala Harris, Cory

Booker, Nancy Pelosi, Maxine Waters, Bernie Sanders, Alexandria Ocasio-Cortez, Pete Buttigieg, Kirsten Gillibrand, Rashida Tlaib, Ariana Grande, Ellen DeGeneres, Cher, and Al Sharpton.

The celebrity call for justice was answered, though not in the way they'd hoped. A few weeks later, Chicago police arrested Smollett after their investigation concluded he had hired two extras from his show *Empire* to stage the attack on him. A grand jury charged him with filing a false police report.

But a month after that, state prosecutors dropped all charges against Smollett for mysterious reasons, and a judge ordered his court file sealed.[6] Perhaps coincidentally, Michelle Obama's former chief of staff Tina Tchen had reached out to the prosecutor overseeing the case to convey Smollett's concerns about the investigation.[7] Perhaps coincidentally, Smollett and Obama were good friends. Who can say why the charges were suddenly dropped? The world may never know.

The story might've ended there, and many notable figures would've been happy. But the Illinois Prosecutors Bar Association released a scathing statement that began, "The manner in which this case was dismissed was abnormal and unfamiliar to those who practice law in criminal courthouses across the State. Prosecutors, defense attorneys, and judges alike do not recognize the arrangement Mr. Smollett received. Even more problematic, the State's Attorney and her representatives have fundamentally misled the public on the law and circumstances surrounding the dismissal."[8] President Donald Trump then directed federal officials to reopen the case and investigate the dismissal, a special prosecutor was appointed, and Smollett was once again charged.

The trial began to go poorly as two of Smollett's friends testified in great detail about how he'd paid them $3,500 apiece to stage the attack. Both are black, and one had an intimate homo-sexual relationship with the accused; nevertheless, Smollett insisted the attack was motivated by homophobia. As his prospects started looking increasingly grim, his lawyer bizarrely asked the judge to declare a mistrial, crying and accusing him of lunging at her during a sidebar and snarling while sustaining prosecutors' objections. She said it was part of a nationwide pattern of disrespect toward black female attorneys.[9]

Despite his attorneys' inventive strategies, Smollett was convicted. One black juror said that the smoking gun for him was Smollett's own testimony that after the attack he returned home and placed the noose around his neck again so the police who came to interview him could see it.[10]

In this single episode, victimhood became a status symbol, a fashion statement, and a (nearly) get-out-of-jail-free card. How did this identity become so prized in our country? When did we stop wanting to be underdogs and start wanting to be victims?

I know, I know. Bringing up the Jussie Smollett case is just a conservative talking point. My liberal friends regularly remind me not to parrot those. Right after the initial staged attack, the standard progressive line when conservatives questioned his account was that we were victimizing him all over again by doubting him. Now that he's been charged, re-charged, and convicted of a hate crime hoax, the standard line is that mentioning any of this is just a conservative talking point.

In this book I hope to present many good conservative talking points, and other talking points as well. Here's one: there's actually not that much difference between an underdog story and a tale of victimhood. They're close cousins, competitors of each other. That's why it's so easy to transition from one to the other.

That's what I think is happening to America today—to liberals, conservatives, and everyone in between.

In both narratives, the protagonist is a sympathetic figure who faces overwhelming odds through no fault of their own. In both, the meat of the narrative involves struggling against an unfair world, and the story can only be successfully resolved once the hero attains the worldly wealth or victory their virtuous heart deserves. A classic Horatio Alger story.

But although underdog stories and victimhood ones follow the same broad outline, the details of the execution are much different. The most crucial distinction is that the underdog struggles and overcomes the forces arrayed against them, but the victim's task is to convince others to overcome adversity for them. The underdog makes a demand of themself; the victim makes a demand of those around them. The underdog's hardships are dealt to them by fate, not by other people, and they make it part of their own destiny to overcome those hardships. The victim's hardships are necessarily created by other people—the evildoers who commit racist acts, the perpetrators who steal elections—who owe them something in return.

An underdog story offers the hope that you can do anything, that no matter your lot in life, your fate is ultimately in your hands, that it's only a question of how hard you work and how long you have to wait for preparation to meet opportunity. That's a naïve view at times, but at least an inspiring one. A quintessentially American one, and true at its core. Maybe people can't do *anything*, but they can almost always do more than they think.

In contrast, although the victim starts in the same destitute position as the underdog, their story is all about what they *can't* do—the odds are too great, the enemies too strong, the circumstances too unjust for the happy ending to be achieved by the hero's own power. The only way to reach a successful resolution is for the victimizers to eventually make recompense to the victim by helping them reach the finish line. The underdog's task is to overcome others' doubt by proving them wrong about what they can do. But the victim's task is to overcome their doubt by persuading them to recognize them as a victim.

Victimhood is often born out of a psychological need created by one's status as an incumbent. If wealthy Hollywood stars and former presidents can be victims, then the greatest country in the world can be one too. The United States has gone from being a nation of insurgents at its founding to a nation of incumbents today. Though the transition hasn't fully eroded its wealth and power, it's already been hell on our national spirit.

In some ways our founding fathers knew we would walk this path. Some of them even hoped for it. John Adams told his wife, "I must study politics and war, that our sons may have liberty to study mathematics and philosophy. Our sons ought to study mathematics and philosophy, geography, natural history and naval architecture, navigation, commerce and agriculture in order to give their children a right to study painting, poetry, music, architecture, statuary, tapestry and porcelain."[11] That was a bit of a humble-brag. It's true that Adams studied politics and war, but he also studied math, philosophy, and poetry, along with Greek and Latin. A little-known fact about Adams is that after serving as our second president, he committed himself to becoming a scholar of Hindu scripture.[12] He wrote to his friend and rival Thomas Jefferson that if he were to live his life again, he'd have been a Sanskrit scholar. Both men continued learning things right up to the day they both died—July 4, 1826—exactly fifty years after they signed the Declaration of Independence together. Jefferson and Adams studied much more than politics and war.

Nevertheless, the quote from Adams expresses a beautiful sentiment. Arguably, it's even played out that way—modern Americans are far more likely to study art and literature than war. But if Adams could've seen even further into the future, he might've wondered what his great-grandchildren would study, and their children, and generations further into the future. Did he imagine that it would all be William Wordsworth and John Keats forever, or that Ibram X. Kendi and Robin DiAngelo would one day supplant them? Mired arm-deep in war and politics as he was, in trying to build a great nation from nothing, Adams could hardly have imagined that one day success would bring its own problems.

The words often attributed to Sheikh Rashid bin Saeed Al Maktoum, the founder of Dubai, come closer to reality: "My grandfather rode a camel, my father rode a camel, I ride a Mercedes, my son rides a Land Rover, and my grandson is going to ride a Land Rover, but my great-grandson is going to have to ride a camel again. Hard times create strong men, strong men create easy times, easy times create weak men, and weak men create hard times."[13]

The viral saying perfectly captures the journey from insurgency to incumbency, from underdog to victim. Today, almost all Americans live far easier and more luxurious lives than our forefathers did. The life span of the average American has doubled since 1776. GDP per capita has multiplied by over forty.[14] An analysis from the Heritage Foundation points out that even poor Americans have things their ancestors wouldn't have dreamed of:

According to the government's own data, the average American family or single person, identified as poor by the Census Bureau, lives in an air-conditioned, centrally heated house or apartment that is in good repair and not overcrowded. They have a car or truck. (Indeed, 43% of poor families own two or more cars.)

The home has at least one widescreen TV connected to cable, satellite, or a streaming service, a computer or tablet with internet connection, and a smartphone. (Some 82% of poor families have one or more smartphones.)

By their own report, the average poor family had enough food to eat throughout the prior year. No family member went hungry for even a single day due to a lack of money for food.

They have health insurance (either public or private) and were able to get all "necessary medical care and prescription medication" when needed.[15]

Don't worry, I'll get to wealth inequality later in the book. But in absolute terms, the average American is doing pretty well compared to the ones who came before us, as you would expect in the richest, most powerful nation in the world. Next to most of the world, we live in a land of milk and honey. Hardworking immigrants should want to be Americans, and we should let them. My parents are still grateful for the chances this country gave them. I'm grateful, too. This is still the land of opportunity.

But it's that very prosperity that now affords us the luxury of seeing ourselves as victims instead of underdogs. Our forebearers in American history (like much of the developing world today) had to focus on surviving and building a future for their descendants. Today we worry about microaggressions, while they were more concerned about regular ones. But when microaggressions are all you've known, those become regular aggressions on the scale you've built for yourself, the same way a well-coddled baby cries over anything they dislike because it's quite literally the worst thing that's ever happened to them. Bickering about pronouns is a classic first-world problem. Americans now worry about finding words to be offended by, while many people in the world still worry about finding food.

Our forefathers didn't have any choice but to embrace the underdog narrative, but we do. That's the crucial difference between a nation of insurgents and a nation of incumbents. The nation as a whole possesses a lot more resources today, so it becomes possible, even logical, for people to overcome adversity by changing the way the pie is distributed instead of by growing it. A story of victimhood would win little in sympathy or reward in the nation's past. But today, it's often the fastest path to greater money and influence.

Underdog stories and victimhood tales are like the light and dark sides of the Force: they have something in common, but the dark side is the easier path to power, even if it leaves you worse off in the end. The underdog's journey is hard; that's what defines it. It's even more daunting set against the backdrop of a long history of people who have made the same journey successfully. That's the historical backdrop of our merit-based culture, one that places a lot of pressure on people today—pressure that the original underdogs in our nation didn't have to face. The high risk of failure in an established merit-based culture provides a powerful incentive for people to take the easier path—say, victimhood—whenever it's available.

Logically, we could resolve that problem either by closing off victimhood as a path to success or by moving away from our merit-based culture. In this book I make the case for the former; in his recent book *The Meritocracy Trap*, law professor Daniel Markovits argues for the latter.[16] Markovits believes meritocracy gives the rich an insurmountable advantage over the poor because it makes education the key to success, and the rich can pay for expensive educations for their children. Those children become successful, educate their own children, and the gap between rich and poor gradually widens into an informal hereditary aristocracy. Markovits also says that even the winners of meritocracy's game are unhappy, because they're placed in a rat race that requires long hours of grueling work, with the constant fear that if they slow down they'll fall behind forever. That's a debate for later.[17]

Nation of Victims

But a victimhood narrative allows one to skip the rat race altogether and jump straight to the cheese at the end. That's the path Jussie Smollett tried to take to prestige and influence. It was working wonders until he got caught, and it even worked for a while afterward, so strong was the narrative and so powerful the people advancing it. Of course, Smollett is just one example, and a mere conservative talking point at that. But look closer at modern America and you'll see people pursuing the path of victimhood everywhere.

Naomi Osaka, formerly the top female tennis player in the world, abruptly withdrew from the French Open. Why? Because of the stress created by press conferences, we're told. Then, less than a year later, in March 2022, she played a match at the famed

Indian Wells tournament in California. In a stadium filled with thousands of fans, she heard one woman scream from the stands "Naomi, you suck!"—and that fan was then shouted down by other fans who were rooting for Naomi. Nothing unheard of at sports games with tens of thousands of fans packed into a stadium. Osaka's response? In the middle of the match, she asked the chair umpire to let her take the microphone and talk to the audience—and then cried before going on to lose that set 6-0, and then eventually the match.[18]

It's particularly interesting that Osaka cited the reason for her trauma at the match back to the moment in 2001 when Serena Williams—and her father, Richard—were booed at the Indian Wells tournament. In that case, there was a real controversy at issue: Venus was supposed to play Serena in the semifinals, yet Venus withdrew from the match due to an injury. Richard Williams was an increasingly prominent and public figure who said all kinds of crazy-sounding things on camera, and there was growing suspicion of foul play of some kind arranged by Richard between the two sisters to give Serena a path to victory at the tournament. In that situation, the entire crowd booed Richard and Serena as they entered the stadium—over ten thousand people jeering against the two of them under suspicion of them having done something wrong.

It might've been unfair. Serena certainly seemed to think so, since she boycotted Indian Wells for fifteen years thereafter. But not after first defeating Kim Clijsters in the championship match at the tournament, without a tear in her eyes at the end of it. It was the inverse of Osaka's situation: a single fan who said a mean thing was shouted down by the rest of the audience, only to have caused Osaka herself to have a meltdown so unprecedented that she begged for a microphone in the middle of the match to address that lone fan.

The new trend toward victimhood isn't limited to sports. It's everywhere.

To begin with one notable example, Rachel Dolezal mastered being a victim. Some people know her as a white woman who posed as black. She rode her civil rights advocacy and her fake race all the way to becoming the president of the NAACP chapter in Spokane, an instructor in Africana studies at Eastern Washington University, and education director at the Human Rights Education Institute as well as securing an appointment to a police advisory commission. She reported numerous hate crimes against her to the police; none panned out.[19] Dolezal's parents eventually outed her as white. She acknowledged that her parents were white but insisted that she still identified as black. She wrote a memoir about it in 2017.[20]

This is only one example. I doubt academics have conducted rigorous studies about how many of them are faking their races—how could anyone know, and who would fund that? But what we can know is that when society attaches massive rewards to being the right race and allows people to self-report it, that provides a powerful incentive for people to lie. I see more and more stories like Dolezal's popping up as time goes on, rarely covered with as much publicity.

Jessica Krug, associate professor of history at George Washington University, had risen to the top of academia by writing about her experiences as an "Afro-Latinx" woman who was an "unrepentant and unreformed child of the hood." When a couple of actual black Latino scholars eventually became suspicious, she admitted she was white. Krug said that her deception was the product of mental health issues.[21] Neuroscientist BethAnn McLaughlin, founder of the MeTooSTEM organization, used the same excuse when she admitted to having created a fake Native American adjunct professor to defend her on Twitter. McLaughlin's followers became suspicious after she held a Zoom memorial for her fake friend, whom she'd killed off with COVID-19.[22] Around the same time, Indiana racial justice activist Satchuel Cole, who uses they/them pronouns, admitted they were a white person who faked being black.[23] Kelly Kean Sharp, a scholar of African American history, resigned her professorship at Furman University after being outed as white instead of Hispanic.[24]

How many academics and activists are faking their racial identities? An article in *The Atlantic* concludes, "You would be surprised at how many there are."[25] Well, I wouldn't. All we can know for sure is that America's new incentive structure, which rewards victimhood narratives, combined with the ease of lying about one's race, ensures that Dolezal is far from alone.

The problem with these false public narratives about racial victimhood is that they create new false narratives in everyday life. I had an Afghani friend who, disappointed to find he'd get no affirmative action boost in his college applications because he counted as Caucasian, told me he was applying as black. I tried to convince him not to. He later told me he'd applied as Hispanic. Considering how competitive college admissions is, how much of a difference race makes, and how easy it is to lie, I would be shocked if it was not very common for people to lie about their race. Colleges certainly have every incentive to turn a blind eye to it; faking your race makes it easier for them to meet their unofficial quotas. It's a win-win. Only dignity and integrity lose, along with the nation.

There's one group that can't fake its race in college admissions and would probably really like to: Asians. In her landmark opinion legalizing affirmative action in *Grutter v. Bollinger* in 2003, Sandra Day O'Connor famously concluded with "The Court expects that 25 years from now, the use of racial preferences will no longer be necessary to further the interest approved today."[26] This is the only time I can think of in all of law when the Supreme Court assigned an expiration date to a constitutional right. We're coming up on Justice O'Connor's deadline, and, right on schedule, the Supreme Court is poised to end affirmative action in lawsuits against Harvard University and the University of North Carolina.[27] But the legal argument is not that affirmative action is unnecessary, but that it causes schools to actively discriminate against Asian applicants.

The evidence is infuriatingly strong. The standard data everyone discusses on this point is Princeton professor Thomas Espenshade's 2009 study finding that Asian applicants had to score 140 points higher than white ones on the SAT to have the same chance of admission to elite colleges, 270 points higher than Hispanic applicants, and 450 points higher than black ones. It is equally standard for progressives to respond that Espenshade himself has said that his evidence isn't a smoking gun because it's possible that Asian applicants tend to be worse than those of other races on all the soft factors beyond GPAs and test scores.[28] I can't help but notice that liberals don't demand a smoking gun when inquiring into racism against other races.

Schools like Harvard have wholeheartedly embraced the idea that Asians have to score higher than every other race and get better grades because our personalities are worse. The group suing Harvard conducted a statistical analysis of more than 160,000 records and found that "Harvard consistently rated Asian-American applicants lower than others on traits like 'positive personality,' likability, courage, kindness and being 'widely respected.'"[29] Harvard disagrees with the methodology of the analysis, yet the lawsuit has revealed that its own private study in 2003 concluded that it appeared to discriminate against Asians:

> University officials did concede that its 2013 internal review found that if Harvard considered only academic achievement, the Asian-American share of the class would rise to 43 percent from the actual 19 percent. After accounting for Harvard's preference for recruited athletes and legacy applicants, the proportion of whites went up, while the share of Asian-Americans fell to 31 percent. Accounting for extracurricular and personal ratings, the share of whites rose again, and Asian-Americans fell to 26 percent.
>
> What brought the Asian-American number down to roughly 18 percent, or about the actual share, was accounting for a category called "demographic," the study found. This pushed up African-American and Hispanic numbers, while reducing whites and Asian-Americans.[30]

It's kind of funny and sad that our antiracist society gives serious consideration to the argument that elite colleges aren't discriminating against Asians because we're just cowardly, unlikeable, unkind worker drones who aren't leaders. It's common knowledge that this is *the exact same argument* that Harvard made when it discriminated against Jews almost a century ago. Harvard wanted to reduce its population of Jewish students from 25 to 15 percent. It called that "the Jewish problem." To accomplish this without imposing a strict quota, it introduced "character" requirements like leadership, which it found Jewish applicants consistently fell short on. It also introduced legacy admissions to further address its Jewish problem.[31]

Look, I don't think we need to bring in Sherlock Holmes on this one. Harvard is discriminating against Asian applicants in exactly the same way it did against Jewish ones, for exactly the same reasons, with exactly the same results, and exactly the same justifications. But when you look at media analysis of the issue, you get a dozen progressive think pieces about how calling this racism is nothing more than another conservative talking point. Jonathan Chait documented this liberal hypocrisy in an excellent article in *New York Magazine*. He begins with this thesis: "The institutions that crafted these policies, and the liberals who have defended them, have relied overwhelmingly on dissembling and lies. Whatever the legal merits, the political case for Harvard's system, and the similar systems used by its fellow elite institutions, has been formed by a stream of insultingly dishonest propaganda."[32] An apt assessment.

What liberals miss in their ruthless pursuit of social justice is that elevating some races above others based on a hierarchy of victimhood inevitably creates new victims. I was giving advice to a bright young Indian guy who wanted to major in computer science. He had a 1550 on the SAT, a 4.5 weighted GPA at a tough school, great essays, and a bunch of extracurricular activities, from editing the school paper to an internship at a top tech company. I foolishly encouraged him to apply to fifteen of the top thirty colleges. He ended up getting rejected from all of them, eventually attending a solid public school where the average GPA and SAT score were significantly lower than his.

It's not the end of the world. He'll likely have a comfortable middle-class life instead of getting on the fast-track to joining America's elites. But as he kept dejectedly informing me of rejection after rejection, I just know that with each one he was thinking, *What's wrong with me?* That's the message an Asian kid gets when they read all their rejection letters and look at how much higher their test scores and GPAs are than the college's averages, when they see their friends getting into those same schools with worse numbers: *What's wrong with me? What do they have that I don't?* That message is reinforced when the media keeps telling them it wasn't about their race, that maybe Asians as a group just deserve to do worse on all the personality-based parts of the application.

I wanted to tell that kid that there was nothing wrong with him at all. I wanted to tell him that people were just holding his race against him, that they just had too many applications from Indian guys who love building robots. But I didn't, because I thought telling him about the racism our society still endorses would've been cold comfort. I've decided to tell the next one.

I raised the issue of anti-Asian discrimination in college admissions in *Woke, Inc.* and was greeted with resounding silence. It was the single least-discussed aspect of that book, and it will likely be ignored again in coverage of this one. For liberals, the anti-Asian discrimination they allow and encourage in college admissions is the ultimate inconvenient truth. Some of you will accuse me of raising this as a conservative talking point meant to advance white supremacy, even as I'm objecting to discrimination against my own race. What a tangled web we weave . . .

Society seems to be going in the direction of handing out education, jobs, honors, and even medical treatment on the basis of race. As I write, New York, Utah, Minnesota, and other states are increasingly allocating scarce lifesaving COVID-19 treatments on the basis of race, explicitly prioritizing nonwhite people above white ones on the FDA's recommendation.[33] The question of whether one can identify as the race of their choice is now a life-or-death issue.

Race-based victim status isn't just a shortcut to education and lifesaving care these days; it's also becoming a qualification for government money. In March 2021, Oakland announced to great fanfare that it was launching a pilot program testing universal basic income, distributing $500 per month to six hundred low-income families for eighteen months. There's a catch: white people weren't eligible to apply.[34] Officials and media justified this discrimination by appealing to gaps in median wealth between races; the editorial board of *the Daily Californian* breathlessly praised "The radical potential of guaranteed income based on race."[35]

But individuals are not mere representatives of their race, and a poor black family and poor white one with the same amount of money are equally poor no matter what's happening to the median white and black family. As the threat of lawsuits rolled in,[36] Oakland quietly changed its eligibility requirements to say that people of all races are permitted to *apply* to the program, though its *focus* is still on helping "BIPOC" people.[37] This is clearly a fig leaf to hide the city's naked discrimination from the equal protection clause of the US Constitution. It appears the city will permit white people to apply and then will prioritize nonwhite ones when approving applications. I don't think the Constitution will be so easily fooled; I hope the same is true for today's judges who interpret it.

We're not a nation that tells itself Horatio Alger stories anymore. Instead we award jobs, educations, medical care, and money—and even vice presidential and Supreme Court nominations—to whoever presents themselves as the right kind of victim. Since race, gender, mental illness, and other preferred victimhood categories are blurrily and subjectively defined, we encourage Americans to lie, stretch the truth, or simply focus on one narrow aspect of their identity to the exclusion of others—we incentivize them to tell stories of victimhood about themselves. There is no need to take the hard road of the underdog. If they can but find the right magic words, their narrative's happy ending awaits.

The insurgent and the incumbent; the underdog and the victim. Two close competitors playing tug-of-war over the American soul. So how did we get here? That story starts farther back than you might think. Turn over the heavy log of a nation's history, and don't be surprised at what crawls out.

Chapter Two

THE CIVIL WAR

Lost Cause

The Civil War was fought over slavery, but the decisive battle was fought over shoes. There began a tale of American victimhood that's still told today.

Instead of looking to America's original founding for the origins of our present-day obsessions, whether 1619 or 1776, this particular story revolves around modern America's founding—the Reconstruction era. The war tore us apart, and as we tried to rebuild ourselves, we fought a cultural battle over the cause of the conflict. The process helped forge us into the nation we are today, establishing our nation's memory and articulating core principles of its identity.

Through this lens, the seeds of modern American victimhood were sown on the fields of Gettysburg, where the South lost the Civil War.

The Confederacy needed to secure the shoe factory in the small Pennsylvanian town to outfit its army to march deeper into Union territory, threatening Philadelphia. The morning of the third day of battle, the South's two best generals were locked in bitter argument. On one side was the great strategist Robert E.

Lee, commander of the Army of Northern Virginia. On the other, his second-in-command, James Longstreet, the Confederacy's top tactician and the leader of Lee's elite First Corps.

Longstreet's subordinate John Bell Hood called him the Confederacy's hardest hitter.[1] Lee chose which battles to fight, but it was Longstreet's job to win them. And win he did. Most of the Confederacy's major victories had Longstreet's fingerprints all over them. He would scout and wait for the perfect moment, test the enemy's strength, then attack the point of greatest vulnerability with tactics designed for the terrain. He'd made a name for himself in the Second Battle of Bull Run by executing the largest flanking maneuver of the war, wheeling with almost thirty thousand men and routing the Union army. It avoided total destruction by the skin of its teeth, escaping encirclement through a narrow gap in Longstreet's lines. He then displayed his trademark calm under fire when his force repelled one twice its size at Antietam, he and his staff personally manning a cannon at the peak of the battle. Later Longstreet distinguished himself with perhaps the best defensive stand of the war, turning Marye's Heights into a killing field at Fredericksburg.

It was partly the memory of his own defense of Fredericksburg that compelled Longstreet to object to the charge Lee ordered at Gettysburg. The two were the preeminent heroes of the Confederacy at the time. Lee had no idea that his order would lead to the Confederacy's demise; Longstreet had no idea that he would take the fall for it, becoming the central villain in the narrative of victimhood the South would concoct to explain its loss of the war.

Lee had grown impatient, made reckless by his successes, believing that the bravery of his troops would allow them to overcome George Meade's large force in a strong defensive position at the top of a ridge. But Longstreet knew that the invention of long-range artillery and rifles had tipped warfare decisively toward the defender. "Conditions were different from those in the days of Napoleon," he later wrote in his memoir.[2]

Longstreet was one of the first to understand that one could now take the strategic offensive by employing the tactical defensive—he agreed with Lee about the necessity of taking the war to the North but advocated fighting the battles by occupying defensible positions and mowing down Union soldiers at long range as they attacked. He often favored maneuvering to threaten Washington, DC, so the Union would be forced to attack him, a tactic he tried to convince Lee to use at Gettysburg. Longstreet's defensive approach didn't stir the popular imagination as much as Stonewall Jackson's bold frontal assaults had, but it was, he calculated, the only way for the South to overcome its numerical disadvantage. At Fredericksburg he'd had his men shelter behind a fortified wall, having the back rows reload rifles and pass them forward, turning his entire front line into an impromptu machine gun. No Union soldier made it within fifty yards of the wall; almost eight thousand were killed or wounded trying.

Now Longstreet feared the same fate befalling his own men as Lee ordered him to have George Pickett lead an assault on Cemetery Ridge, the center of the Union line. Longstreet told Lee such a brazen attack would require at least thirty thousand men; Lee said he'd have half that number. Longstreet replied, "General, I have been a soldier all my life. I have been with soldiers engaged in fights by couples, by squads, companies, regiments, divisions, and armies, and should know, as well as any one, what soldiers can do. It is my opinion that no fifteen thousand men ever arrayed for battle can take that position."[3]

Lee ordered the assault anyway, the rare time he overruled his top lieutenant. Longstreet waited as long as he could before complying, searching for a way to get out of the order without disobeying but finding none. When Pickett finally asked if it was time to attack, unable to speak, Longstreet could only nod grimly. As the Confederate soldiers marched toward Cemetery Ridge under withering artillery fire, Union troops chanted "Fredericksburg! Fredericksburg! Fredericksburg!" to let them know what awaited them in rifle range.

Pickett's Charge has become synonymous with a brave but doomed attack. Confederate troops evaporated under fire. More than half were killed, wounded, or captured. A couple hundred momentarily broke through the Union line before falling. As the assault's survivors fled in disarray, Lee rode out to meet them. "This is all my fault," he told them over and over. "It's all my fault."

History didn't see it that way. That's because, common wisdom notwithstanding, the history of the Battle of Gettysburg was written by its losers. As the war wound down, the cultural battle over American history was about to begin, and victimhood would take center stage.

The Army of Northern Virginia slowly bled out after Gettysburg, too many men lost, too many of its best officers. Ulysses S. Grant took the fortress city of Vicksburg by siege shortly after, sealing the Confederacy's fate in the Western Theater by controlling the Mississippi, cutting the South in two. Then he took command in the East and waged a bloody war of attrition against the outnumbered Lee, who surrendered at Appomattox two years later. The small patch of Cemetery Ridge that Southern troops briefly occupied is now known as the high-water mark of the Confederacy.

Pickett's Charge came to stand for a valiant but hopeless attack largely because embittered Southerners made it the centerpiece of the Lost Cause narrative, making the charge not just the proximate cause of the Confederacy's defeat but a microcosm of the entire war. Many still remember the Lost Cause today, associating it with the claim that the war was fought not over slavery, but states' rights—mainly the right to secede from the Union and the right to decide the legality of slavery. On this telling, which some still believe, the South began the war as the plucky underdog standing up to the overbearing North. Lost Cause disciples dubbed the Civil War "the war of Northern aggression" to make clear that the South was fighting not for slavery, but freedom.

Pickett's Charge fit perfectly as a symbol of the tenacious underdog fighting an uphill battle against overwhelming odds. There came to be a certain romanticism about the ill-fated assault, captured well by William Faulkner:

> For every Southern boy fourteen years old, not once but whenever he wants it, there is the instant when it's still not yet two oclock on that July afternoon in 1863, the brigades are in position behind the rail fence, the guns are laid and ready in the woods and the furled flags are already loosened to break out and Pickett himself with his long oiled ringlets and his hat in one hand probably and his sword in the other looking up the hill waiting for Longstreet to give the word and it's all in the balance, it hasn't happened yet, it hasn't even begun yet, it not only hasn't begun yet but there is still time for it not to begin against that position and those circumstances which made more men than Garnett and Kemper and Armistead and Wilcox

look grave yet it's going to begin, we all know that, we have come too far with too much at stake and that moment doesn't need even a fourteen year old boy to think *This time. Maybe this time* with all this much to lose and all this much to gain: Pennsylvania, Maryland, the world, the golden dome of Washington itself to crown with desperate and unbelievable victory the desperate gamble, the cast made two years ago.[4]

The South had always known the odds were against it, but so what? The deck is always stacked against an underdog; they must overcome them with bravery and skill. The South knew it had both, with legendary generals and valiant soldiers fighting to defend their homes and their liberty. It not only hoped for victory; it thought it deserved it.

But when an underdog is defeated and their hopes fail, the narrative must shift and become one of victimhood to explain why the protagonist was unable to complete their hero's journey. The new story required a villain—while an underdog story simply requires a favorite to oppose the hero, a tale of victimhood requires a culprit. The story could not simply be that the Union had won because it had a larger population with more industry; it had to be that someone had actively undermined the Confederacy's deserved victory.

To achieve this transition from plucky underdog to cheated victim, Lost Cause mythology turned James Longstreet into the South's abuser. It became gospel that Gettysburg had been lost not because Lee's orders were wrong, but because Longstreet sulked over being overruled and delayed too long in implementing them. But Lee's orders were wrong. Dwight Eisenhower once visited the site of Pickett's Charge and, at a loss to explain Lee's tactics, told British general Bernard Montgomery, "The man must have got so mad that he wanted to hit that guy with a brick."[5]

Though some contemporary Americans still remember the Lost Cause story's central claims, they have forgotten the means it used to prove them. Every time someone knows Stonewall Jackson's name but not James Longstreet's, that's the Lost Cause narrative still telling itself. It's elevating the daring, cruel, devout Christian above the proud, deliberate master of tactics. Even remembering Jackson by his Confederate nickname instead of his given name, Thomas, is the Lost Cause mythology still at work. By valorizing Jackson's skill as a lieutenant, it could avoid giving Longstreet any credit for the Confederacy's major victories. But there's a reason Lee promoted Longstreet to lieutenant general one day before Jackson and gave him the First Corps and Jackson the Second Corps—he wanted to make it clear that Longstreet was his right-hand man. But history cannot remember. "My old war horse," Lee had called Longstreet ever since his stand at Antietam.[6]

Lee himself never uttered a harsh word about Longstreet's performance at Gettysburg, but he died five years after the war, allowing the Lost Cause a head start on making him a legend. Jackson, too, was dead, lost to friendly fire in the dark before Gettysburg, and so he too was slated for martyrdom instead of villainy. It had to be Longstreet.

He did himself no favors when he became a Republican after the war, supporting Reconstruction and rekindling his friendship with Grant. They'd attended West Point together, and Grant had married one of Longstreet's cousins; most accounts agree Longstreet was either his best man or a groomsman. On the way toward Appomattox Court House, Longstreet told Lee that Grant would offer generous terms of surrender, and that if not, they ought to fight it out. Once they arrived, Grant proved him right, greeting Longstreet like the old friends they were and inviting him to play cards.[7]

Grant urged President Andrew Johnson to grant his friend a pardon, but Johnson refused, telling Longstreet, "There are three persons of the South who can never receive amnesty: Mr. Davis, General Lee, and yourself. You have given the Union cause too much trouble."

"You know, Mr. President, that those who are forgiven most love the most," replied Longstreet, appealing to his Christian nature.

"Yes," said Johnson, "you have very high authority for that, but you can't have amnesty."[8]

Congress re-granted Longstreet full citizenship a few years later, and once Grant was president, he gave him a series of government jobs. Longstreet was, in the parlance of the times, a scalawag, a fact that earned him little love in his community. Nor did he win many friends when he led an outnumbered mostly black state militia to defend New Orleans from the White League, a paramilitary army of five thousand white supremacists who marched on the state capitol in revolt over the disputed 1872 gubernatorial election. Unlike its more secretive rival, the Ku Klux Klan, the White League did its violence openly. Longstreet was shot with a spent bullet and captured in the Battle of Liberty Place as the terrorists seized control of Louisiana's government, inflicting a hundred casualties. They melted away a few days later once President Grant's federal troops arrived, deciding the KKK's furtive approach was better. It had been founded by another gifted Confederate general, Nathan Bedford Forrest.

Surprisingly, in the eyes of the defeated South, fraternization with the enemy was not even Longstreet's greatest sin. No, his unforgivable sin was resisting the Lost Cause narrative. For that, the narrative first made him the whipping boy for the Confederacy's loss, then erased him from American history.

First, Longstreet flatly rejected the noble story that the South had been fighting for states' rights: "I never heard of any other cause of the quarrel than slavery," he said.[9] But second, and worst of all Longstreet's offenses, he laid the blame for Gettysburg squarely at Lee's feet.

The Lost Cause's argument was easy: Lee was an unimpeachable hero. Longstreet blamed him for the loss at Gettysburg, and therefore implicitly for the loss of the war. To do so was to impeach the unimpeachable, therefore Longstreet was wrong, and simply trying to blame a dead hero for his own failings. Jubal Early and other senior Confederate officers who'd fought at Gettysburg eagerly spread the story that jealousy and resentment had made Longstreet insubordinate, ruining Lee's battle plan as he pouted about being overruled.[10]

Historians perpetuated the story for decades. In particular, Douglas Southall Freeman, who wrote what stood for a long time as the definitive biography of Lee, portrayed Longstreet as a talentless, insubordinate, cowardly general.[11] He and his disciples entrenched Longstreet as the villain in the Lost Cause narrative, the one who had deprived the underdog of their hero's journey and turned them into a victim. They portrayed him as a general who always deliberated too long, squandering the opportunities Lee's brilliance created.

But in fact, Longstreet's methodical style of waiting, scouting, and striking served the South well on many occasions, like the

Battle of Chickamauga, the Confederacy's greatest victory in the West, where one of Longstreet's signature counterattacks once again broke a Union army. After he returned east, he extended the Confederacy's life for a year in the Battle of the Wilderness when his flanking maneuver down an unfinished railroad he'd reconnoitered rescued Lee's army from Grant's in the nick of time. As one of Lee's soldiers put it, "Like a fine lady at a party, Longstreet was often late in arrival at the ball. But he always made a sensation when he got in, with the grand old First Corps sweeping behind him as his train."[12] Before he could complete his rout of Grant's army, he was severely wounded by friendly fire as he led a scouting party on the front lines, just miles from where Jackson had fallen.

Far from being a coward, Longstreet was a superior tactician who recognized the way new technology had changed warfare and valued the lives of his men highly, spending them to maximum effect on both defense and offense. It was that desire that made him resist Lee's fatal orders at Gettysburg, not cowardice or jealousy. Cadets at West Point could learn from his example today.

Though baseless and self-serving, the strategy of blaming Longstreet's generalship for the Confederate loss in the Civil War worked like a charm. It was the shared fiction that made the Lost Cause plausible. Longstreet was widely reviled throughout the South for the rest of his life, spending much of it fruitlessly trying to defend his military record.[13]

And then he was forgotten. No forts were named after Longstreet, though two were named after his subordinates Hood and Pickett. Others were named after incompetents like Braxton Bragg, who lost almost every battle he fought with the exception of Chickamauga, which Longstreet won for him. Although some modern historians now believe James Longstreet was the best tactician on either side of the war,[14] only two statues of him exist today—one in his hometown of Gainesville, and a recently created one in an out-of-the-way spot at Gettysburg.

Unlike Longstreet, the Lost Cause narrative was never forgotten. It is America's past and present. This mythology of Confederate victimhood was given a prominent voice as recently as 2003 in the film *Gods and Generals*, a celebration of Stonewall Jackson that portrayed slaves as happy with their lot and rebel soldiers as defenders of freedom. Historian Stephen E. Woodworth wrote that "The result is the most pro-Confederate film since *Birth of a Nation*, a veritable celluloid celebration of slavery and treason."[15]

Perhaps in part because of Longstreet's defense of New Orleans from the White League, it was Lee, who had no particular connection to the city, who had a statue built in his honor there. After Lee, too, eventually became controversial, his statue was moved to an undisclosed location in 2017.[16] But as America tries to forget the Confederacy's greatest champion, it fails to remember its greatest villain. Both great generals are now, in the words of one beloved Lost Cause story, gone with the wind.

Lost Memories

As you know, something important happened in 1776: Hume died.

David Hume is often considered the greatest philosopher to have written in English. Though still an important figure in academic circles, he's not quite as well known as he used to be. It turns out he's in the process of being canceled just as Longstreet was, which is one reason he's been on my mind lately. More on that in a bit.

Hume's quietly becoming a your-favorite-player's-favorite-player kind of philosopher. Immanuel Kant said Hume's skepticism "awakened me from my dogmatic slumber." Hume often grasped at a theory of evolution by natural selection but didn't quite get there;[17] fortunately, he was one of Darwin's favorite writers.[18] Albert Einstein said that without reading Hume's *Treatise on Human Nature,* he might've never arrived at the theory of relativity, since Hume's skepticism about all things extended to doubting the existence of an objectively correct, universal time. He argued that time was an illusion created by subjective impressions.[19]

Hume was also one of the first intellectuals to attempt to rigorously define the mental processes that govern the direction of thought; we call the field that descended from his principles of association cognitive science. As part of that, he gave what still stands today as one of the best accounts of causation, saying that cause and effect are illusions our minds create from the constant conjunction of one event and another. This theory also led Hume to raise the problem of induction, pointing out that inductive reasoning, which presumes that unknown information resembles known information, is hopelessly circular: the only reason we think induction will work well in the future is that it's worked well in the past. The first sentence of this section is actually a little joke about the pitfalls of induction: obviously, 1776 wasn't just the year that Hume died. It was, of course, also the year that his friend Adam Smith published *The Wealth of Nations.*

I respect Hume's contributions to human thought. That's why I was surprised and disappointed to find out that he got caught up in the cancellation craze that swept the Western world after George Floyd's death. Outraged Black Lives Matter protesters got the University of Edinburgh to change the name of its David

Hume Tower to 40 George Square.[20] Why did valuing black lives end up demanding the cancellation of a long-dead Scottish empiricist? The problem came down to a footnote.

In 1753 Hume revised his essay "Of National Characters" with a footnote saying he suspected that nonwhite races were naturally inferior to white people because white civilizations had produced greater achievements. In another revision published a year after his death, he changed the footnote to limit his criticisms to black people. Because of Hume's towering stature as an intellectual, racists in later generations would sometimes appeal to this footnote. A century after Hume wrote it, some of Longstreet's fellow Confederates would cite it to defend slavery.[21]

Though Hume was expressing the conventional view of mid-1700s British society, some scholars pointed out its flaws even at the time. I winced when I read the end of the footnote, where Hume references a respected black thinker in Jamaica and argues that it's "likely he is admired for very slender accomplishments, like a parrot, who speaks a few words plainly."[22] It's jarring to hear those words come from one of your intellectual idols, the man who inspired entire fields of modern science even as he questioned its foundations. The great skeptic, the great empiricist, seems to have drawn strong conclusions about race from very little evidence.

There's actually a lesson there: even the most critical thinkers have their blind spots, and race can easily be one of them. If only Hume had been as skeptical of his thoughts on race as he was of his belief in induction. As some defenders of David Hume Tower noted, although Hume had racist beliefs, they stood in isolated opposition to his own theories and methods rather than being entailed by them. If Hume had been able to follow his own commitments far enough, his philosophy would've allowed him to

escape his own racism as surely as it freed him from his precon-
ceived notions of time and causation. It could help people escape
their biases today.

Should David Hume Tower have been renamed 40 George
Square over that footnote? Ironically, the first time the University
of Edinburgh canceled Hume was in 1744, when because of his
religious skepticism it denied his application to become a professor of moral philosophy. He was a famous atheist at a time when
no one was open about their atheism. That's why he only allowed
his *Dialogues Concerning Natural Religion* to be published post-
humously. It's why Adam Smith was risking his reputation and
career when he published a defense of Hume's character after his
death, endangering the success of his recently published *The
Wealth of Nations*.[23] Because of his reputation as an atheist, David
Hume, the greatest philosopher to write in English and possibly
any language, was never allowed to become a professor anywhere.

So Hume was canceled during his life for his atheism, a view
ahead of its time, and is being canceled today for his racism, a
view that was a product of his times. That's why he reminds me of
Longstreet: a traitor to the Confederacy because he opposed the
Lost Cause narrative, a traitor today because he's just another
Confederate. Freethinkers tend to be canceled in every time, just
for different reasons; the only way to avoid that trap is to avoid
canceling people at all.

Postwar Longstreet was no storybook redemption on the subject of race either, by the way, even if he did advocate equal rights
for black people. He argued that if white people didn't join Southern black people in the Republican party, they'd simply be handing them unchecked political power.[24] That argument earned him

the scorn of racists in his time, but antiracists would be the ones to despise him for it today.

Should we have statues of neither Longstreet nor Hume, then? Before the most recent wave of partisan division, liberal media outlets like CNN and the *Washington Post* actually published articles supporting creating statues of Longstreet.[25] I wonder if their readers would allow them to express that view today. If David Hume cannot have a tower named after him, it's hard to imagine anyone building statues of any Confederate general. The University of Edinburgh renamed Hume's tower; should it take down its statue of him, too? Should there be no more statues of Hume or buildings named for him anywhere? Philosophers are debating that very question, with some saying yes.[26]

Of course, everyone will argue, as the University of Edinburgh does, that one can refuse to honor Hume while still teaching his influential ideas. That's certainly logically possible, but I suspect that as Hume becomes controversial, professors will quietly decide not to teach his views unless necessary. He will go from a figure who's casually mentioned in many classes to one who's discussed mostly in Hume courses. Those will become fewer as interest in him lessens, and teachers who fear their students will ask whether it's worth risking mentioning Hume himself when they could simply find other thinkers who had similar ideas, people of color or women if possible . . .

We are witnessing the beginnings of the erasure of a great thinker from human thought. The next Charles Darwin or Albert Einstein may have to come up with their revolutionary theory without the benefit of being inspired by Hume's skepticism. The next Immanuel Kant may have to sleep in his dogmatism for a while longer, waiting for someone less problematic to wake him. David Hume. Your favorite thinker's favorite thinker, but not yours.

I started thinking of Hume's connection to modern America at first because the BLM protests of him forced me to. He seemed so disconnected, someone from a completely different part of my life, yet American victimhood somehow ended up reaching even him. American grievance has become like a black hole dragging the rest of the world into its maw, warping time and space to capture everything that offends it. James Longstreet is stuck deep in that singularity, so far gone that no light from him can escape. Now I see David Hume beginning the same journey, slowly being dragged to the event horizon, the point where the gravitational pull of American victimhood is too strong for even his great ideas to break free.

That's one reason I go into some depth about figures like Hume and Longstreet in this book. I don't want to just argue that we ought to remember our history; I want to remember it. We're a nation that's losing its memory, rewriting and sanitizing its own history to fit preapproved victimhood narratives. We suffer from our own version of Alzheimer's. As we lose our memory, we lose our national identity. Instead of arguing in the abstract that we shouldn't cancel people, I've told you about a great general we've canceled and a great philosopher we're in the process of canceling. You can judge for yourself whether they're worth remembering.

In this chapter I presented an account of one strand of American victimhood, one that focuses on the way it arose as America fought over the memory of the Civil War during the Reconstruction era. But my story was never just about our nation's history. Once again, William Faulkner put it well, so well that Barack Obama quoted him in his celebrated speech "A More Perfect Union": "The past is never dead. It's not even past."[27]

The Lost Cause narrative is not past, nor is the Civil War. A 2021 Harvard poll found that the majority of young Americans believe American democracy is either in trouble or failing; only 7 percent described it as healthy.[28] Thirty-five percent expected to see a full-scale civil war within their lifetimes. That was one of the more optimistic polls. A different 2021 survey found that 46 percent of Americans felt civil war was likely, with 43 percent thinking it unlikely and the remainder unsure.[29]

Lee's statue was removed from New Orleans just a few years ago, in 2017. That same year, Charlottesville's city council narrowly voted to remove statues of him and Stonewall Jackson, prompting a white supremacist protest that culminated in violence, with one man ramming his car into a crowd of counter protesters, killing one and wounding thirty-five.[30] The statue was finally removed in 2021.[31] Meanwhile, the question of whether forts should be named after Confederate generals has surged to the forefront of the national consciousness, with President Trump arguing in favor of keeping the names, claiming that attempts to rename them were part of cancel culture. He even advocated maintaining the name of Fort Bragg, saying "Fort Bragg is a big deal. We won two world wars, nobody even knows General Bragg."[32] Well, those who do know about Braxton Bragg know he was a hapless general who lost almost every battle and had to endure the embarrassing spectacle of watching all his top subordinates implore Jefferson Davis to remove him for incompetence.

Personally, I think Fort Longstreet would be a much better name, one that would remind American officers to update their tactics to respond to new technology and to value the lives of the soldiers under their command. As I finish this book, the congressionally appointed Naming Commission has proposed renaming

Fort Bragg and others after a variety of figures, including Dwight Eisenhower and Harriet Tubman.[33] Unsurprisingly, James Longstreet's name is not on the list.

If Fort Bragg is to be renamed, name it after the true winner of the Battle of Chickamauga. Remember the Confederate general the ghost of the Confederacy made America forget. It would be a step toward unity. It would also remind American citizens that humans are complex beings, capable of change, who seek atonement and sometimes deserve forgiveness. As Longstreet would tell us if he were here today, those who are forgiven the most love the most. If we allow history to erase those nuanced men and women who struggled to do the right thing, sometimes failing, sometimes succeeding, we will fail to look for the nuances that exist within each other. If we divide the world into black and white, virtuous victims and evil oppressors with no shades of gray, we will create the nation that we see.

We remind me of the dystopia predicted in the young adult novel *The Giver*, where a community achieves an artificial tranquility through a philosophy called Sameness.[34] The false utopia makes everyone equal by eliminating all the features of life that could make them different: color, memory, individuality, and even family are all sacrificed to guarantee that everyone has the same experiences, to remove the possibility of pain. Only one member of the community, the Giver, is allowed to remember the world as it really was, so that he can share those memories with the rest of the community when disaster threatens.

Disaster is at the doorstep. It's opening the front door. I think every American who remembers the way things used to be has a duty to share those memories. Otherwise, we too may find ourselves lost by history, following Longstreet and Hume into the dark.

Chapter Three

THE CONSTITUTIONAL WAR

No Nation of Citizens

America's first civil war never really ended. It just entered a new phase. There were two fronts in this more genteel stage of the war: one over America's past, and one over its future. The Lost Cause fought a cultural battle for America's memory, turning Robert E. Lee and Stonewall Jackson into martyrs who'd defended states' rights and the Confederacy into an underdog that never had its day. Meanwhile, an even more consequential battle unfolded in courtrooms as the two sides fought to rebuild the nation with new principles.

The moment the Civil War ended, the constitutional war began. The story of that shadow war was the most important thing I learned in law school.

The first major blow was struck in New Orleans in 1873, a year before the White League's revolt. It came in the *Slaughterhouse Cases*, in a decision that is now universally regarded as incorrect by legal scholars across the political spectrum.[1] With this, Southern efforts to rebuild the nation in the image of the Confederacy intersected with the Constitution; together, the two birthed many hideous offspring.

What does it mean to be a citizen, and what does it mean to be a victim? The law had a golden opportunity to make the first of those questions the foundation of our civil rights jurisprudence. Instead, through a series of moves, the Supreme Court deprived the nation of a conversation about the meaning of citizenship and created one about the meaning of victimhood. That choice left our country worse off for more than a century afterward, all the way to the present day, with implications for American law and culture.

Toward the end of *Woke, Inc.*, I argued that identity politics flourishes when people embrace their tribal identities to fill the void left by the absence of national identity.[2] In this chapter, I explain how constitutional law encouraged that transition. The Constitution, after all, literally defines what it means to be American. So before I explain the constitutional story of how we became a nation of victims, I'll tell you why we never got to be a nation of citizens.

The Constitution's Fourteenth Amendment begins by telling us who counts as a citizen and saying citizens have certain fundamental rights, but it says virtually nothing about what those rights are. Today, we ask what constitutional rights people have instead of what constitutional rights citizens have. This section explains how that happened.

The *Slaughterhouse Cases* concerned the interpretation of the privileges and immunities clause, a key part of the Fourteenth Amendment. As the dust settled on the Civil War, America began redefining itself by amending the Constitution, passing the Thirteenth, Fourteenth, and Fifteenth amendments in rapid succession. The Northern states passed them, that is, and required the

Southern ones to accept them as a precondition for full readmission into the Union.

The Thirteenth Amendment outlawed slavery, and the Fifteenth protected former slaves' right to vote, but it was the Fourteenth where the Northern states did most of their work reinventing America. The framers put the most important parts at the beginning: "All persons born or naturalized in the United States, and subject to the jurisdiction thereof, are citizens of the United States and of the State wherein they reside. No State shall make or enforce any law which shall abridge the privileges or immunities of citizens of the United States; nor shall any State deprive any person of life, liberty, or property, without due process of law; nor deny to any person within its jurisdiction the equal protection of the laws."

The *Slaughterhouse Cases* forced the Supreme Court to interpret the Fourteenth Amendment five years after it was ratified. Some poor butchers in New Orleans sued some rich ones, saying they were creating a monopoly preventing them from practicing their trade, an activity the plaintiffs claimed should be an unbridgeable privilege of citizens of the United States.

In a 5-4 decision, the Court reasoned that the privileges and immunities clause didn't protect the butchers because the rights it covered didn't include ones that people might have in virtue of being *citizens* of the United States, but only ones they had in virtue of being citizens of the *United States*. It's a very fine distinction, one only a lawyer could love. Instead of asking the straightforward question of what rights American citizens had, the Court asked what rights citizens had to possess in order to unify the states they belong to. That meant that the Court understood the privileges and immunities clause to protect only certain rights to travel around the nation—the rights to travel between states; to travel to Washington, DC; and to use navigable rivers.[3]

The bottom line? With the privileges and immunities clause, the Fourteenth Amendment's framers included broad language to protect citizens' rights, but the Supreme Court immediately transformed it into very narrow language protecting their right to travel around the United States.

If you're wondering why the Court erased the privileges and immunities clause right after it was written, you're not alone. The answer is that it felt that protecting the rights of citizens was a job for the states they belonged to, not the federal government, so the federal government could only be in charge of protecting their right to move around the states. The Civil War had ended, but the battle between state and federal power immediately resurfaced in constitutional law.

I looked up the histories of the nine justices and discovered that one of the ones in the narrow majority, Nathan Clifford, was pro-slavery. Justice Clifford was appointed in 1857, shortly before the war. Afterward, he did his best to defuse the Reconstruction Amendments. He coined the phrase "equality is not identity," arguing that treating races equally didn't require treating them identically; his theory later became known as "separate but equal" in *Plessy v. Ferguson*.[4] We defeated the Confederacy's generals, but we never defeated its Supreme Court justice. Supreme Court justices, as we keenly appreciate today, are appointed for life.

The Fourteenth Amendment had begun by specifying who counted as a citizen, and then with the privileges and immunities clause attempted to ground Americans' fundamental rights in their citizenship. If that key plank of the Fourteenth Amendment had survived Justice Clifford and the *Slaughterhouse Cases*, our nation would've evolved a jurisprudence clarifying the relationship between citizenship and fundamental rights—for instance, one of the first things the Court would've had to do would be to distinguish the privileges citizenship grants from the immunities it entails. Such distinctions about the benefits of citizenship would likely have evolved side by side with an account of its duties; one cannot develop a theory of what one is owed by others without simultaneously developing a theory of what one owes them.

Instead of illuminating the rights of citizens, as the years went on, the Court gradually located fundamental rights in the remaining two clauses from the second sentence of the Fourteenth Amendment. With its due process jurisprudence, it made the Fourteenth Amendment protect the fundamental rights of people instead of citizens. With equal protection doctrine, it gave instructions about which groups of people ought to be regarded as victims deserving of special protection.

The privileges and immunities clause was gone, but judges saw convenient language right after it in the due process clause, saying that states couldn't deprive people of life, liberty, or property. This seemed like a promising location for rights that were fundamental but unspecified elsewhere in the Constitution.

The problem was that the due process clause, in the end, was meant to provide only procedural protections, not substantive ones. It said not that states couldn't deprive people of life, liberty, or property, but that they had to provide timely notifications and hearings first. It was an attempt to prevent America from recreating one of English law's greatest mistakes: the Star Chamber.

The Star Chamber was a secretive English court that wielded vast power from its seat in the Palace of Westminster. Until it was abolished in 1641, it would frequently haul nobles in without notice, representation, or charges and assign them whatever punishment it wanted, sometimes ignoring the law to do so. It did all this to fight the nobles' privilege in the name of a nebulous legal concept called equity, which was vague enough to mean whatever the Star Chamber wanted it to. Remind you of anyone else?

The US Constitution's guarantee of due process was meant to prevent the Star Chamber from being reborn in America. It may have been unsuccessful; these days, I think the Star Chamber goes by "Twitter." But the thought was good. Getting timely notifications and hearings about judicial acts that might deprive you of life, liberty, or property is actually pretty important. The Fourteenth Amendment's due process clause was always meant to protect those boring procedural rights, not juicy substantive ones. That's why it's called the due process clause.

The justices solved this problem by saying that the due process clause protects not only procedural due process but also substantive due process. If the term sounds strange, that's because it's an obvious contradiction, Orwellian doublespeak. Antonin Scalia spent his entire judicial career railing against substantive due process, claiming it would be the death of democracy.[5]

According to Scalia, the way substantive due process works is basically this: a judge looks at a law and thinks really hard about whether they like it or not. If they don't, most of the time, they say that it deprives people of a fundamental liberty without due process of law.

The legal fiction justifying substantive due process is this: fundamental rights are so important that no number of timely notifications or hearings could be sufficient to justify the government in taking them away. So if the government has taken away a fundamental liberty, it doesn't matter how good the process it used was: we can deduce that it wasn't the amount of process that was due because no amount of process could be good enough.

If that argument doesn't make sense, don't worry about it. It's legal nonsense, meant to sound impressive, but ultimately meaningless—full of sound and fury, but signifying nothing. What it comes down to is that the Court felt the Constitution ought to have some clause protecting fundamental rights, and it wrapped itself into knots trying to find a way to say those rights came from the due process clause, because they were actually located in the privileges and immunities clause but an earlier Supreme Court had killed that.

But the privileges and immunities clause protected the rights of citizens, while the due process clause protected people. The Supreme Court's flailing efforts to locate fundamental rights in the Fourteenth Amendment's due process clause, then, made the question come down not to the nature of citizenship, but to a single issue: what fundamental rights do people have?

In contrast, suppose that we had framed the analysis of fundamental rights through the privileges and immunities clause, as the framers of the Fourteenth Amendment intended. Instead of taking the due process clause, cutting out the process part, and asking judges to decide which rights the single word "liberty" entails, there would've been at least two important guardrails to guide judicial inquiry. First, since the law would've had to wrestle with the difference between the privileges and immunities of citizenship, the question for judges would be more specific than what they thought the word "liberty" meant. Second, even more importantly, while today's judges ask what fundamental rights people have, in a world without the *Slaughterhouse Cases*, they'd ask what fundamental rights citizens have.

These are completely different questions. If all people have a fundamental right that derives from their humanity, that right does not in fact derive from their citizenship. There are probably many fundamental human rights—like, perhaps, the rights to due process and equal protection of the law—but the privileges and immunities clause doesn't attempt to protect them. I like Kant's account of what human beings owe each other, but I've never thought the Fourteenth Amendment enshrined the categorical imperative in the Constitution.

So, counterintuitively, if Fourteenth Amendment jurisprudence had evolved in the way it ought to have, we might be making the opposite of the legal arguments we make today. Today, we argue that people possess fundamental rights and make grand, sweeping claims about human rights in court. But if the privileges and immunities clause replaced substantive due process, those arguments would be losers, not winners. If a right is fundamental for all humans, it cannot be one of the privileges or immunities conferred by American citizenship.

Of course, one could argue that some fundamental human rights are protected through the privileges and immunities of American citizenship. In a world without the *Slaughterhouse Cases*, this argument likely would've been one of the first ones lawyers raised—in fact, it might have sprung up under a doctrine of immunities. One could attempt to argue that the privileges of American citizens involve some special rights beyond what all humans possess, and the immunities of American citizens involve things that can't be done to them because they shouldn't be done to any human. This would have been an interesting and complex question for constitutional law.

Although a worthy question, this argument that human rights are included among the immunities of American citizens would've had to contend with the troubling fact that the structure of the Fourteenth Amendment seems to deliberately distinguish between the protections it gives citizens and the ones it affords all people. The amendment begins by saying who's a citizen and immediately follows that by protecting two classes of rights citizens have. It then shifts its focus from citizens and explicitly says that all people have the rights to due process and equal protection of the law. This structure suggests that the privileges and immunities of citizenship were meant to entail rights beyond the ones offered to everyone. If the privileges and immunities clause was meant to protect rights all people have, why not just use the word "person" like the remaining two clauses of the same sentence?

Elucidating the differences between human rights and the privileges and immunities of citizens would've raised difficult and fruitful questions in constitutional law—for instance, the exploration might have begun by asking what duties citizens have that noncitizens lack. The legal concepts raised by the resulting jurisprudence would've inevitably trickled out into American culture, the same way constitutional doctrines about the value of diversity have after being introduced by equal protection analysis of affirmative action law, or the way debates over liberty have shaped culture through due process law.[6]

Imagine how different the nation would be if we discussed citizenship with the same seriousness with which we discuss diversity, the same fervor with which we debate fundamental liberty. That was supposed to be our path. Talking about the nature of citizenship sounds lofty and abstract, while talking about diversity sounds practical and pressing. But there's actually greater constitutional justification for discussing citizenship, and if it weren't for the *Slaughterhouse Cases*, those discussions would've seemed very practical.

But the privileges and immunities clause now stands for nothing. And so instead of having the Fourteenth Amendment pose the intriguing question of what rights citizenship confers that humanity itself does not, we are left with the highly subjective question of what fundamental liberties all people possess.

As an illustration of the costs of this unguided subjectivity, consider that the substantive due process doctrine was actually created in *Dred Scott v. Sandford*, when in 1857 the Court ruled that for the federal government to side with a state that freed an escaped slave was a violation of his owner's right to not have his property taken away without receiving due process of law under the Fifth Amendment. The Fifth Amendment requires the federal government to give due process, while the Fourteenth requires it of states.[7] The right to own a slave struck the Court as so fundamental that no number of notifications or hearings could justify taking the owner's property away.

A conservative Court then resurrected substantive due process in the early 1900s in the Lochner era, a legal civil war where for four decades the Court struck down whatever progressive laws it disliked, saying they infringed on some fundamental liberty, usually the liberty to make contracts. In *Lochner v. New York* itself, for instance, the Court ruled that a New York law setting maximum working hours for bakers violated the bakers' Fourteenth Amendment substantive due process right to freedom of contract.[8]

The conservative era of substantive due process ended only when President Franklin D. Roosevelt threatened to pack the Court, tired of it derailing the New Deal. He came up with some story about needing to add more justices to the Supreme Court to help the older justices carry the workload. It was obviously bullshit, but substantive due process was also bullshit, so the morality of all this is unclear.

Incidentally, as I wrote this, Microsoft Word informed me that the word "bullshit" might be offensive to my reader and I ought to reconsider using it. As I said in the last chapter, America's victimhood complex drags everything into its grasp. I will use the word and trust you to be brave and strong. Anyway, one reason we don't have fifteen justices right now is that Justice Owen Roberts defected from the conservative wing in what's now called "the switch in time that saved nine." After that, the conservative justices gave up their arms and stopped using substantive due process to do whatever they wanted.

But three decades later, a liberal Court used substantive due process in *Roe v. Wade* and created a constitutional right to have an abortion.[9] The monster was back. Scalia devoted his life to fighting it.[10] He died of natural causes, but sometimes I think that somehow, it must've been substantive due process that killed him.

I wish I could at least hear the arguments that once we fully understand what it is to be a citizen, it's clear that citizenship entails an unenumerated privilege or immunity to control one's body through having an abortion. I wish I could hear the arguments about whether it's a privilege or an immunity or, as some lawyers would no doubt argue, both. And I want to hear a judge question them about what theory of the relationship between the privileges and immunities of citizenship allows them to say that the choice of abortion is protected by both.

That's the kind of thing judges should be asked to do. Having judges decide what fundamental rights people have is—if you'll pardon my language—balderdash.

The Constitutional Oppression Olympics

After the Supreme Court ended one conversation about American identity, it began another. We never got to find out what it means to be a citizen. But the Court told us exactly what it means to be a victim, and we listened carefully.

Consider, for example, the most famous footnote in constitutional law, *Carolene Products* footnote 4, the progenitor of modern equal protection jurisprudence. *United States v. Carolene Products* was decided in 1938, one year after the switch in time that saved nine. The newly compliant Court dutifully upheld the federal government's power to prohibit certain kinds of milk from being shipped in interstate commerce, holding that the kind of economic regulation it had struck down for decades under substantive due process was now presumptively constitutional because Congress only needed to have a rational basis for passing such laws.[11]

Hardly anyone remembers the substance of *Carolene Products*. What's more important is that, just as it gave up its arms on adjudicating economic regulations, the Court snuck in a key footnote that opened the door for it to possess broad authority on civil rights. Writing for a plurality, Justice Harlan Stone wrote that the Court would employ a stricter form of judicial review on some laws, concluding that "prejudice against discrete and insular minorities may be a special condition, which tends seriously to curtail the operation of those political processes ordinarily to be relied upon to protect minorities, and which may call for a correspondingly more searching judicial inquiry." This more searching form of judicial review came to be known as strict scrutiny.

As later Courts fleshed out the meaning of the footnote, it grew into the "suspect class" doctrine, laying out the criteria that would presumptively make laws affecting certain groups merit strict scrutiny instead of the rubber stamp of rational basis review. Such protected groups were to be recognized if they were discrete and insular (meaning relatively powerless to mobilize their fellow citizens to protect them through the political process), if they had historically been discriminated against, and if membership in the group was based on immutable characteristics.

Constitutional scholar Bruce Ackerman argued in an influential article that *Carolene Products* was the Supreme Court's attempt to redefine itself as a cog in the system of democracy instead of its overlord. With the rational basis review's rubber stamp, the Court abandoned its Lochner-era power to strike down any law it disliked; it presumed that a democratically passed law was constitutional. But, Ackerman said, with footnote 4 the Court identified the rare times judicial activism was appropriate: to correct defects in the democratic process that had allowed majorities to oppress minorities. The idea is that some groups of minorities, like black people in the Antebellum South, were likely to face prejudice so strong that it could prevent them from protecting themselves using normal political processes. Since groups especially likely to be victimized couldn't fully protect themselves, it became the Court's job to guarantee them equal protection.[12]

The equal protection clause did in fact play this role sixteen years after *Carolene Products*, when the Court applied it to find that segregation was unconstitutional. *Brown v. Board of Education* was a case where the Constitution worked as intended and the equal protection clause really did bring justice to a historically oppressed minority group that had been disempowered by the majority. But as the decades went on, the Court kept looking for new victim groups to protect, and it started using the framework outlined by *Carolene Products* to find them.

So black people were enshrined by precedent as the gold standard of constitutional victimhood, the ideal suspect class—any law that treated them differently was automatically suspect. For all other groups seeking to fight discriminatory laws, to get special constitutional protection, they had to prove to the Court that they met the requirements of *Carolene Products* footnote 4: that they were "discrete and insular," that they were politically powerless, that they'd been discriminated against historically, and that their group identity was based on immutable characteristics.

In other words, to get coveted suspect class status, groups had to do their best to argue that they were like black people, the paradigmatic victims. Otherwise, they'd be consigned to rational basis review, and the Court would reflexively approve of almost any law treating them differently from other groups. The Oppression Olympics was born in equal protection law, and suspect class status was the gold medal.

Some groups made it. Along with race, today national origin, religion, and status as an alien are called suspect classifications. Any law treating a group differently on the basis of one of those categories faces the harsh light of strict scrutiny, and the government must prove that the law is narrowly tailored to achieve a compelling state interest. As a demonstration of how demanding strict scrutiny is, consider that only two policies treating people differently on the basis of race have ever survived it: the internment of the Japanese during World War II, and affirmative action.

After a long battle, women eventually won something called intermediate scrutiny and gender became known as a quasi-suspect classification. The basic problem was that women could prove some elements of the *Carolene Products* criteria, but not others. They could show they'd experienced a history of discrimination and that their identities were based on immutable characteristics. But they weren't politically powerless, since they controlled about 50 percent of the nation's votes, and they were by nature the opposite of a discrete and insular group. So eventually gender became a quasi-suspect classification, along with legitimacy of birth. Women got a silver medal.

After that, the Court felt that constitutionally recognized victim groups had flourished enough and that suspect classes ought to be kept scarce. There could only be so many spots on the victimhood podium, and groups had to compete with each other to get them. There have been no new suspect classes in decades. Among the many groups who sought precious suspect class status and lost were the poor, the intellectually disabled, and the elderly. And, so far, gay people.

The final groups to win the Oppression Olympics were, ironically, white people and men. They won a sneaky come-from-behind victory that has hardly been noticed even to this day. Legal scholars often use the terms "suspect class" and "suspect classification" interchangeably. But in fact there's a big difference between the two, one law professor Jed Rubenfeld identified in an article on affirmative action.[13] Equal protection law initially focused on identifying suspect and quasi-suspect classes like black people and women. But as time went on, conservative justices gradually broadened the language so that instead of saying laws treating black people differently were automatically suspect, equal protection doctrine said that laws treating races differently were. Today, instead of saying that black people are a suspect class, we say that race is a suspect classification. So laws treating white people differently from others also face strict scrutiny.

We kept using the *Carolene Products* criteria to identify victim groups like women. But once we identified and protected them, men got that protection too, because we now say not that laws treating women differently are suspect, but that laws treating genders differently are. With this judo-like legal move, a national history of discrimination against women became a legal reason to protect men. A history of discrimination against black people was rephrased as a history of discrimination on the basis of race, so now all other races share black people's spot at the top of the victimhood podium. It was an incredible last-minute legal maneuver before the race for victimhood status ended and the hierarchy was frozen. Equal protection law had been about protecting victimized minorities, but the majority struck back and subtly protected itself from victimization too.

Much of the legal history of the fight for gay rights can be understood as the struggle for gay people to win recognition as a suspect class or, as we put it today, to make sexual orientation a new suspect classification. Much hinges on achieving constitutional recognition as a victim group—preferably prototypical victims like black people, winning coveted strict scrutiny, or at least plausible victims like women, getting intermediate scrutiny. Failing that, gay people would be relegated to dreaded rational basis review like the elderly, intellectually disabled, or poor, and laws treating them differently would be rubber-stamped.

Indeed, that's how the early gay rights cases went, as in *Bowers v. Hardwick*, when in 1986 the Court applied rational basis review to find a Georgia law banning gay sex constitutional.[14] Gay people couldn't prove a history of discrimination anywhere near that experienced by black people, the paradigmatic victims. The discrimination was in the present, with laws like Georgia's ban on gay sex, but the constitutional definition of victimhood provided by equal protection law required the Court to look at the past.

So gay people have done their best to meet as many of the *Carolene Products* criteria as possible, creating a discrete and insular group identity, establishing a history of discrimination, arguing that they're politically powerless, and claiming that homosexuality is an immutable characteristic. The Court told everyone how to shape their group identities to receive constitutional victim status, and gay people have dutifully crafted their group identity around its requirements. Their efforts have not yet been rewarded on the federal level, but some state laws have granted gay people suspect class status.

As law professor William Eskridge noted, this need to be seen as politically powerless created strange incentives: "Gay rights advocates have spent a generation seeking political advances for sexual minorities—yet now find themselves arguing that gay men, lesbians, and bisexuals are 'politically powerless.' During the same time period, traditionalists have sought to block gay power—yet now say that 'homosexuals' are political powerhouses."[15]

The more effective gay rights advocates are in the political arena, the less effective they are in the legal one. Each minor political victory sets them further back in their effort to reach the ultimate constitutional prize, suspect classification status. The

Court's victimhood-centric approach to equal protection ensures that gay people have an incentive to portray themselves as victims no matter how many political victories they achieve. It gives them an incentive to pursue the big win of victimhood instead of the slow win of politics. They must always be victims.

Carolene Products footnote 4 also created a world where gay people would have more legal protection if they argued in court that being gay was an immutable characteristic that they could never change—that they'd been born that way.

As Douglas Murray points out in *The Madness of Crowds*, to this day science is undecided on the question of whether homosexuality stems more from nature or nurture. Nevertheless, he writes,

> The single factor that has most clearly helped to change public opinion about homosexuality in the West has been the decision that homosexuality is in fact a "hardware" rather than a "software" issue. Some people—mainly religious conservatives—continue to try to smuggle in their contrary view on this matter. For instance some of them still like to describe homosexuality as a "lifestyle choice"—a phrase insinuating that homosexuals have chosen their own programming.
>
> Countries and times in which this attitude predominates tend to coincide with periods of repressive laws against homosexual activity. And so there is an understandable push to reject the "lifestyle choice" claim and encourage the recognition that homosexuality is a hardware matter or, as Lady Gaga would put it, a matter of being "Born this way."[16]

When the Court's equal protection jurisprudence evolved to grant groups more judicial protection if they argued their identity was immutable, it put two thumbs on the scales in favor of the "born this way" view of homosexuality. Murray observes that, conflicting scientific evidence notwithstanding, the narrative of immutable gayness became so powerful that it quickly became a sign of bigotry not to accept it.

Ironically, now that the gay rights movement has rode the wave of immutability to great victories, progressive society is contemplating a new dogma: sexuality is fluid. We occupy a strange moment where social norms still demand we think gayness is innate, but also demand we think sexual orientation is fluid. Speaking on the issue is therefore like navigating Scylla and Charybdis; best to wait ten years until the trends settle before opining.

In the introduction, I observed that Americans often fight each other by attempting to use language to control thought. Law controls both language and thought. In my last book, for instance, I showed how our nation's obsession with diversity stems from a piece of dicta in *Regents of the University of California v. Bakke*, a plurality opinion on affirmative action.[17] As you can see, those bits of nonbinding judicial commentary in Fourteenth Amendment equal protection jurisprudence tend to wield outsized cultural influence: you can trace a direct line between *Carolene Products* footnote 4 and the modern insistence that homosexuality is innate. The Supreme Court writes a footnote in 1938 in a case about milk, and seventy years later Lady Gaga is telling you gay people are born that way.

All of this maneuvering has been done to get the Court to declare that gay people meet its victimhood criteria. And the funny thing? If gay people *do* succeed in getting sexual orientation declared a new suspect classification, a history of discrimination against gay people, their political powerlessness, and the immutability of gayness will ultimately justify making laws about *straight people* receive strict scrutiny too. Under the old regime, gay people would've been a suspect class, and only they would receive special protection; under the new regime, sexual orientation would become a suspect classification, and straight people would receive special protection too.

The moves and countermoves in the constitutional war for victim status have led equal protection law to a strange place. It is a hodgepodge of rules reflecting little more than the efforts of each identity group to seize power by claiming victimhood. In the Oppression Olympics, ironically, might makes right.

Equal protection law's three-tiers-of-scrutiny approach is famously bad.[18] Groups have to compete with each other to win scarce victim status, it's not clear how many *Carolene Products* criteria they have to meet or what the criteria mean, past discrimination matters but present discrimination doesn't, and if a minority group somehow succeeds in proving victim status, the corresponding majority then gets the same protections.

Fighting discrimination doesn't have to be a competition for victim status. Legal scholar Susannah W. Pollvogt has outlined a theory by which equal protection law could focus not on identifying special victim groups but on making sure individuals don't have their merit burdened by being reduced to mere members of groups they belong to. She begins with this observation:

> [I]s it the nature of the group being discriminated against that makes the discrimination [wrong], or the nature of the discrimination itself?

By comparing social groups to one another and sorting them into suspect, quasi-suspect, and non-suspect classes, the Court itself engages in discriminatory, hierarchical ordering of these social groups with respect to one another. Worse yet, this ordering is virtually permanent. Rather than analyzing the relevance of a particular trait in the context of a specific discriminatory action, the Court declares certain classifications suspect for all time and in all circumstances.

And although this designation is based on history, it then becomes permanent and ahistorical, applied with symmetry to subordinated and non-subordinated groups, and unlikely to be subject to reexamination.[19]

Pollvogt explores a variety of interesting cases in equal protection jurisprudence to divine a new theory. Some of the most informative ones are those very rare cases when the Court has denied a group suspect class status, but still struck down laws burdening them as discriminatory. In *City of Cleburne v. Cleburne Living Center, Inc.*, for instance, the Court ruled that people with cognitive disabilities weren't a suspect class, but still struck down a regulation denying a company the right to build a group home for them.[20] Although rational basis review is virtually always a rubber stamp, the Court found it so obvious that the city simply didn't want cognitively impaired people to live near nonimpaired ones that it struck the law down. The trait of cognitive disability had nothing to do with the government's interest in regulating housing, so the only plausible explanation for the law was prejudice. The impaired individuals were being denied housing based on disdain for their group. They weren't given the chance to be good neighbors.

This is the true heart of the equal protection clause, Pollvogt argues, not all that stuff about finding special victim groups and arranging them in a hierarchy. When the government burdens individuals on the basis of their membership in some group, the question is simply whether the nature of that group is relevant to the purpose the government is trying to achieve. In *Brown v. Board of Education*, for instance, there was simply no connection between race and public education, so the only plausible explanation for why a law would put black people in different schools is that the lawmakers didn't like black people. A black person with many identities beyond their race would be sent to a school on the basis of their blackness, even though blackness has nothing to do with school. Pollvogt sums up her theory this way:

> Thus, the political theory underlying much of the Court's post–*Carolene Products* jurisprudence actually focuses more on the individual than on the group. Specifically, it seeks to preserve (1) an ethos of self-determination based on individual merit and, in connection with this, (2) a modicum of social mobility in which individuals can express that merit.[21]

When a law targets a group for unfavorable treatment, Pollvogt says, instead of asking whether that group has special protected-victim status, equal protection law should simply require the government to prove that there's a connection between the trait that defines the group and the interest the government's trying to achieve. Otherwise, it's interfering with individuals' self-determination on the basis of their membership in some group with no proof that belonging to that group is relevant to anything.

That's just prejudice. Instead of forcing everyone to demean themselves by playing the Oppression Olympics, we can refocus equal protection law on ensuring individuals don't have their merit burdened by arbitrarily being reduced to irrelevant group identities.

Modern Victimhood

The evolution of Fourteenth Amendment jurisprudence saw America wage an endless battle over how to redefine itself after the Civil War, and its choices were often very poor. But the constitutional origin story of our present identity is not just a tale about how the law incentivized us to present ourselves as victims instead of citizens; it is simultaneously a tale about how judges gave themselves more and more power to decide who counted as a victim.

And in doing so, the Court gradually gave itself near total power over the most important questions about American identity. This was fine with liberals when it used that power to create a right to abortion and protect gay rights, just as substantive due process was fine with conservatives when the Court struck down economic regulations for decades during the Lochner era. But now we once again have a strongly conservative Court wielding the power to decide who is oppressed.

This is the lesson about law I learned from Antonin Scalia: the tools you create to fight oppression will one day be used by your enemies to oppress people. Both sides need to remember that when building their tools. The equal protection doctrine liberals built up to protect their favored minorities was adapted by conservatives to protect majorities. The due process doctrine conservatives built to fight progressive labor laws was used by liberals to allow abortions.

Now it will fight progressive laws once more, unless conservatives abandon substantive due process and resurrect the privileges and immunities clause, which they ought to do but probably won't. Just as FDR was driven to threaten court packing to respond to the Lochner Court, we see liberals talking themselves into packing the Court more and more with each passing day.[22]

White liberals, you see, suffer from their own victimhood complex today. Their oppressor is not any particular race, gender, or class, but they do have a hated overseer. Their abuser is the Constitution itself—the power of a Supreme Court that disagrees with them, the ability of the president to nominate members of that court, the ability of the Senate to confirm them, and looming behind it all, the Great Compromise that gave small states disproportionate representation in the Senate and therefore disproportionate votes in the Electoral College.

Liberals have increasingly taken to arguing that there is something presumptively wrong about presidential, congressional, and judicial power not reflecting the will of the popular vote. But, of course, this is only wrong if you begin with the premise that our national identity ought to be determined by popular vote, which is precisely what the constitutional compromises between large states and small ones were meant to deny. The increasing sense of grievance among white liberals, then, really reflects a sense that the Constitution's form of republican government has trapped them in a bargain they are unwilling to accept.

It is a great irony that while modern America's victim complex began as a tale of conservative white victimhood after the Civil War, it has evolved through the constitutional war into an ongoing story about liberal white victimhood. Just as the South seceded from the Union when the Constitution began to threaten its perceived interests and it couldn't muster the electoral votes to resist, we face the specter of blue states doing the same today. Imagine we had another Lochner era, forty years of a conservative Court using substantive due process to decree who is the victim and who is the oppressor; imagine it applying equal protection to decide which groups have faced historical discrimination and which traits are immutable; imagine more Republicans win the presidency while the population of coastal states grows quicker than their electoral power.

We are left with a constitutional impasse. Can a nation survive under these conditions, where small states would never give up the concessions that were necessary to induce them to join the Union while modern large states would never agree to make those concessions? Do states have a right to secede if they grow unhappy with the Constitution? Why should we expect the Union to remain whole?

The best answer I have sometimes seems naïve: the Union can only stay intact this time, and perhaps should only stay intact, if Americans come to see themselves as fellow citizens rather than each other's victims. Otherwise we will continue to be locked in endless cultural and legal warfare, like the Hatfields and the McCoys, always avenging the last generation's grievances, fighting to control the future but never looking forward to it. How could we? We've already had one civil war, and we're still fighting it. The past is not past.

Chapter Four

RACE THEORY

Two Stories

A few years ago I visited my aunt's house for a family reunion. She still lived in the heart of the Rust Belt, in the same community where I'd spent so much time that it was practically my second home.

As my uncle drove me to his home from the airport, there was only one change that I noticed. Their former neighbors were no longer there. As we arrived, my uncle made an offhand comment that he was annoyed that their new neighbor repeatedly covered their driveway in grass whenever he mowed the lawn—something that could've easily been avoided if he'd simply mowed in the opposite direction. It was frustrating for my uncle since several members of my visiting family were allergic to pollen and it was high springtime.

The next morning, I saw the new neighbor mowing his lawn. There was indeed a mess of grass spilling onto the driveway. I walked out and waved, inviting him over for a chat. I had no idea how much I'd come to regret that.

I asked him if he lived next door, a question that seemed to annoy him, and in retrospect a piece of small talk I wish I'd skipped. I introduced myself, and after a couple more botched attempts at small talk asked him if he could mow his lawn in a way that didn't jettison the cut grass onto my aunt's driveway. He stuck his hand into my face, as if to signal an end to the conversation. When I asked him why he couldn't just mow so the clippings went on his lawn, he turned his back on me and started walking back to his yard, visibly upset.

That's when I made my big mistake. I said, "Look, I'd prefer to resolve this in a friendly way, but if we need to get a third party involved, then we can do that." I didn't have a particular solution in mind—asking another neighbor to weigh in on lawn-mowing etiquette, maybe.

The man charged at me, gesturing wildly and spewing curses. He came right up to my face, screaming so loud that my entire family came outside. Race played a strange part in his profane monologue. He shouted several times that my skin was three shades darker than his and I shouldn't forget that; he kept calling Indians "you people" and saying we were the racist ones. And he yelled that if I said another word, he would go get his gun to "come back and end this motherfucker."

I backed away, shocked and fearing for my life. My aunt had broken down in tears. The man finally declared that her presence was the only reason there wasn't blood on the ground. Then he stalked away, leaving everyone in my family victimized—but feeling oddly victimized in his own right, it seemed, as well.

That experience changed me in many ways. I've thought about it many times. I felt frustrated and powerless, concerned for the safety of my aunt and uncle who still live there, but too intimidated to report the incident to the police. At first I thought maybe I'd been the victim of racism; it seemed like a natural inference. But as I told other people about what had happened, I was surprised to find that some of them thought I'd been the racist one.

You see, this time I left out one detail: the guy was black. Apparently three shades lighter than me, in his opinion. But he was black, and I was not.

That detail changes everything for some people. I told the story to you the way I experienced it, and I hadn't thought his race was an important element at the time. But my well-educated liberal friends told me there was a different narrative I'd been missing, one that revolved around his race and mine.

A black guy was out peacefully mowing his lawn. Maybe he was having a bad day, or a bad lifetime. Some Indian guy he'd never seen before came over and demanded he mow his lawn differently. Then when he refused and went back to his business, the other guy threatened to call the cops on him. The black guy understandably blew up when a nonblack stranger threatened to sic a racist police force on him, endangering his life over a gardening dispute. So the black guy met the threat of violence with his own threat of equal violence.

I didn't recognize that story at all, and I was the one who'd been there. Yet, after I thought about it, I realized that my friends were at least right about the other guy's perspective. I'd been seeing him as a guy mowing his lawn, not a black guy mowing his lawn. I had no idea how race entered into things when he started yelling about how my skin was so much darker than his. I had no idea he might interpret my vague talk about bringing in a third party as a threat to call the police—I was thinking more of the homeowner's association. And I definitely had no idea he might've thought I was threatening him with police violence over how he mowed his lawn.

But that story revolving around me using some superior position in a racial hierarchy to threaten him with police brutality is the only thing that makes sense of his overreaction. Realizing that made me think that these kinds of misunderstandings must happen all across the nation, even if they don't usually go so far. My aunt's neighbor—her black neighbor—saw the world through the lens of a particular narrative of black victimization that I was hardly aware of, and he thought I was attempting to use that narrative against him as a casual display of power.

I came to blame the victimhood narrative that made us talk past each other more than I blamed him. I wish I could do that day differently, and he probably does too. I should've taken no for an answer; he shouldn't have threatened to hurt me over failing to. Neither of us covered ourselves in glory, but the racial lens he was seeing the world through didn't even give us a chance to get things right. We couldn't disagree with each other over the simplest of things without being brought to the brink of violence. That's America, these days.

I wanted to understand where the racial narrative that almost got me killed over a lawn came from. I wanted to know whether there was any truth to it, and whether the nation had any path forward to a world where these misunderstandings don't happen. That's what this chapter is about.

Critical Race Theory

It turns out the idea that any police interaction with a black person puts their life in mortal danger stems from a particular school of

Critical Race Theory. CRT is a term that's often used these days, but seldom defined. Many conservatives fear that some version of it is being taught to their children in schools, leading to a wave of bills meant to prevent that: seven states have banned teaching CRT, and more than a dozen have bans pending in their legislatures.[1] For their part, most liberals say fears over CRT in school are just— my favorite argument—a conservative talking point. They add that these bans are really just thinly veiled attempts to prevent schools from teaching America's history of racial discrimination.

Given the extent of these disagreements and the stakes, it's important to define terms, so I want to get clear on what CRT is and the varieties it comes in. What all forms of CRT have in common is that they divide the world into oppressors and their victims; they simply disagree on the mechanisms of oppression.

Critical theory traces its origins to the Frankfurt school, an early 1900s philosophical movement that sought to apply Karl Marx's theories to social systems instead of economic ones. While Marx understood post–Industrial Revolution history as a class struggle, many of his intellectual descendants understood it as a racial one. When you hear conservatives call CRT "cultural Marxism," they're referring to this intellectual lineage. Today, all that really unites socialists and critical race theorists is broad agreement that the world should be understood primarily in terms of power structures, with dominant groups always seeking to construct the economic and legal rules of society to maintain their privileged position.

This way of thinking is actually a very old one, though it's gained new prominence in recent years. At the beginning of Plato's *Republic*, when Socrates first begins to muse on the nature of justice, he's immediately met with a challenge from the sophist

Thrasymachus, who claims that there's no point in wondering what justice is or what it calls for: justice is just the rule of the stronger.[2] Society's principles about right and wrong, claims Thrasymachus, are nothing more than rules that the strong impose on the weak to protect their wealth and social status. The strong then build up grand institutions like religion, law, and ethics to convince the weak that they ought to accept the status quo. In other words, from the first moment humans started thinking about justice, people argued that it was just a sucker's game meant to create willing victims.

Two and a half millennia later, modern critical theorists have come full circle and concluded that Thrasymachus was right: what we call justice is nothing more than the rules the privileged have imposed on the oppressed. The rules are then dressed up with lofty language to get the victims to embrace them.

At first, the modern version of the ancient argument went by the name "critical legal studies." In the 1970s, a coalition of leftist scholars argued that law was really just politics in disguise, a way for the powerful to control the weak. Critical legal studies concerned itself with many disempowered groups: the poor, the working class, the disabled, racial minorities, women, sexual minorities. But after only a decade, critical theorists began to focus their attention on race and gender. Discussion of class dropped by the wayside, and modern feminism and critical race theory were born. The Marxists splintered off and went their own way, abandoned by the academy. This, by the way, is an important distinction most conservatives miss in their effort to brand any idea they dislike Marxism: they have no idea how much Marxists resent identity politics for ignoring class issues in favor of race and gender. Wokeness isn't Marxism; it's the movement that replaced it.

Critical race theory sprang up in legal academia when American law professors interpreted US law as a subtle system of racial control meant to replace the overt oppression of slavery and the Jim Crow era. After being introduced by scholars like Derrick Bell and Kimberlé Crenshaw, CRT really took off in academia in the 1990s. Interestingly, while critical legal studies had been broadly skeptical of all law, its successor CRT had to grapple with the fact that some doctrines, like equal protection law, had been a powerful force for racial civil rights. To address this phenomenon, Bell advocated an idea called "interest convergence" theory, arguing that legal victories like *Brown v. Board of Education* only came about when protecting racial minorities happened to serve the interests of white people.[3]

Even in the 1990s, CRT was only a niche academic theory, fashionable mostly in the halls of Ivy League law schools. All that changed in May 2020, when police officer Derek Chauvin killed George Floyd. In the height of the pandemic lockdown, the murder gave millions a cause to rally behind and a public-health-approved reason to take to the streets. Floyd became far more than the victim of murder—he was turned into a *martyr*, one who becomes a victim to further a worthy cause. To turn victim to martyr, politicians portrayed Floyd as a Christlike figure who'd sacrificed himself for racial justice,[4] although his death was involuntary and his personal history checkered.[5] As activists turned Floyd's murder into a potent symbol, public interest in CRT skyrocketed. The academic theory promised a path to ending injustices like police brutality.

This is how modern CRT's most well-known practitioners suddenly rose to fame. In the month after Floyd's death, sales of Robin DiAngelo's *White Fragility* and Ibram X. Kendi's *How to Be an Antiracist* spiked several thousand percent.[6] Overnight, a once-niche academic theory became the prevailing wisdom. DiAngelo popularized the idealist school of CRT, focusing on changing *beliefs* about race, while Kendi popularized the competing materialist school, emphasizing eliminating disparities in racial *outcomes*.[7]

DiAngelo and her disciples, often found in corporate boardrooms and universities, are the ones who carefully monitor language and thought—by eliminating biased words, they hope we can eliminate biased beliefs. This branch of modern CRT implores people to constantly check their privilege and tells them they're obligated to check the privilege of others. It is a religious approach that treats racism as a sin that all people must recognize in themselves so they can be cleansed. DiAngelo's main solutions to racism essentially involve confessing sin, encouraging others to do so, and self-flagellating in public.

In contrast, Kendi focuses almost entirely on eliminating racist *outcomes* instead of racist thoughts. According to him, any practice that leads to unequal racial material outcomes is racist by definition: "A racist policy is any measure that produces or sustains racial inequity between racial groups. An antiracist policy is any measure that produces or sustains racial equity between racial groups . . .There is no such thing as a nonracist or race-neutral policy." The remedy to policies leading to unequal racial outcomes, says Kendi, is countervailing racial discrimination: "Someone reproducing inequity through permanently assisting an overrepresented racial group into wealth and power is entirely different than someone challenging that inequity by temporarily assisting an underrepresented racial group into relative wealth and power until equity is reached. The only remedy to racist discrimination is antiracist discrimination."[8]

A terrifyingly simple view to some; appealingly so to others. DiAngelo holds that the system the strong use to control the weak is linguistic; Kendi says it's political. Both their antiracist theories are watered-down versions of CRT meant to increase the ease of public transmission. Liberal pundits love to mock concerned parents as country bumpkins who don't understand that CRT is only taught in law schools, but this is only a semantic shell game. You don't have to get a law degree to know that the divisive way race is taught to children has something to do with academic theories about race. The popular versions are crude, but they're straightforwardly derived from academic CRT.

There are more sophisticated, rigorous versions of CRT, particularly in the materialist school that Kendi draws from. One of these is responsible for the belief that the criminal justice system is biased against black people from top to bottom. This narrative of black victimhood is called "the New Jim Crow." It's the one my aunt's neighbor must've been taking as gospel.

The work that popularized this narrative, appropriately enough, is called *The New Jim Crow*, and was written by Michelle Alexander. The book was highly influential when it came out in 2010; it brought an existing strand of CRT to public attention. Though more popular among journalists and academics than suburban book clubs, sales still rose from five thousand to sixty thousand in the month after George Floyd's murder. Like Kendi, Alexander argues that racist policies create unequal material outcomes for black people, but while Kendi stipulates that all policies leading to unequal outcomes are automatically racist, Alexander presents a narrative of intentional racism in the US criminal justice system, grounding it in history and empirical data.

The New Jim Crow story of black victimization begins at the same place the victimhood narratives from the last chapter did: the Reconstruction era. In the last chapter, I gave you my story of how the Oppression Olympics developed out of this period. Now I'll tell you the other side of the story, the narrative critical race theorists offer to explain how modern oppression came about.

The Reconstruction Amendments tried to fix the flaws in the Constitution, but it quickly became clear they could be circumvented. After the *Slaughterhouse Cases* rendered the privileges and immunities clause toothless, former Confederate states created literacy tests and poll taxes to disenfranchise former slaves and their descendants for more than a century. The Fifteenth Amendment said that states couldn't deprive anyone of the right to vote over their race or status as a former slave, but that left plenty of room to deny it for other reasons.[9] These pretexts ended up inadvertently disenfranchising poor and illiterate white people too, so a half-dozen states created "grandfather clauses" in the 1890s, allowing men to vote if their ancestors had been able to.[10] The biggest remaining obstacle to efforts to recreate the Antebellum South was the Fourteenth Amendment's guarantee of equal protection of the law. For this, former Confederate states turned to Jim Crow laws, on the theory that statutes could make black and white people separate but equal.[11]

Almost sixty years later, Thurgood Marshall struck a major blow against Jim Crow laws when he successfully won a unanimous Supreme Court opinion declaring separate but equal inherently unequal in *Brown v. Board of Education*.[12] But the Court said little about when and how states ought to enforce desegregation; that was the main task of the civil rights movement. Led by Martin Luther King Jr. and his method of nonviolent resistance, the civil rights movement brought down the Jim Crow era for good over the next decade and a half, culminating in the Civil Rights Acts of 1964 and 1968 and the Voting Rights Act of 1965.

All of that is accepted history, but here's where CRT comes in: while for many decades the prevailing wisdom was that equality under the law had finally been achieved with the civil rights movement, some critical race theorists began to argue that just as Jim Crow laws had been a backlash to the Reconstruction Amendments, there was a subtle but powerful legal resistance to the civil rights acts of the 1960s. Legal scholars like Michelle Alexander argued that immediately after the civil rights acts, conservative politicians like Barry Goldwater[13] and Richard Nixon[14] attempted to appeal to racist white people by oppressing black people under the guise of tough-on-crime laws, especially the war on drugs that began in earnest under Ronald Reagan.

Alexander assembles detailed empirical evidence to show that the war on drugs harms black people more than white ones. In particular, she focuses on the harms of mass incarceration, arguing that the American criminal justice system disproportionately labels black men criminals, which then creates a racial undercaste that faces discrimination in arenas such as housing, employment, voting, welfare programs, and education. Mass incarceration, she says, creates "a stunningly comprehensive and well-disguised system of racialized social control that functions in a manner strikingly similar to Jim Crow."[15] While Americans of all races consume illegal drugs at similar rates, black people are arrested for it far more often. Alexander points out that in some states, black men are imprisoned on drug charges twenty to fifty times as often as white men.[16] Other sources reach similar conclusions, although less extreme: one DOJ report examining some of the same data sets Alexander uses found that black people constitute 13 percent of illicit drug users but 36 percent of drug-possession arrests, with differences in frequency of use, type of drug, and place of use only accounting for 10 percentage points of the gap.[17]

This is where police abuse against black people enters the New Jim Crow narrative: "The absence of significant constraints on the exercise of police discretion is a key feature of the drug war's design."[18] Alexander argues that the war on drugs caused the Supreme Court to erode the Fourth Amendment's protections against unreasonable searches and seizures until police were able to stop and interrogate black people with few restrictions, often stopping them on the pretext of minor traffic violations and intimidating them into granting consent.[19] To encourage police departments to wage the war on drugs, she says, the federal government shoveled tons of cash and military equipment their way, often tying funding and equipment to high drug arrest rates.[20] As another powerful financial incentive, civil asset forfeiture laws allowed police departments to keep most of the cash and assets they seized in raids of suspected criminals, in most cases without even charging anyone with a crime.[21]

In the decade since *The New Jim Crow* was released, the narrative of US police being at war with black people has only grown stronger as a series of cases of police violence have received intense media scrutiny. Michael Brown, Eric Garner, Tamir Rice, Freddie Gray, Sandra Bland, Breonna Taylor, and George Floyd were among those who died at the hands of police officers. In some cases, as with Floyd, the killings were later found to be murder; in others, like Brown, the officers' use of force was deemed justified. But the facts of individual cases hardly mattered, set against the backdrop of the story that a racist police force was the latest tool of oppression in a centuries-old system of white supremacy.

In fact, when an officer kills a black suspect, no matter what the facts of the case are, the default presumption these days is that the officer is guilty until proven innocent, especially if they're white—and then if the criminal justice system does find them innocent, that's simply taken as evidence that the system itself is racist. This new dogma was displayed vividly in the case of Ma'Khia Bryant, a sixteen-year-old black girl who was fatally shot by a white police officer moments before she could stab another black girl. Coming right on the heels of the conviction of Derek Chauvin for Floyd's murder, the narrative of police brutality was at its strongest: LeBron James immediately posted a picture of the officer who'd shot her with the caption "YOU'RE NEXT #ACCOUNTABILITY."[22] White House press secretary Jen Psaki told press that President Biden had been briefed and the shooting underscored the need to address systemic racism in policing.[23]

White House officials, media, and celebrities didn't feel any need to wait for facts to emerge; the now-entrenched narrative that police violence is the newest form of systemic racism told them all they needed to know. It's become part of the fabric of America, something everyone is expected to know, accept, and apply to every police interaction with black people. That's how we got today's "defund the police" movement. It's probably also how my aunt's neighbor thought I was threatening his life when I spoke vaguely about having a third party help us resolve our lawn-mowing dispute; it's why he threatened mine.

Black Victimhood

The New Jim Crow narrative is worth taking seriously. It's certainly a more rigorous version of CRT than the trendy antiracist theories that are taking the academic and corporate world by storm. DiAngelo and Kendi's theories are characterized by how they define opposition to them as racist. To DiAngelo, when a white person disagrees with her claims about systemic racism, that's just proof of their white fragility, and when a nonwhite one does, that's proof that they're white-adjacent. To Kendi, any policy that permits unequal racial outcomes is by definition racist, so any critic of his antiracist solutions is also necessarily racist; an anti-antiracist must be racist, the argument goes. It is a vast improvement that theories like the New Jim Crow rely on historical and empirical claims and are falsifiable through data.

But it's still designed to be a narrative of black victimhood, and that exposes it to certain weaknesses. To make a neat analogy between the criminal justice system and Jim Crow laws, New Jim Crow theorists have to emphasize whatever similarities they can find and deemphasize differences. Because of its rhetorical success, the metaphor is expanding beyond criminal justice and becoming ever looser; President Biden often casually labels Republican-led voting reform "Jim Crow 2.0."[24] Democrats have taken to calling the filibuster part of the New Jim Crow too. While the Jim Crow analogy makes black victimhood narratives powerful and easy to understand, it always obscures relevant facts.

The biggest failing of the approach is that the Jim Crow analogy requires writers like Alexander to argue that the criminal justice system not only disproportionately harms black people, but that it's intentionally designed to do so. This is the provocative claim that really animated public interest in the cause, but that same incendiary nature is also divisive. There are two main flaws with the idea that the war on drugs and mass incarceration were created by white backlash to the civil rights movement: first, violent crime skyrocketed in the years before tough-on-crime laws, and second, black people were often the ones pushing for them.

Legal scholar James Forman Jr. offers one of the most compelling critiques of the New Jim Crow narrative in general, and of Alexander's account of it in particular.[25] He writes,

> But in emphasizing mass incarceration's racial roots, the New Jim Crow writers overlook other critical factors. The most important of these is that crime shot up dramatically just before the beginning of the prison boom. Reported street crime quadrupled in the twelve years from 1959 to 1971. Homicide rates doubled between 1963 and 1974, and robbery rates tripled. Proponents of the Jim Crow analogy tend to ignore or minimize the role that crime and violence played in creating such a receptive audience for Goldwater's and Nixon's appeals.[26]

Alexander mentions these increases in reported crime rates, but she glosses over them, saying there was controversy over their accuracy and calling them "fairly significant" instead of conveying their full scope.[27] Interestingly, in later editions of *The New Jim Crow*, the phrase is changed to "fairly dramatic," perhaps in response to Forman's criticism.[28] He goes on to observe that the white backlash narrative requires New Jim Crow theorists to ignore, understate, and explain away strong black support for tough-on-crime laws:

> In *The Politics of Imprisonment*, Vanessa Barker describes how, in the late 1960s, black activists in Harlem fought for what would become the notorious Rockefeller drug laws, some of the harshest in the nation. Harlem residents were outraged over rising crime (including drug crime) in their neighborhoods and demanded increased police presence and stricter penalties. The NAACP Citizens' Mobilization Against Crime demanded "lengthening minimum prison terms for muggers, pushers, [and first] degree murderers."[29]

Black support for being tough on crime isn't just a thing of the past; it's still present today. It is a bitter irony that the white liberals loudly pushing the "defund the police" movement on the basis of the New Jim Crow victimhood narrative are drowning out black communities who want to keep police present constant or even increase it.

In Minneapolis, for instance, after Floyd's death, black residents were the driving force defeating a proposal to replace the police department with a public safety agency; in one poll, 75 percent of black residents opposed cutting the size of the police force while only 51 percent of white ones did.[30] A national poll found that 81 percent of black people wanted police to spend the same amount of time in their communities or more—blacks and Hispanics had the highest support of all demographics for *increasing* the police presence in their communities. This is a recurring pattern: in 2015, shortly after the Ferguson protests, 38 percent of black people wanted more police in their communities, while only 18 percent of non-Hispanic whites did.[31]

This consistent pattern reveals one of the biggest dangers of black victimhood narratives like the New Jim Crow: as the victimhood narrative becomes common wisdom, it replaces the voices of black people themselves. Eventually, well-educated white people end up making policy decisions on behalf of black ones, so confident in what they want that they see no need to listen to them. Even worse, on the occasions when black people do speak out against the victimhood narrative, politicians, media, and activists will be tempted to say that they don't really know what they want, that their desires have been corrupted by white supremacy. This is how dark-skinned people who resist progressive views on criminal justice end up getting called Uncle Toms.

The New Jim Crow narrative of systemic racism infecting the criminal justice system also obscures relevant facts by implying that mass incarceration, rather than the root causes of it, is the biggest problem facing black communities. Because civil rights activists are constrained by their analogy, they frame mass incarceration through the lens of drug use, where they can make the clearest statistical case that black people are treated unfairly because all races use illegal drugs at the same rate while black people are arrested more for it. But violent crime is another major cause of imprisonment, and the evidence suggests that black people commit violent crimes at higher rates than other races. As Forman notes, "the African American arrest rate for murder is seven to eight times higher than the white arrest rate; the black arrest rate for robbery is ten times higher than the white arrest rate. Murder and robbery are the two offenses for which the arrest data are considered most reliable as an indicator of offending."[32] Since people of all races commit crimes most often against members of their own race,[33] the victims of these disproportionately high violent crime rates are overwhelmingly black.

Black people are therefore harmed twice by the New Jim Crow victimhood narrative's focus on drugs instead of violent crime. First, that focus leads activists to ineffectively try to reduce mass incarceration through addressing drug offenses instead of violent ones. Second, since the only reasonable way to reduce incarceration for violent crimes is to reduce the crimes themselves, the victimhood narrative prevents society from helping black people by fighting violent crime. Instead of doing the hard work of addressing the educational, economic, and cultural causes of violent crime, the Jim Crow analogy offers the false hope that we can reduce mass incarceration simply by remedying inequitable drug laws.

In fact, New Jim Crow theorists have already succeeded in plucking the low-hanging fruit of reducing incarceration by addressing imprisonment over drug offenses. In his 2017 book *Locked In: The True Causes of Mass Incarceration*, criminal justice expert John Pfaff points out that most US jurisdictions have already slightly reduced incarceration rates by modifying sentencing laws. Pfaff criticizes the New Jim Crow's focus, calling it "the Standard Story," and argues that further decreases in incarceration will have to come from addressing violent crime.[34] Notably, a couple years after Pfaff wrote, President Trump signed the First Step Act into law, which reduced federal prison sentences for nonviolent crimes in a variety of ways.[35]

Although addressing the root causes of violent crime is a complex task, there is still low-hanging fruit to be picked here: shift money from prisons to policing. Pfaff argues that "Hiring a police officer is probably about as expensive as hiring a prison guard, for example, but investing in police has a much bigger deterrent effect and avoids all the capital expenditures of prisons." He points to estimates that money spent on policing is at least 20 percent more effective than money spent on prisons. So there's one easy starting point to reducing both incarceration and crime: fund more police instead of more prisons.[36]

The real solutions to the violent crime that disproportionately harms black communities, though, have to be cultural. Ensuring equal access to education and economic opportunity will go a long way, and these are race-neutral policies we ought to be pursuing anyway to create a fair merit-based society; I discuss how to do this later in the book.[37] But in my opinion, the single biggest cultural cause of black Americans' problems is our country's lack of emphasis on stable families.

This is the account given by Adam B. Coleman in *Black Victim to Black Victor: Identifying the Ideologies, Behavioral Patterns, and Cultural Norms That Encourage a Victimhood Complex.*[38] Coleman argues that narratives like the New Jim Crow and Kendi's and DiAngelo's theories make black people see themselves as victims. This sense of victimhood then makes them attribute their hardships entirely to others, not recognizing that they have the capacity to improve their own lives.

Writing from personal experience, Coleman begins his critique by saying that the root of the problem comes down to absent fathers. He points out that a whopping 70 percent of black households have a single parent, usually a mother.[39] In contrast, only 38 percent of white households are single parent, and 20 percent of Asian ones.[40] Coleman then traces the absence of black fathers to a host of evils for their children. He writes about how this abandonment creates lost boys and lost girls who grow up feeling unwanted and fill that need for approval with the cheap substitutes of sex and gang violence. When they grow up, "These lost men find lost women and create children who will subsequently struggle with finding acceptance in the world."[41] In other words, when black fathers abandon their children (as Richard Williams allegedly abandoned his first family) that creates a vicious cycle of abandonment that perpetuates itself.

No doubt critics would object that Coleman is wrong to place the lion's share of the blame at the feet of black fathers instead of inquiring into the forces that make black men leave their children in disproportionate numbers. We face a chicken-and-egg question: did mass incarceration cause black men to leave their children behind, or did paternal abandonment create the violent conditions that caused mass incarceration? Coleman takes the latter view, arguing that the absence of a paternal authority figure causes young black men to lack respect for the authority of law.[42] He also argues that a single mother simply doesn't have the time to both support and discipline her children.[43] While boys perpetuate the cycle of single-parent families by embracing crime, he claims, girls do so through promiscuity—Coleman cites evidence that girls whose fathers left them before the age of five are seven to eight times more likely to become pregnant as adolescents, while those abandoned by their fathers between six and thirteen are two to three times likelier than average to become pregnant.[44]

The causes of America's high number of single-mother black families are complex, multifaceted, and interlinked, and Coleman grounds his argument more in personal experience than rigorous statistical evidence. It may be that the chicken and egg both played important causal roles in the high level of violent crimes committed by black people, regardless of which came first. But I do agree with Coleman's diagnosis that the root cultural cause of the crime problem is the lack of a stable family structure among black Americans. Regardless of how the cycle of absent fathers started, the important thing is that it be resisted, not encouraged. The official Black Lives Matter website, for instance, originally had a statement saying the movement stood for "disrupt[ing] the Western-prescribed nuclear family structure requirement by supporting each other as extended families and 'villages' that collectively care for one another, especially our children, to the degree that mothers, parents, and children are comfortable."[45]

Knowing the cause of black violent crime is important, because you need an accurate diagnosis to get an effective policy treatment. Modern America's victimhood-narrative mindset suggests that we ought to embark on an endless debate about which came first, mass incarceration of black men or their abandonment of their children. That's because the most crucial question from the perspective of a victimhood narrative is who to blame—do we blame black fathers or white cops? Or maybe white voters? In the eyes of a tale of victimhood, carving up causal origins and divvying up the right share of blame is the most important task, because it establishes who is the victim and who is the villain, which in turn establishes who bears the burden of remedying the plight of black Americans.

But the divisive, impossibly difficult question of deciding who's to blame and how much only seems like the crucial task if you view the world through the lens of victimhood. There are other questions we could ask, like "How can I help?" Knowing that absent black fathers cause violent crime, which in turn causes mass incarceration, which in turn leads to unequal material outcomes in many walks of life gives everyone a head start on figuring out how the nation can move forward. We can know that we ought to reject BLM's leap to suggest the nuclear family just simply isn't part of black culture; we can know that we ought to tailor our economic and educational efforts at ensuring equal opportunities to address the harms created by single-parent families.

My family and my aunt's neighbors are haltingly finding a way to move forward without debating who's to blame for our argument. Everyone still has to live together, after all. A couple of years after that guy blew up at me, my aunt got a knock on her door one evening. She answered it and was surprised to see it was the neighbor's wife. She apologized for what he'd done that morning, saying that as they'd gotten to know everyone in the neighborhood, they heard a lot of good things about our family and came to the conclusion that everything must've somehow been a big misunderstanding. It was a big misunderstanding; I wasn't thinking even a fraction of the things he thought I was about the relation between black people and police.

I'm still not sure why it was his wife that did the apologizing. I think the guy himself must've been embarrassed. I'm a bit embarrassed about it all, too; everyone I tell this story to gently tells me never to put it in print. Next time I see my aunt's neighbor—her black neighbor—I'm leaving the subject of his lawn alone. I'll probably just nod at him, he'll nod at me, and we'll take it from there.

Chapter Five

CONSERVATIVE VICTIMHOOD

Sore Losers

It was a dark day for democracy. The loser of the last election refused to concede the race, claimed the election was stolen, raised hundreds of millions of dollars from loyal supporters, and is running for executive office again.

I'm referring, of course, to Stacey Abrams.

Abrams ran as the Democratic candidate for governor of Georgia in 2018. She lost a hard-fought election to her Republican opponent Brian Kemp, who was then Georgia's secretary of state. She lost by about fifty-five thousand votes out of almost four million cast, a margin of 1.4 percent. Abrams immediately rejected the legitimacy of the election.

First she gave a speech announcing that Kemp would become the governor, but making it clear she didn't consider his win legitimate: "This is not a speech of concession, because concession means to acknowledge an action is right, true or proper," she said. "As a woman of conscience and faith, I cannot concede that. But, my assessment is the law currently allows no further viable remedy . . . I don't want to hold public office if I need to scheme my way into the post."[1] She added that "Democracy failed Georgians."

To this day, even as Abrams campaigns for governor again in the 2022 election, she still refuses to concede that she lost the last one. Half a year after the lost election, she gave an interview to the *New York Times* explaining at length why she still wouldn't concede: "It was largely because I could not prove what had happened, but I knew from the calls that we got that something happened. Now, I cannot say that everybody who tried to cast a ballot would've voted for me, but if you look at the totality of the information, it is sufficient to demonstrate that so many people were disenfranchised and disengaged by the very act of the person who won the election that I feel comfortable now saying, 'I won.'"[2]

Abrams's case that the election was stolen from her rests on the claim that Kemp abused his power as secretary of state to suppress votes. Her first argument is that his office delayed approving fifty-three thousand voter registrations, disenfranchising them. Her second is that he also disenfranchised hundreds of thousands of citizens by removing them from the list of registered voters. After looking at the facts, I find both allegations exceedingly weak.[3]

The first charge is especially misleading. Abrams's account, with the help of media, would lead one to believe that the fifty-three thousand pending voters were prevented from voting, but that's not true at all. In Georgia, citizens whose registrations are on hold are still allowed to vote as long as they just show a photo ID. Kemp's office had put their applications on hold to comply with Georgia's "exact match" law passed a year earlier—as the office sorted out minor discrepancies between information on the voter registration and other government records, people were still allowed to vote. In response, critics claimed that the pending voters were disenfranchised because they may have *believed* they were unable to vote.[4] No one alleges Kemp did anything to try to convince pending voters they couldn't vote; I suppose the claim is that he suppressed their votes by not screaming the law from the rooftops.

Abrams's second charge of voter suppression is equally unpersuasive. Along with members of the media, she claimed that Kemp had "purged" more than 1.4 million people from voting rolls since 2012. In actuality, he was simply following a law Georgia and eight other states have removing voters from the rolls after long periods of inactivity, a practice upheld by the Supreme Court. The law Kemp was enforcing was actually passed by Georgia *Democrats* in 1997. The *Atlanta Journal-Constitution* frequently referred to this practice as a purge, but when it tracked down deregistered voters, they simply said they didn't care about voting.[5] Basically, just about anyone who was remotely interested in voting was able to.

The old fight for civil rights involved sit-ins and marches. The new one requires Google searches and photo ID, and apparently that's too much to ask. Here's a test you can apply anytime you hear a Democrat call a policy voter suppression: can this supposed Jim Crow law be defeated by googling "how can I vote?" If so, it's probably not the death of democracy.

What does threaten democracy, though, is for political parties and their candidates to deny the legitimacy of elections. It reminds me of another story.

It was a dark day for democracy. The loser of the last election refused to concede the race, claimed the election was stolen, raised hundreds of millions of dollars from loyal supporters, and is considering running for executive office again.

I'm referring, of course, to Donald Trump.

Conservatives have their own victimhood complexes these days; we are, after all, a nation of victims now. All that differs is whom we see as our oppressors. The worst victimhood narrative that afflicts modern conservatives is their budding belief that any election they lose must have been stolen. Instead of distinguishing ourselves as the party that strives for excellence and rejects the easy path of victimhood narratives, we simply created our own.

I voted for Trump in 2020. I had some policy disagreements with him—for example, I disapproved of his large-scale government spending and his tariff policies—but I voted for him anyway because he refused to apologize for the things that make America great. Like many Americans, I hungered for the unapologetic pursuit of excellence in our nation. To me, that was something worth voting for. Donald Trump was, notwithstanding his shortcomings, the candidate who best embodied American greatness. He was unafraid to stand up for it, and I respected that.

But while Trump promised to lead the nation to recommit itself to the pursuit of greatness, what he delivered in the end was just another tale of grievance, a persecution complex that swallowed much of the Republican party whole.

When my candidate lost the election, I was dissatisfied, but I also felt a sense of peace. The election was done, and it was time to move on. No one likes a sore loser; that's one of the worst victimhood complexes of all. Accepting the outcomes of elections and having a peaceful transition of power is part of what it means to be a constitutional republic: sometimes your team loses, but if you accept the result and prepare for the next election, eventually the scales will tip your way again. We fought, we lost, and I accepted the result.

So I was especially disappointed when I saw President Trump take a page from the Stacey Abrams playbook. His claims were just as weak as Abrams's. She claimed voter suppression, he claimed voter fraud. He filed scores of lawsuits over various claims of fraud, as was his right, but they came nowhere close to changing the outcome in a single state, let alone the several swing states whose results he needed to overturn. In many cases, judges the president himself had nominated ruled against him, a sign of health in our nation's institutions. Of the sixty-two lawsuits he and his supporters filed, he lost all but one, a minor victory in Pennsylvania that affected few votes. A Supreme Court with a strong conservative majority ruled against President Trump twice.[6]

Top election officials in virtually every state, regardless of party, said they'd found no evidence of any significant level of fraud.[7] The Cybersecurity and Infrastructure Security Agency issued a statement saying "The November 3rd election was the most secure in American history...There is no evidence that any voting system deleted or lost votes, changed votes, or was in any way compromised."[8] The president fired the agency's director a few days later.[9] In a call with Georgia's secretary of state, the president implausibly claimed to have won every single state—something unprecedented in the nation's history, and a sign that his claims weren't grounded in fact.[10] Mike Pence, a man I have great respect for, decided it was his constitutional duty to resist the president's attempts to get him to unilaterally overturn the results of the election, even in the face of the January 6 Capitol riot.[11] Our institutions did hold, in the end. But they shouldn't have been tested.

I won't go into the details at length. The fact that all of our governmental institutions so unanimously found no evidence of significant fraud is telling. Furthermore, I've talked to many Republicans at all levels of government, and not one has ever presented convincing evidence that the 2020 election was stolen from President Trump; very few have seriously tried. I don't believe that most Republican politicians actually think the election was stolen. Lately, more of them have started admitting that in public.[12]

I recognize that this is not a typical conservative talking point. I'm committed to following the evidence, not blindly rooting for any one person or party. The pursuit of excellence requires that beliefs be determined strictly by evidence, not loyalty to one group or animosity for another. I'm simply not convinced the election was stolen.

As this book went to press, Dinesh D'Souza released a documentary called *2000 Mules*, using geolocation data to argue that operatives illegally carried ballots from nonprofits to drop boxes.[13] As Ben Shapiro has noted, even if ballots were illegally delivered, that wouldn't make the votes themselves illegal. And I wasn't convinced of the film's central claim.

The organization D'Souza worked with, True the Vote, counted someone as a mule if they stopped near a drop box at least ten times and a nonprofit at least five times in the month before Election Day. How near? According to the Georgia Bureau of Investigation, within one hundred feet. Presumably the hundred feet of wiggle room was meant to account for the inaccuracy of geolocation—but if someone geolocated one hundred feet away from a dropbox could've actually been standing right next to it, by the same token, they could've been two hundred feet away from it. To prove their method wasn't picking up lots of false positives, True the Vote should've applied it to red states and shown that it identified fewer mules there.

D'Souza really needed substantial video evidence to tie it all together. He claims to have surveillance tape showing the same people stuffing multiple drop boxes, but the documentary never shows that. If he releases this footage, I'll find his argument more compelling.

Beyond all the court decisions, statements from election officials, and a general lack of evidence of fraud, what I keep coming back to is this: why do I see Republicans insisting that the presidential election was stolen, yet accepting the legitimacy of the congressional ones? It all happens on the same ballot, and Republicans netted twelve seats in the House of Representatives, setting themselves up to easily claim a decisive majority in 2022.[14] Yet I saw some of the very congresspeople who won their races deny the validity of the presidential one.[15] None suggested that their own election had been tainted by fraud in any way. I can't see how anyone could hold both those views with a straight face. Of course, it's a free country, and President Trump and those who agree with him should be allowed to argue his case on platforms like Twitter.

At times, the Republican party seems to be moving toward the position that any races it wins are legitimate and any it loses were stolen. That's not a tenable view. It's just the preferred conservative brand of victimhood, a knee-jerk kind of sore losing more common to playgrounds than great republics. Republicans could've become the one major party that moved beyond grievance and aimed only for greatness; instead we placed grudges about elections at the core of party identity. Once victimhood becomes part of the essence of both parties, it's just a national identity.

Arguing over the 2020 election is starting to feel a bit like debating *Roe v. Wade*: if you're already in one camp, you're never going to switch to the other. But even those who genuinely believe the 2020 election was stolen should at least be amused by Trump's comments after losing the 2016 Republican Iowa Caucus to Ted Cruz: "Ted Cruz didn't win Iowa, he stole it," Trump tweeted at the time. "Based on the fraud committed by Senator Ted Cruz during the Iowa caucus, either a new election should take place or Cruz results nullified," Trump added.[16] No word yet on whether Dinesh D'Souza has located Ted Cruz's mules.

Or consider Mr. Trump's comments about the 2022 Republican US Senate primary in Pennsylvania, which is headed for a recount as this book goes to press. Trump had the following to say about his endorsed candidate: "Dr. Oz should declare victory. It makes it much harder for them to cheat with the ballots that they just 'happened to find.'" He later added: "The Pennsylvania Oz race is ridiculous . . . Stop FINDING VOTES in PENNSYLVANIA! RIGGED?"[17]

So for the purpose of our discussion here about conservative victimhood, forget the 2020 presidential election. Apparently even Republican primaries across space and time are specially rigged against Trump and his endorsed candidates. Maybe Stacey Abrams is a Republican at heart.

Being a sore loser is a danger to democracy no matter which party it comes from. It chills me to see the Democratic Party moving in the same direction. In part in response to the victimhood narrative of a stolen election, Republicans in many states passed a variety of voter reform laws, so far at least thirty-three bills in nineteen states.[18] In truth, many of these reforms strike me as minor tweaks that won't affect elections much one way or the other; some of them seem to be symbolic gestures that legislators are "doing something."

But President Biden and other top Democrats call them Jim Crow 2.0.[19] I guess that's because "the New Jim Crow" was already taken by one of their other victimhood narratives. They apply the Jim Crow label to a number of Republican-led voting reforms, most of them pretty innocuous. Claremont McKenna College professor of government Andrew E. Busch sums it up by saying, "Jim Crow 1.0 entailed widespread murder and violent intimidation, onerous taxes, rigged literacy tests, and a flat prohibition on blacks voting in the primary elections of the dominant party, leading to results such as Mississippi's 7% voter-turnout rate for African Americans. 'Jim Crow 2.0,' mean[while], requires that voters show proper identification, vote in the correct precinct, and request their absentee ballot every two years instead of every four. Someday, historians will marvel that anyone ever took seriously the argument that these two regimes bore any relation to one another."[20]

The Jim Crow analogies don't stop there. Democrats are still making hay of it. The latest story is that the filibuster is also a form of Jim Crow when it's used to stop their own voter reforms.[21] Presumably Democrats didn't think the filibuster was a Jim Crow relic when they used it a record-breaking 328 times in the 2019–2020 congressional term.[22] I'm not sure whether we're on Jim Crow 3.0 or 4.0 now. Regardless, the power of the well-worn analogy allowed President Biden to say that the 2022 midterms will be illegitimate if Republicans win: "I'm not going to say it's going to be legit," he told a reporter. "The increase [in] the prospect of being illegitimate is in direct proportion to us not being able to get these reforms passed."[23]

Ironically, Republicans and Democrats are converging. Maybe no one likes a sore loser, but it seems everyone likes being one. The new wisdom for both parties is that any election you win is legitimate, and any you lose must've been stolen. Wallowing in this shared victimhood narrative may soothe the sting of defeat, but it's poison to the rule of law. Republicans were in prime position to reject identity politics, including the game of identifying as a victim, but instead we used stolen election stories as a back door to embracing our own victim identity, pursuing the easy path to power. Fighting fire with fire may sound appealing, but water's actually the better choice.

It reminds me of the final passage of George Orwell's *Animal Farm*: "Twelve voices were shouting an anger, and they were all alike. No question, now, what had happened to the faces of the pigs. The creatures outside looked from pig to man, and from man to pig, and from pig to man again; but already it was impossible to say which was which."[24] That, I fear, is the destiny that awaits a nation of victims. We'll become indistinguishable, someday soon, low creatures yelling the same tired victimhood narratives at each other and filling in the variables of victims and villains with our preferred names.

Sarah Palin's libel lawsuit against the *New York Times* exemplified America's disturbing trend toward mutually assured victimhood. As she'd no doubt say, the *Times* started it. In 2017, after a Bernie Sanders supporter shot Republican congressman Steve Scalise and several others at a baseball practice, the *Times* wanted to run an editorial connecting the shooting to conservative violence. It had to make multiple leaps in logic to do so. First, the writer brought up a shooting six years earlier when a mentally ill man wounded Representative Gabrielle Giffords and killed six others, vaguely suggesting that he might have been motivated by a map Palin's PAC had released putting competitive electoral districts like Giffords's under crosshairs. Then *Times* editor James Bennet, dissatisfied with mere insinuation, added multiple lines saying that the map had clearly and directly incited the shooting of Giffords. That claim was utterly false, with no evidence to support it except the *Times'* own wishes. It quickly realized its mistake after a conservative outcry and issued a series of corrections, though none mentioned Palin by name.[25] A couple weeks later, Palin sued for libel.

But she lost. As the jury deliberated, the district court judge said that no matter the verdict, he would dismiss Palin's suit because she hadn't met the very high bar public figures must meet to win defamation cases. A public figure has to prove not just that the defendant made false statements about them, but that they acted with actual malice—that they knowingly or recklessly said something false intending to cause harm. This legal standard was established, ironically, in the landmark case *New York Times v. Sullivan*.[26] The judge said that the *Times'* speedy efforts to check and then correct its article mentioning Palin were evidence it lacked actual malice. The jury ended up reaching the same decision as the judge, although, as Palin's lawyers will no doubt point out on appeal, a few jurors received news alerts on their phones informing them of the judge's decision as they deliberated.[27]

Not only did Palin lose; she deserved to lose. What the *Times* did was sloppy, arrogant, and prejudiced, and it's understandable that she was angry. But at the end of the day, it did quickly notice and correct its mistake, and defamation law is clear. We value free speech highly in America, and that includes the freedom to harshly criticize the public figures that have so much influence over the direction of the country. As the Court pointed out in *Sullivan*, with so much speech flying around, it's inevitable that some of it will be false. To keep spirited debate about public figures going, we have to give them less protection from false claims. The deal in America is that if you want to be famous, you have to have thick skin. Sarah Palin chose to play the victim instead, spending millions of dollars and several years hounding the *Times* over a mistake it had immediately acknowledged and fixed. She should've just moved on.

There are only two ways to win a culture war: defeat the other side, or infect it with your own values. No matter who wins the next few elections, Republicans are losing the culture war, and it's not just because liberals control the media, universities, Hollywood, or even business. Republicans aren't just losing to wokeness and its many victimhood narratives. They're losing because they've adopted the tactics and principles of their opponents and, in doing so, stand for nothing but the pursuit of power. Democrats may have been the first to master telling tales of victimhood, but lately Republicans have decided to join them in spinning out stories of persecution. They sacrifice core principles for short-term political gain.

It's easy to be a sore loser; it's harder to figure out how to win. The comforting blanket of stolen-election stories allows those who embrace them to avoid self-examination and introspection and place all their electoral shortcomings at the feet of others. This is how the woke left wins—not with a bang, but with a whimper. Not by winning a battle of arguments with the other side, but by getting the other side to adopt its own values and methods without even realizing it, even as they continue to battle one another.

Legitimate Grievances

When I say that a group has embraced the mindset of victimhood, I don't mean it has no legitimate concerns. Part of my whole point is that many groups of Americans *do* face real hardships; the question is which mentality best helps us overcome them. One problem with viewing the world through the lens of victimhood is that it forces you to look for an oppressor—it's easier and more viscerally satisfying to blame people than policies or trends. The mindset of victimhood makes you look for an enemy to punish; the mindset of an underdog makes you look for which parts of the world you can change.

But none of that is meant to be an excuse for ignoring the hardships people face and the legitimate complaints they have. Moving past America's fixation on victimhood doesn't require sticking your head in the sand. It's not about being ignorant of people's struggles; it's about opening your eyes to their capabilities. It's about opening your eyes to your own capabilities.

We can't let our grievances define us, or let others' define them. That doesn't mean we need to pretend grievances don't exist. Really, the most effective way to help someone move past their victim identity is to demonstrate that you understand where they're coming from and still don't see them as a mere victim. I tried to use that mindset in the last chapter—not once did I see black people as victims, but I did try to understand why some of them see themselves that way. Learning the victimhood narrative of the New Jim Crow and how it extended to one of police brutality allowed me to get closer to the heart of things, seeing that addressing violent crime and strengthening families would help the nation move forward. I couldn't get to the truth without the stepping-stone of seeing that black people really *are* treated unfairly in the war on drugs; that kernel of truth is what lends plausibility to the larger narrative of black victimhood.

In the same way, conservatives have valid grounds to feel aggrieved, even if they sometimes give them a poor outlet through anti-immigrant sentiment or stories about the 2020 election. In fact, the reason these false victimhood narratives are able to take root is that parts of them are grounded in truth. Many white industrial workers *have* unfairly lost jobs, just not to immigrants. There *was* an election that was stolen from President Trump, just not the one many people think.

The election that was stolen from Trump wasn't the 2020 one that he lost; it was the 2016 one that he won.

No Collusion

The 2016 election wasn't stolen in a literal sense. Donald Trump was sworn into the office of president of the United States of America. But he was immediately robbed of the ability to execute the duties of that office effectively.

Throughout his campaign, Trump was dogged by allegations that he was "colluding" with Russia to win the election. Much of the media frenzy about this conspiracy theory stemmed from the Steele dossier, which was ultimately discredited. But the sensationalist opposition research did its work in shaping public and governmental opinion. It contributed to FBI investigations of Trump's campaign that cast a pall over most of his four years in office. When Robert Mueller finally concluded the investigation more than halfway through Trump's term, by that time it didn't matter that his report found that the evidence was insufficient to establish criminal conspiracy—Trump was already guilty in the court of public opinion. To this day, liberal media commentators still take it as gospel that Trump's 2016 win was the product of collusion with Russia.[28]

Rumors of collusion had been swirling for years, but was *Buzzfeed*'s publication of the Steele dossier in January 2017 that launched public speculation into the stratosphere.[29] The report offered everything a Trump critic could hope for. It had a credible author: Christopher Steele was a former head of the Russia desk for fabled British intelligence agency MI6. It told the story many liberals wanted to be true: it said Russian intelligence had been cultivating Trump as a Russian asset for at least five years and that he'd closely coordinated with them, including by supporting Russian hacking of the Clinton campaign. And, best of all, the dossier had salacious details to make its allegations spread like wildfire. It said that Russian intelligence had Trump under its thumb because it was blackmailing him with tapes of embarrassing sex acts—the infamous "pee tapes." The Steele dossier was a conspiracy theorist's dream come true.

Too good to be true, in fact. It turns out that it was just opposition research. Crucial information has surfaced in Special Counsel John Durham's ongoing investigation, which recently resulted in a criminal indictment of Igor Danchenko, the key source behind the dossier. Kimberley Strassel sums up the current state of play in an article in the *Wall Street Journal*:

> It took a year for congressional investigators to reveal the dossier had in fact been commissioned by the opposition-research firm Fusion GPS, working for the Democratic Party and Hillary Clinton's campaign. It took two more years for Justice Department Inspector General Michael Horowitz to expose that Mr. Steele had relied on a Russian source who said he'd never expected Mr. Steele to present his info as facts, since most of it was "hearsay." Two more years on, Mr. Durham's indictment says this source—Mr. Danchenko—obtained material from a longtime Democratic operative who was active in the 2016 Clinton

campaign. Clintonites here, Clintonites there, Trump "scandals" everywhere.[30]

Danchenko was the main source of the Steele dossier's information, and he in turn got much of his information from Democratic PR executive Charles Dolan, who had deep ties to both the Clintons and Russia. Dolan later told the FBI he'd just made up a GOP friend as a source for rumors he'd actually heard in the press.[31]

So not only was the Steele dossier funded by the Clinton campaign, but one of its main sources was an actual member of the campaign, who was himself just repeating rumors he'd heard in liberal media outlets. The Steele dossier was a circle of paid-for disinformation reporting on itself to itself, a snake eating its own tail and liking the taste.

But as the saying goes, a lie travels halfway around the world while the truth's still lacing up its boots. Not only did much of the public treat the Steele dossier's allegations as fact, but the FBI itself relied heavily on them in applying for and renewing its application for a FISA warrant authorizing it to surveil Carter Page, a member of Trump's campaign. In part on the basis of the Steele dossier, it even hired an informant to spy on Page.[32] A review conducted by the Department of Justice's inspector general, Michael Horowitz, found that the FBI had made seventeen errors or omissions in its FISA warrant applications.[33] The DOJ later declared two of the four FISA warrants invalid.[34]

The FBI investigation of Trump's campaign, and later Trump himself, was given the code name Crossfire Hurricane. Its origins are contested and still under investigation. The dominant narrative from media, the FBI, and the inspector general's review is that the Steele dossier played no role in the launch of the investigation, although it was used during the course of it. Special Counsel Durham is currently leading his own investigation into the origin of Crossfire Hurricane, and he has disagreed with the inspector general's conclusions about the importance of the Steele dossier.[35]

What can be known with certainty is that the first two years of Trump's presidency were beset by a shamefully political and fact-disconnected investigation. Trump's presidency was bedeviled even before it began by accusations that he'd colluded with Russia to steal the 2016 election. The entrenched narrative of Trump's collusion with Russia even contributed to his eventual impeachment. The Mueller report, the most impartial assessment we have, found that there was insufficient evidence to conclude Trump's campaign conspired with Russia to interfere with the election. The report implies that if Trump was guilty of anything, it was of obstructing the FBI investigation itself, not of the underlying crime he was being investigated for.[36]

So Trump fell into a host of difficulties that consumed his presidency as he raged against an investigation that was motivated in large part by a scam. My party's candidate won, and he never got a fair chance to do the job because Democrats couldn't accept that he'd won. That's my own grievance. For my part, I'm ready to move on. It's in the past. There are other conservative grievances, though, that we can't simply move on from, that aren't in the past.

Left Behind

Liberals often say that conservatives voted for Trump as part of some white backlash against an increasingly diverse nation. I do think the nation has left many conservatives behind, including many white ones, but the problem has nothing to do with race. It's a changing *economy* that's abandoned many Americans. Once we accurately diagnose the source of the hardships aggrieved conservatives face, we can figure out together how to address them.

The heart of the problem is that the US economy is booming, but many workers in our industrial sectors haven't shared in the good times. Unemployment is at 3.9 percent, but that figure doesn't include people who have given up on looking for work, and more and more Americans have stopped trying to find jobs over the last two decades. Many of them used to work in manufacturing, one of the only sectors that has failed to add jobs lately. During the 2008 recession the US lost 1.6 million manufacturing jobs that require only high school diplomas, and during the recovery it replaced them with jobs in different places that require more education.[37]

When faced with past economic disruptions, Americans who lost their jobs eventually relocated to find new ones or changed careers. For many, that's no longer an option. People without a college education often stay where they are and resign themselves to joblessness as they watch a thriving nation leave them behind.

Classical conservatives ignore this crisis among blue-collar workers because their commitment to growing the economic pie outweighs their commitment to making sure everyone gets a piece. Modern liberals think these particular victims—mainly white working-class Americans in the Midwest and South—are simply a low priority because we should spend our limited resources remedying more problematic injustices. Some liberals even think these displaced workers deserve their fates, a belief in some kind of racial karma where fairness requires that white privilege be balanced by financial hardship. Many white working-class

Americans flocked to Donald Trump in 2016 because he at least paid lip service to their plight.

But the election of President Trump still failed to address the underlying issues causing these Americans to struggle. While illegal immigration is a major problem, it's far from the source of the lean times for US manufacturing workers. Blaming immigrants for lost jobs is a textbook example of the biases imposed by a victimhood mentality. Lambasting immigrants does little for American workers while sowing discord and alienating a growing segment of our population.

Blaming robots isn't much better. Automation *is* one factor that displaces some workers from manufacturing jobs, but blaming it prevents us from seeing less obvious issues. Enacting tariffs on foreign goods isn't the answer to our problems either: while this may provide a short-term boost to American manufacturers, it comes at the cost of making American-manufactured goods less competitive globally, shrinking the entire global economy in the process. That's one of the economic policies I disagreed with President Trump about. Putting America first isn't worth much if it means everyone has less.

The real root cause of the problems facing American manufacturers are the conscious policy choices we've made to advance America's economic growth and geopolitical position: perpetuation of the US dollar as the world's reserve currency, a prioritization of knowledge-based industries over others, and a free trade agenda that grows the global economy for all countries. Don't get me wrong—these are indeed the right policy choices for America to make. But we also owe it to American workers in our manufacturing sector to acknowledge that their plight is a direct consequence of these policy choices.

Collectively, we've sacrificed America's blue-collar workers to grow the pie for everyone else. We win half the battle if our professional political class and intellectual elites simply recognize this reality. We win the other half by doing something about it.

First, let's recognize the real causes of manufacturing workers' difficulties, starting with the strong US dollar. The US dollar is the reserve currency of the world, the backstop currency that citizens and banks around the world trust most. This puts the US in an extraordinarily advantageous economic and geopolitical position. We control the global financial system. We alone can freeze a terrorist's assets on demand. We alone can borrow inexpensively precisely when other countries would face difficulty. This is an incredibly precious position, and one that we as a country should be careful not to lose.

However, these policy choices—even if right for America overall—have unfair distributive consequences at home. The US dollar's status as the reserve currency of choice creates constant global demand for it. Because they're always in high demand, our American dollars allow us to purchase goods from other countries cheaply, while their weaker currency makes it harder for them to buy goods from us. American consumers benefit from being able to buy cheap imported products, but American manufacturers pay the price by being forced to export products that may be too expensive to compete in the global market.

It would be a mistake to retreat from policies that expand the size of the overall economic pie, like ones favoring free trade or promoting research-driven American innovation. Global free trade allows each country to focus on where it has a competitive advantage, enriching all countries who capture the benefit of those efficiencies. American leadership in technological innovation is therefore good for America and the world: we're able to focus on our competitive advantage in the knowledge economy, while supplying the fruits of those industries to consumers around the globe. America's position on the global economic stage is strengthened, not weakened, by focusing most on our greatest relative strength compared to other nations.

We should be proud of our strength in innovative, knowledge-based industries. But we should also recognize that it comes at a cost, and that we've asked the manufacturing industry to bear too much of that cost by giving knowledge-based industries more favorable treatment to encourage their growth. We favor them, for instance, by using our strong patent system to protect intellectual labor, government support that amounts to a subsidy since it allows producers of ideas to make more money.

We focus more on regulating producers of goods than protecting them. We currently ask them to bear most of the costs of fighting climate change by placing strict environmental regulations on factories. Even if limiting climate change is worthwhile, society gets to choose who ends up paying for it. Just as having a strong dollar is a policy that benefits America as a whole at the expense of its manufacturers, environmental regulation benefits us all, but we once again ask manufacturers to shoulder the costs. Those costs ultimately fall on blue-collar workers who belong to physical industries that struggle more than more profitable, less-regulated knowledge-based ones.

So we should keep a strong dollar, a policy of free trade, and our growing focus on a knowledge economy. Those weren't mistakes. At the same time, we have to recognize who bears the costs: American manufacturers and the workers they employ. This unfairness is amplified by the consequences of American technological innovation. While advances in automation have reduced the cost of producing goods (in ways that can be shared with the consumer in the form of lower prices), workers in the manufacturing sector face declining wages and job security.

Most workers in America's manufacturing sector were taught by their parents' generation that if you work hard and make your contributions, you'll be rewarded eventually. It's the promise of a Horatio Alger story. It may have been true a century ago, but the modern economy makes that promise a lie. While left-behind workers in the Rust Belt may not be able to articulate exactly why they've fared poorly despite doing their part, they certainly know it to be true. And they're frustrated that the intellectual elites fail to recognize the consequences of their policy choices, even as those same elites are increasingly woke to other injustices that are decades or centuries past.

Our twenty-first-century economy has left American manu-facturing workers behind, and our politicians and pundits say it's wrong to recognize that fact. There's always someone more deserving of help than white guys, no matter how destitute. They're always the lowest priority. They watch their proud cities waste away into ghost towns as coastal elites tell them to apologize for their privilege.

If half of the battle is to recognize the problem, the other half is to give American manufacturers back what they're owed. We need to do more to help blue-collar workers thrive in the world our policies have created instead of acting as if they're the inevitable victims of progress. Maybe you can't make an omelet without breaking a few eggs, but people deserve more; they're not just means to an end, no matter how good the end. As a nation, we can't take peoples' livelihoods from them then just point to the rising GDP. Part of moving on from America's various victim-hood complexes involves making sure everyone's got a fair chance to find their way back to their feet.

The right way to go isn't to subsidize the manufacturing industry through tools like tariffs, which reduce the overall economic pie. Instead, we need to bring these displaced workers into the new economy and reward them for doing so in new ways—addressing the crisis of shortages in teachers, elder care workers, and other much-needed service-oriented jobs. We can start by radically overhauling our patchwork system of job-retraining programs, which is currently inefficient and ineffective.[38]

To understand how to create a well-oiled job-retraining machine, we need to think about why so many Americans have left the workforce and stayed in increasingly desolate communities instead of pursuing the traditional options of relocating or retraining. Part of the answer is that it's more difficult than it used to be to move to areas with higher wages thanks to increased land and zoning regulations. Studies suggest that even relatively modest housing deregulation would make housing in wealthy areas of the country much more accessible. Another part of the answer is that occupational licensing laws have proliferated in recent years—in the 1950s, 5 percent of all US workers had to meet a licensing requirement before practicing their trade. Today, 33 percent do. We need to make sure jobs with licensing requirements really need them to keep people safe. We can't let the market alone determine who gets to be a doctor, but we can allow it to choose who gets to be a hairdresser.[39]

Removing unnecessary regulations that prevent workers from finding new careers will help, and we should pick that low-hanging fruit, but in the end we will have to rethink how our country educates people in order to make it easier to reeducate them. These days, a college degree is more necessary than ever to get a job in virtually any industry. Manufacturing workers who dropped out of college decades ago and find themselves unemployed today are reluctant to spend several years as a middle-aged college student. They fear that they'll spend time and money in school only to see younger graduates hired instead.

These are reasonable fears, and to assuage them we'll have to take up the difficult task of reshaping America's colleges. That's something we have to do anyway as part of rededicating ourselves to a merit-based culture. I take that task up in the next part of the book.

The Missing Shade of Red

I became a conservative in sixth grade. That's a little young to be getting into politics. It was my dad's fault. He might not appreciate taking the blame, since he's liberal. We can say it was Jack Welch's fault, then.

Jack Welch was a guy I heard a lot about growing up, a guy who seemed to have a lot of control over my family's destiny, although he knew nothing about us. He was the CEO of General Electric, where my dad had worked as an engineer for twenty years. Welch turned GE's share price into a one-way rocket ship, a fact that made him beloved among shareholders. But his employees felt more fear than love. Jack Welch was legendarily good at cutting costs. He didn't really take a chiseled approach; he preferred the chain saw.

I remember one night my dad came home and told my mom what they'd said to him at work that day. "Look to your left, look to your right. After the layoffs, only one of you will be left here." It was a scary proposition. We were a comfortably middle-class family with two incomes, but the threat of layoffs hung over our head after that, a sword of Damocles that would change our lives in an instant whenever it finally fell. Both parents worked harder, and, like Jack Welch, we cut costs wherever we could. My mom no longer had time to drive me to basketball games and my brother to soccer, so she switched us both to tennis.

Meanwhile, my dad tried to make himself indispensable. He heard there was a shortage of patent attorneys at GE, so he found a company program that would pay for him to pursue a degree in law through taking night classes. But that meant my dad had to work a full-time job while also going to law school at night, in addition to finding time to do the copious reading. On top of all that, he had to do an extra hour-and-a-half commute to school each night.

Since both my parents were working more, my brother and I usually tagged along with one or the other. My mom was a geriatric psychiatrist, so I ended spending a lot of time at nursing homes during her extra hours. I'd do my piano practice there, which became a hit with the patients. The Alzheimer's patients especially loved listening to me practice. My time playing for them inspired me to pursue a therapy for Alzheimer's as my first major project at Roivant, although it wasn't meant to be.

On other days, it was my dad who took me in the car with him on his long drive to his law classes. I'd sit in the back of the classroom while my dad sat closer to the front. I remember my surprise at how actively my dad participated, and the fact that I was so proud of him for doing it, while at the same time being ever so slightly embarrassed at his thick Indian accent. I didn't really follow much of those exchanges, but my dad would explain the gist of them during the long ride home late at night, and I'd mull it over as I looked out at the stars.

He got most animated when discussing two guys in particular—Clarence Thomas and, above all, my dad's arch-nemesis Antonin Scalia. My dad loved complaining about them. I quietly wondered how much he actually detested them, since those were the only opinions he ever made me read. I had no idea who Scalia was, but I decided that if he was so important in my dad's mind, he must've been a pretty cool guy. I slowly started making whatever argument was the opposite of my dad. Typical preteen move. So I became a conservative because I was a bratty kid taking Scalia's side against my dad.

That's the cute little story I give in interviews, at least. There's a kernel of truth to it. But, looking back on it, the financial insecurity my family faced and watching my parents do whatever they could to fight it played at least as big a role as those Scalia opinions. A bigshot CEO had casually made us live under the constant threat of layoffs, but those days watching my mom put in extra hours at the nursing homes, those nights watching my dad take on law school . . . it convinced me that our destiny was in our own hands, that our fate wasn't ultimately up to other people. Other people may get the opening move, but hard work and the choices we make determine victory. That's what being a conservative always meant to me.

Once I looked past the standard story I usually tell, I realized that there were other moments during that time that pushed me toward the conservative worldview.

In sixth grade I'd had a teacher, Mr. B, who had a real bone to pick with me for some reason I couldn't explain. I'd get bad grades on assignments where I'd obviously done nothing wrong. After my parents got home from a conference with him, it turned out the problem had something to do with race; he kept telling them they focused too much on math and science and closed the conversation with a lecture starting "This is what's wrong with you people." To tell the truth, I thought they did spend too much time making me take torturous supplemental math tutoring, but that still didn't explain the bad grades. The upshot of it all was that my parents transferred me to a different school, where I spent some time being bullied for being the new kid.

The bullying took a darker turn once I got into high school, where most of the kids were bigger than me, partly because many of them had been held back a grade or two. When I was in eighth grade, I was making my way in a rush from one class to another, dutifully carrying my large stack of books as I always did, when I approached a staircase. That's when a big black kid thought it would be amusing to push a nerdy high-achieving Indian kid down the stairs. Whether our races were relevant, I don't know, but I've learned that others think it's part of these stories. It was a traumatic incident physically—I ended up having hip surgery later that year. Middle school had taught me to stand up to social bullying, but the moment I learned to do that, it was physical force that confined me. No more basketball or tennis for a long while.

So it's true that I became a conservative during middle school, in those years when I took long car rides to and from law school with my dad. But it wasn't just the conversations with my dad that did it. It was also everything else that was going on in my life at the same time.

I didn't select conservatism from an intellectual menu of options. It started as the emotional choice of a teenager. Part of it was the emotive choice to stand up to my dad. But part of it was also a psychological defense mechanism for a thirteen-year-old who was drawn to a worldview—and even an identity—that centered on self-reliance rather than dependence. A teenager who didn't want to be weak, even though he sometimes was. A teenager who didn't want his family to feel vulnerable, even though they sometimes were. My path to conservatism was an emotional choice first, a reasoned one second. Though I have some trouble admitting it to myself, it was, at its core, a psychological defense mechanism against being victimized myself at a vulnerable time. By Mr. B. By the kids in middle school. By the black kid who pushed me down the stairs. By the white guy that might have fired my dad.

Psychologists say that people don't arrive at their moral beliefs through reason, but through emotions, and they just use reasons to justify those emotions.[40] I buy that. I'd like to think I'm an exception to that rule, but I'm probably not. My own journey to becoming a conservative traversed the path of, I guess, victimhood. Maybe that's why I so badly want conservatism itself to become the path of deliverance from it.

That's why I take it personally when I see conservatism becoming just another brand of victimhood. It feels like a betrayal. To me, conservatism always stood for the idea that you're responsible for your own life, but everywhere I look these days, I see conservatives blaming other people for their problems. We preach personal responsibility, but we no longer take it.

It reminds me of the illusion I experience whenever I look at the sky from my backyard on a rare clear night. I see countless stars and believe that they exist just because I see them—even though they may not, because a faraway star burns out long before its light stops traveling across the galaxy to reach Earth. Like I read somewhere, all we ever see of stars are their old photographs.

I call myself a conservative, and I still feel like one at my core. But maybe I'm just basking in old light from a star I first saw when I was in sixth grade. Like all dead stars, there's now a black hole left in its wake, devoid of meaning, devoid of content, pulling people in with the gravitational force of grievance and then trapping them in victimhood's grasp. Unlike stars, though, ideologies can be reignited.

One of David Hume's famous thought experiments is called "the missing shade of blue." Hume was a die-hard empiricist who thought you could only imagine ideas that were based directly on sensations you'd experienced. One counterexample bothered him: if he saw a spectrum of shades of blue, from light to dark, but one shade in the middle was missing, Hume was certain he could imagine exactly what the missing shade of blue looked like, even though he'd never seen it before.

What haunted Hume can save me and other conservatives who feel lost these days and wonder what the Republican Party stands for. Sometimes I feel like I'm trying to imagine the missing shade of red. I look to the past, and I see all these different shades of conservatism that influenced me: Scalia's dogged originalism, Reagan's resistance to government regulation, Trump's insistence in American greatness. But when I look at modern conservatism, there is only a void, an absence of content covered with the thin veneer of victimhood. When I listen to conservative pundits and politicians, they offer only grievances, not meaning. They define conservatism only as the negation of liberalism, which is no definition at all. There is nothing in my experience that tells me what it really means to be a conservative these days.

But maybe Hume was right. Maybe we can imagine the missing shade of red even if we've never seen it before, even if no one's ever seen it before. We have to look to the past, to all the shades of conservatism we have seen, and find a way to extend them into the present. Even when I don't say it, that's the way I think of much of my writing on America. I'm searching for the missing shade of red.

Chapter Six

EMPIRE IN DECLINE

Are We Rome?

These wall-stones are wondrous—
calamities crumpled them, these city-sites crashed, the work
*   of giants*
corrupted. The roofs have rushed to earth, towers in ruins.
Ice at the joints has unroofed the barred-gates, sheared
the scarred storm-walls have disappeared—
the years have gnawed them from beneath. A grave-grip holds
the master-crafters, decrepit and departed, in the
*   ground's harsh*
grasp, until one hundred generations of human-nations have
trod past.

Those are the opening lines of an Old English elegy called "The Ruin," written more than a thousand years ago by an anonymous poet contemplating the remains of a once-great Roman city, most likely Bath.[1] Although he was probably speaking metaphorically, his line about the ruins being the work of giants fired up modern popular imagination, leading some to believe that English commoners in the Middle Ages regarded Roman ruins as the literal work of giants.[2]

It's difficult to piece together what the common folk actually knew or believed of Rome, but the clergy and nobility never forgot it. All across Europe, Rome loomed large in their consciousness ever since the Western Roman Empire's fall late in the fifth century CE. For more than a thousand years after, virtually every empire great or small fashioned a narrative portraying itself as the inheritor of the Roman tradition. That's why words like "kaiser" and "tsar" all derive from "Caesar." As Voltaire famously quipped, the Holy Roman Empire was neither holy, nor Roman, nor an empire.

I wonder what Voltaire would think of the United States of America, which he helped inspire but didn't quite live to see. I suspect his judgment would be harsh, both on the appropriateness of the name and because he was a valiant defender of free speech. We've come a long way from "I disapprove of what you say, but I will defend to the death your right to say it." That belief is part of our classically liberal intellectual lineage. We remember the words, and that they once seemed praiseworthy, but modern America seems to have watered it down to "I disapprove of what you say," not nearly as good a foundational principle for a nation.

The work of intellectual giants decays, too, when it's not remembered. Maybe that's what happens first when a great nation falls. Sometimes the United States of America strikes me as a set of ruins in the making.

I first started thinking about the parallels between the fall of Rome and the fall of America because of something San Antonio Spurs coach Gregg Popovich said. I'm a fan of Pop, despite some political disagreements. He's been around so long he's practically an American institution himself, an elder statesman of sorts. He's known for making his players think. He quizzes them on history and current events, as if he's trying to make them not just basketball players, but citizens.[3] Pop made me think, too, when I saw this quote from him a few years ago: "I worry that maybe I'm being a little too pessimistic, but I'm beginning to have a harder time believing that we are not Rome. Rome didn't fall in twenty days or thirty years. It took a couple hundred years. The question is: Are we in that process and we don't even know it?"[4]

It's a fair question, one that's lingered with me. I've noticed others making the Rome comparison more often over the last few years. Maybe that's one of the few things us Americans still agree on, one of the things Pop and I would agree on. Most of us share the sense that our place in history is at the end of a grand story, not the beginning or middle, the disappointing outcome to a great experiment.

That's a kind of victimhood that Americans share: we're victims of history, born too late, trapped in the middle of a decline ordained by forces we didn't create. We find ourselves the inheritors of grievances that predate us, just playing out our assigned roles at the conclusion of a narrative written long ago.

The American experiment was always a test of whether a diverse group of people could govern themselves and be free, and many of us have decided that the results are in and the answer is no. As I pointed out in chapter 2, more and more Americans expect to see another civil war during their lifetimes. Perhaps some Americans don't expect another civil war simply because they hope to end the American experiment through peaceful secession. A YouGov survey found that almost 40 percent of the country favors secession, splitting the Union into several regional nations.[5] Sixty-six percent of Republicans in the South favored forming a confederation of some sort. In the Midwest, the largest group in favor of secession was independents at 43 percent. Forty-seven percent of Democrats on the West Coast favored striking out on their own. Governor Gavin Newsom has taken to calling California a nation-state, while the Constitution regards it more as a state, as I understand it.[6]

Newsom appears to have retired this rhetoric for the moment—it seems that California is a state when we have a Democrat in the presidency, and a nation-state when a Republican is in office. It's Schrodinger's state: you cannot know whether California is still a member of the Union until you peer inside the ballot box. Imagine what will happen once every state acts that way, or when too many people do. I have to admit my faith in the nation was shaken when I saw the Capitol riot and its aftermath. I started to wonder if this was going to happen after every election from now on, no matter who won. Rome fell to invading barbarians, but us Americans have become our own barbarians, sacking ourselves.

Have we had our long decline already, and is this the beginning of our fall? The middle, even, or somehow the end? Popovich thinks so. A few months after he raised the question, he gave another interview where he expressed his dismay at the election of Donald Trump and delivered his answer: "And so, my final conclusion is—my big fear is—we are Rome."[7]

I'm not so sure. These questions, though thought-provoking, aren't well formed. Inevitably, the answer is that we resemble Rome in some important ways but not others. The only place I ever properly studied Latin was during my tenure in a relatively less well-off public school in southwest Ohio. It's the place where I was pushed down a flight of stairs as my punishment for being an overachiever, but I took a lot away from those years too. The kids in my Latin class used to incessantly make fun of the plump young woman who taught the class, and of me, the nerdy Indian kid who used to stay long after class ended during lunch break and recess to hear stories about Roman history. In class she'd call me by my Latin name, Tiro.

Most of what I'm going to share about Rome came from back then. I brushed up on some of the facts in preparation to write the book, but one of the good things about Roman history is that our view of it hasn't changed nearly as much since 1997 as our popular understanding of American history. In some ways Popovich flatters us too much; Rome appears on track to have lasted a lot longer. Hundreds of years from now, historians may regard the United States of America as just another short-lived empire that during its brief peak fashioned itself the successor of Rome.

Are we Rome? We should be so lucky. At the same time, there's a lot we can learn from it. Over the next couple of chapters I'll take you through several key moments in Rome's rise and fall and show you how America's arc parallels Rome's. I'll also analyze a couple of other great empires that fell. The first fallen giant I want to assess is Carthage, the Mediterranean superpower that had to fall for Rome to rise. More and more Americans these days are wondering if we're Rome, but sometimes I think we're more like Carthage, the great power that had to make way for an even greater one.

The Thucydides Trap

One of Rome's first real crises of faith came when it faced its great enemy Hannibal in the Second Punic War.

Rome was just spreading the wings of its empire. By 264 BCE it had come a long way since its founding almost five hundred years earlier, which legend has it came from a pair of boys raised by wolves, or perhaps refugees escaping the fall of Troy.[8] We speak today of a Roman republic and the empire it became, but the moment one became the other is blurry and disputed. People often point to Julius Caesar's crossing of the Rubicon, the first time a Roman general took his army into the city, as the moment when republic took its first steps toward empire. But Rome truly began to pursue imperial ambitions centuries earlier, when its ships and trade routes stretched out across the Mediterranean, past Sicily, and it brushed up against a more established power.

Carthage was the preeminent power in the Mediterranean at the time, a proud North African city-state with a history and influence that surpassed Rome's. The two had cooperated for a time, finding each other useful trade partners. But there came a point when both civilizations had prospered and their world had grown small. Things came to a head when they fought over the island of Sicily, the gateway between the eastern and western halves of the Mediterranean. Carthage's position on the opposite shore of that naval choke point had allowed it to flourish, and now Rome wanted its turn as the Mediterranean's gatekeeper.

Its reach almost exceeded its grasp. The First Punic War was inconclusive, twenty-three years of bloody naval warfare. Carthage had begun the war as the far superior naval force, supported by its stronger civilian fleet, but Rome learned from it, used its powerful industrial base to outbuild it, and eventually defeated it. The war's end saw Rome in control of Sicily, and Carthage smarting from its wounds but still dangerous.

It bode its time for twenty years and then struck back. Hannibal launched the Second Punic War when he took his army across the Alps and invaded the Roman heartland. The Romans had thought the mountains were impassable, especially in winter. Hannibal brought war elephants over.

He ran rampant for fourteen years, occupying vast swaths of Italy without defeat. Hannibal stunned the Romans early on with his total victory at the Battle of Cannae, still taught to cadets at military academies across the world today. In military tactics, "Cannae" has come to stand for a complete victory on the battlefield, the envelopment and total destruction of an enemy army using a numerically inferior force. Eisenhower wrote, "Every ground commander seeks the battle of annihilation; so far as conditions permit, he tries to duplicate in modern war the classic example of Cannae."[9]

One of Hannibal's greatest talents as a general was his ability to know the strengths and weaknesses of his eclectic army, a motley of troops drawn from across Carthage's expansive empire, united mostly by loyalty to him and enmity of Rome. Hannibal's victory at Cannae was in some ways the product of his understanding of the value of diversity, combined with his exploitation of Roman conformity.

He knew that as the Roman army outnumbered his eighty-six thousand to fifty thousand, it would attempt to concentrate its forces into a deep column and break his center so that it could quickly flood in reinforcements to separate the wings of his army. So Hannibal placed his most battle-tested troops there, a mix of lightly armored but experienced Hispanics and Gauls backed up by Balearic slingers. The Romans underestimated them as cannon fodder and advanced, not realizing that Hannibal had entrusted his best infantry with conducting a controlled retreat, drawing the Romans deeper into the Carthaginian formation. Rome still had the numbers, but as Carthage gradually formed a concave around its column, it gained something better: surface area.

Meanwhile, Hannibal sent his Numidian light cavalry to keep the Roman horse occupied while his brother Hasdrubal led his medium Hispanic and Gallic cavalry to defeat one flank of Roman cavalry, then wheel to help the Numidians defeat the other. As the light cavalry hunted down the routed Romans, the medium attacked the main force from the rear, Hannibal's African reserve infantry closed in from the sides, and the Roman army was completely encircled, then utterly destroyed. About six thousand Carthaginians died; perhaps fifty thousand Romans were killed, with another twenty thousand captured. The remaining Romans had been at camp, away from the battle.[10]

For the first time in its history Rome felt true fear, even panic. Its leaders looked for answers in the Sibylline Books, ancient prophecies inherited from its last king; its emissaries consulted the oracle at Delphi. It buried four people alive to appease its angry gods.[11]

But in the end, though Hannibal was a great general, able to unite and employ a diverse array of forces, he could only forestall Rome's rise, not prevent it. Rome had won the First Punic War by outbuilding the Carthaginians; it won the Second by outwaiting them. Fabius adopted the unpopular but effective strategy of avoiding open battle with Hannibal, always moving the Roman armies to wherever he was not, knowing that Hannibal could win anywhere, but couldn't be everywhere. Hannibal lost his grip over Italy over the next dozen years without losing a battle, never reinforced by Carthage, and was eventually recalled to defend against a Roman invasion of Africa. He was finally defeated at the Battle of Zama at the hands of Scipio, afterward named Scipio Africanus, the son of the first Roman general Hannibal had defeated. Rome finished off Carthage fifty years later in the Third Punic War, razing it and enslaving its citizens, bringing its near-thousand-year history to an end.

So are we Rome? Sometimes I think we're Carthage, the great power coming into conflict with the rising one, being surpassed as the world suddenly grows small. The conflict between Rome and Carthage can be seen as an example of what American political scientist Graham T. Allison calls the Thucydides trap, a theory that holds that an established empire is doomed to go to war with a rising one as their ambitions put their interests at odds.[12] Thucydides himself was describing the Peloponnesian War between Athens and Sparta, but I think the later Punic Wars are the more instructive examples for the modern day, with China standing in for Rome and the United States assigned the unenviable role of Carthage.

Taiwan is the main island that might draw us into conflict, not Sicily. But this is where modern considerations change the parameters of the problem. Though Taiwan is just off China's coast, the way globalization has connected the world means that from an economic perspective, Taiwan is just on the US doorstep. That tiny island is the hub of global semiconductor chip production. The Taiwan Semiconductor Manufacturing Company produces the vast majority of the world's most advanced chips, with the US far behind in capability and China even further. State-of-the-art chips are increasingly necessary for a range of civilian and military applications such as data centers, automobiles, drones, missiles, and anything else involving artificial intelligence—as I finish writing this book, Russia has invaded Ukraine, and one of the most effective tactics the civilized world has used against it is starving it of advanced chips, depriving it of the ability to replenish lost tanks and missiles. While Sicily was the gateway to the rest of the world between Rome and Carthage, Taiwan is for the US and China. The question of who controls it seems to be coming to a head.

But while Sicily could not be moved, Taiwan, in a sense, can—or at least global semiconductor manufacturing can be moved away from it. Such a project is imperative for national security, but more easily said than done. It takes years of development and billions in funding to build new semiconductor foundries, often called fabs, and train skilled workers to operate them. China has embarked on its own effort to create a domestic semiconductor fab industry as part of its Made in China 2025 plan, which aims to meet 70 percent of China's domestic semiconductor demand within the next few years. But China's effort is at least ten years behind TSMC's capabilities, which may help explain its renewed interest in Taiwan.[13]

The US is faring little better. Our own leading semiconductor manufacturer, Intel, has fallen at least five years behind the state-of-the-art, with its ten-nanometer node just reaching production at scale after facing years of delays,[14] even as TSMC brings the three-nanometer node to market—smaller processes allow chips to be faster and more energy efficient.[15] The machinery of the US government is ponderously turning to solve this problem. TSMC and Samsung are spending $12 and $17 billion, respectively, building fabs in Arizona, and the CHIPS Act recently passed by the Senate would provide $52 billion to stimulate US semiconductor production. Publicly, Intel argues that money ought to go to domestic manufacturers like itself even as it quietly asks TSMC to build its advanced chips.[16]

The unfortunate truth is that this is all too little, too late. The production from those Arizona fabs will be a drop in the bucket in the face of the US's ravenous demand for semiconductors. And while $52 billion is a lot of money, the fact of the matter is that it will take hundreds of billions to turn the US into a semiconductor manufacturing superpower. We don't need $52 billion and a couple of factories. To remain competitive militarily and economically, we need a Manhattan Project for semiconductor fabrication. We need to dramatically increase funding for semiconductor fabrication into the hundreds of billions, not tens, and recruit Taiwan's top engineers for starters. But the project will require more than time and money—it will require us to refocus our educational system to produce more engineers than activists. Believe me, China's teaching its kids calculus.

We aren't doomed to fight our own version of the Punic Wars with China to control the gateway to the global economy. The modern-day chokepoint is technological, not geographical. The problem simply seems to be one of geography, because we've outsourced excellence in a key technology to a small island just off China's coast. That means we can avoid fighting a bloody naval war over Taiwan if we find a way to bring the best things about it here.

We need to avoid fighting that naval war, because if we fought it today, we'd probably lose, as virtually all of our own war games conclude.[17] The problem runs deep. One of the main lessons we should learn from the conflict between Rome and Carthage is that wars are not necessarily won or lost with great generals or decisive battles; more often they're won or lost by economies. Russia is currently learning that lesson the hard way. But America may face its own hard lesson soon. Just as Carthage began the First Punic War as the vastly superior naval power but lost because Rome out-built it for twenty years, the US has rested on its laurels as it fought the War on Terror and given China a twenty-year head start in outbuilding our navy.

That task has already been accomplished. The PLAN, the People's Liberation Army Navy, is now the largest navy in the world, with 360 ships to the US's 297, and most of its ships are new, while the US relies on ones that are decades old. Only 25 percent of the US Navy's capital ships were built during the last ten years, compared to more than 80 percent of China's.[18] The US wasted time and money developing its toothless and vulnerable Littoral Combat Ship, the first of which was recently retired after just thirteen years of service.[19] China has seventeen naval shipyards.[20] The US Navy relies on four, all of them more than a century old.[21] In 2020, it made six warships to China's twenty.

This numerical gap widens even more when you consider that the US Navy has defense commitments around the world, so could only send a portion of its strength to fight any naval war with China. We do have powerful allies in the region, especially Japan, which is converting its so-called helicopter destroyers to light carriers capable of carrying American-made F-35s (Japan doesn't call them aircraft carriers because its constitution prohibits offensive weapons).[22] We just inked a deal with Australia to help it build eight nuclear attack submarines, a sign of the gravity of our naval disadvantage, because no nation shares such dangerous technology lightly.[23] But China has a capable ally too: it's been rapidly building its military ties with Russia, with the two recently sending a sizable joint fleet to menace Japan.[24]

The US still calls its navy the most powerful in the world, exemplifying the American faith that naming yourself something makes it so. As a particularly cutting analysis from naval historian Claude Berube assessed the balance of power:

> Secretary of Defense Lloyd Austin [testified to Congress], "certainly we have the most capable and dominant navy in the world, and it will continue to be so going forward." While the secretary's support of the Navy is laudable, this statement is contrary to quantifiable trends and the future based on the continuing shipbuilding gap.
>
> It is natural for any organization to claim that it is the best business, sports team, or school. It is understandable that public affairs officers build Potemkin-like propaganda machines to support their established organizational narratives and promote their brands regardless of what it is. However, rose-colored statements that ignore addressing challenges actually weaken the military and its goals...The nation and its military need to operate on facts, not hyperbole. The same joint culture that produced optimistic projections regarding the Afghan National Army and its efficacy now threatens to undermine its justification to the administration and Congress for a sufficiently sized U.S. Navy.[25]

The thought that the US military's assessments of its own strength might resemble its assessments of the Afghan National Army is alarming, but probably apt. While the US spent twenty years orienting its military around occupying Middle Eastern nations, China spent that time building ships and shipyards.

Warships take several years to build, test, and commission; building a shipyard, of course, is an order of magnitude more difficult. As Marine Corps commandant general David Berger put it, "Replacing ships lost in combat will be problematic, inasmuch as our industrial base has shrunk, while peer adversaries have expanded their shipbuilding capacity. In an extended conflict, the United States will be on the losing end of a production race— reversing the advantage we had in World War II when we last fought a peer competitor."[26]

To be fair, one could argue that the focus on the number of hulls a navy has is misleading and that what's more important is the tonnage, which correlates with how many missile tubes the navy has. On both counts the US Navy more than doubles China's.[27] Much of that tonnage comes from our eleven nuclear super-carriers, capable of carrying eighty fighters each, and our nine amphibious assault ships, which can function as light carriers with a complement of about twenty F-35s.[28] Each of those fighters adds to the missile count the US Navy could theoretically bring to bear in a conflict. On the face of it, our carrier fleet makes our navy unmatched. At least, that has been the conventional wisdom for decades.

Conventional tactical wisdom is likely to serve us about as well as it did the Romans at Cannae. These navy-to-navy comparisons that focus on tonnage and missile tubes miss a crucial factor: if we fight China anywhere within three thousand miles of its shores, it gets to use its vast, rapidly growing arsenal of DF-26 antiship ballistic missiles, which it calls carrier killers. It's been practicing killing American carriers on full-scale moving targets in one of its remote deserts.[29] This is part of China's anti-access/area denial strategy, which seems to be working. When the

US Air Force learned China is now capable of hitting our military bases in Guam, it stopped stationing bombers there.[30]

Arithmetic is against us. Carrier-killing missiles are much cheaper than carriers and have a much longer range. The Ukrainian use of missiles to sink the Russian flagship *Moskva* was our hint that the nature of naval warfare has changed. Our massive, expensive carrier fleet is a paper tiger that can't even get close to Guam, let alone Taiwan. If we tried, there's a good chance that China would get to live the dream of recreating Cannae in modern warfare, overwhelming our ships with long-range missiles and annihilating them without taking significant losses itself.

None of this is even to mention China and Russia's several-year lead on cutting-edge hypersonic missiles, which are fast, agile, and hard to detect or shoot down. They each began deploying hypersonic missiles years ago, while the US aims to develop and deploy its own by 2023.[31] This is merely aspirational; our tests usually fail.[32] Meanwhile, in summer 2021 China flew a hypersonic glide vehicle around the world. Chairman of the Joint Chiefs of Staff General Mark A. Milley said "I don't know if it's quite a Sputnik moment, but I think it's very close to that."[33] Later, we learned that China had launched a separate missile from the first one while it was moving at Mach 5, defying DARPA scientists' understanding of physics.[34]

For its part, Russia's actually the leader in hypersonic missile technology, achieving speeds up to Mach 9 on its Zirkon missile, which it's placing on ships and submarines in 2022.[35] We claim to be in an arms race with China and Russia, but this is just American pride speaking. In terms of actual results, our progress is closer to North Korea's: like them, we're at least several years away from deploying hypersonic missiles, and our tests only succeed once in a while.[36] This is the kind of thing that happens when a nation stops prioritizing education in math and science. It's the kind of thing that happens when an empire declines.

The bottom line? If we fought a naval war with China over Taiwan within the next few years, we would almost certainly lose, reprising Carthage's loss from the First Punic War as Rome outbuilt it. China's already outbuilt us. Instead we should take a page from Rome's playbook when it faced a seemingly unbeatable military power in Hannibal: avoid open conflict and outwait our opponent, rebuilding our diminished industrial capabilities. We have to recognize our weakness so that we can become strong. The US economy is still the world's juggernaut, and our greater freedom and diversity give us a capacity for innovation that China doesn't always allow. If we bide our time and devote ourselves to reclaiming global leadership in semiconductor and ship manufacturing, we may yet become Rome instead of Carthage.

In the best of all worlds, though, we wouldn't become either.

Ladders of Power

There's a crucial question most people don't ask when they wonder if we're an empire in decline: so what if we are? Why should we care about being the most powerful country in the world, and why should we mourn losing that status?

Certainly we'd rather not be conquered like Carthage, but why not be content to diminish and become a lesser power like Britain? The sun did finally set on the British Empire, but it's still a first-world country with a high quality of life. The world didn't stop turning when America, India, and many others started controlling their own destinies. If anything, most people were better off. Maybe it wouldn't be such a bad thing for the sun to set on American empire as well.

The question of why anyone should care about whether the United States of America declines gets to the heart of the nature of excellence, both in nations and individuals. Ultimately, I don't think pursuing national excellence requires that we be the strongest, most powerful country in the world. It would be a mistake for any country to make being the biggest and best a core part of its identity. Ernest Hemingway once said, "There is nothing noble in being superior to your fellow man; true nobility is being superior to your former self." That insight doesn't stop being true when individuals form nations.

Victimhood and hegemony actually have a lot in common: they're the products of hierarchical worldviews. Both ways of thinking structure the world according to networks of power. Critical race theorists believe in a ladder of oppression where white people are at the top, followed by Asians, then Latinos, with black people and Native Americans at the bottom. That's what the term "BIPOC" is meant to remind people of—it separates out black and indigenous people for special recognition, lumps all other people of color like Asians and Latinos together, and further separates all those groups from white people. Meanwhile, Marxists say the ladder of oppression is constructed by degrees of wealth. Feminists see a sex-based pecking order. The concept of intersectionality introduced by UCLA professor Kimberlé Crenshaw allows one to blend all these ladders together, constructing a complex web of power where people fall or climb the rungs of power based on who they're interacting with, as context renders different hierarchies salient.[37]

So-called realists about international relations actually see the world in a similar way, except they build their hierarchy out of pure power itself, skipping the middlemen of race, sex, and wealth. This school of thought developed from the nineteenth-century German approach of *realpolitik*, which itself had roots in ancient theorists like Thucydides and Sun Tzu. While critical race theorists and Marxists tend to conduct their analysis on the scale of nations, a realist just applies the same hierarchical thinking on an international scale. A realist, like a critical theorist, divides the world into weak and strong. From there, it's just a short step from realist to imperialist: if that's all there is, might as well be one of the strong.

What you have to understand is that each of these worldviews claims not to *want* to think hierarchically—they claim to have been *driven* to it. No one wants to see their national or global community so cynically, driven just by the raw exercise of power as dominant groups write the rules to keep their privileges. These are views that people reluctantly conclude are necessary to fully explain the phenomena they observe. A critical race theorist, for instance, starts by describing the real racism of the past and the way it ordered society, such as with Jim Crow laws, and then they simply keep applying the same method, using the lens of racism to describe the social structures of the present. Although CRT proponents, feminists, and Marxists all spend a lot of time describing the world in terms of dominant groups and subordinate ones, their stated goal is to dismantle the power structures they see.

But if all you can see is a ladder of power relations, that's all you'll be able to create. If you see a nation where a racial caste system orders everything, you'll think that equality requires an even balance of power. And then because the old ladder of oppression had a long reign, you'll think the only way to get an even balance of power is to create a new hierarchy that simply inverts the old one. A female student I talked to in law school, for instance, insisted that because we'd had so many male Supreme Court justices in the past, equality required that we have an all-female Supreme Court for the foreseeable future. It's the same thinking that makes it seem obvious equity requires a black female vice president or justice. When you describe the world's evils in hierarchical power structures, you're prone to thinking the best you can do is flip the ladder of oppression on its head.

The same danger awaits when you see international relations as a zero-sum game for power and influence. When all you've trained yourself to see is strong and weak, oppressors and their victims, all you can think to do is claw your way to the top of the food chain. Unlike the British Empire, modern Americans don't seek hegemony simply because we feel some kind of white man's burden; we don't see it as our sacred duty to civilize the rest of the world by bringing it under our dominion. In the modern era, we seek to preserve American power mainly because we fear that if we aren't the hegemon, some other nation will be. It's a relic of Cold War thinking that rears its head again as China rises and Russia stirs.

Both critical theorists and realists are vulnerable to the blinders they place on themselves. The realist becomes an imperialist because they fear that if their nation doesn't dominate others, it must be dominated by them. For the same reason, the critical theorist can only imagine liberating themself from the oppression of others by subjugating them—like Kendi, they conclude that the only possible solution to discrimination is discrimination.

This is a trend Douglas Murray zeroes in on. He points out that the gay rights movement has led not to the claim that gay people like himself have the same rights as straight ones, but that they deserve a little bonus, too. For instance, he observes that gay people are often granted license to make jokes that'd be called sexual harassment when uttered by straight ones.[38] Making irreverent sexual comments is just part of being gay. Likewise, he notes that feminism has arrived at the belief that women are not only just as good as men, but probably at least a little better; he cites feminists who argue the world would be better off if women were in charge of financial institutions.[39]

You can easily prove this yourself: you can't get away with claiming that men are naturally better than women at anything, but say that women are inherently better than men in some ways and most circles will applaud your enlightenment. But if women are at least as good as men at everything and better at some, they're just the true superior sex. Society's mistake was not in thinking the sexes were unequal, then, but simply in elevating the wrong one. Say that men are the weaker sex, and many feminists will nod approvingly.

This is the danger of hierarchical worldviews made vivid: the natural response is not to eliminate the existing hierarchy, but invert it. If you try to counterbalance discrimination with discrimination, knowing that it's hard to hit any target perfectly, you're liable to think justice requires you to overshoot.

Kantian Fishermen

Chief Justice John Roberts once said that the way to stop discrimination based on race is to stop discriminating based on race.[40] That's true, but it's only a corollary of a more general principle: the way to end a world defined by power relations is to stop defining all relations by power. Of course, there are real injustices out there, real power imbalances between groups, but you can't make identifying them the foundation of your worldview. If you spend all your time thinking about how people are unequal, you won't even know what it would mean to be equals. You'll think that justice is nothing more than the absence of injustice.

That's one reason I'm drawn to Immanuel Kant's ethical theory: he gives a coherent account of how rationality itself commands us to treat each other as equals. I've mentioned Kant a couple of times in this book and my last one, but until now I haven't had reason to describe his theory in any detail. The time for that has finally arrived, because Kant gives us the missing piece we need to escape seeing the world as a mere network of power. His categorical imperative provides a road map for what it would look like to have a world where everyone was fundamentally equal—no victims, no oppressors, no battles for individual supremacy or international hegemony, just human beings pursuing excellence together.

Kant advocated just one ethical rule that had to be applied to all people in all times and places; that's why he called it the categorical imperative. Most people who have heard of him will have heard the version of the rule that goes "Act in such a way that you treat humanity, whether in your own person or in the person of another, always at the same time as an end and never simply as a means."[41] In other words, never use a human being as a mere means to an end; don't even use *yourself* as a mere means to an end.

That's an idea I'll keep coming back to, because pursuing victimhood as a path to power runs afoul of it. In some cases, like the Rachel Dolezals of the world, it's blindingly obvious that someone is playing the victim card to profit from someone else's suffering. She used black people's problems as a means to gain employment and wealth, and they got nothing out of it. But in most cases, the central problem with victimhood complexes is actually that someone uses their own pain as a mere means to an end. Consider the Ben Simmons saga for an exemplar.

The Philadelphia 76ers took Simmons with the first pick in the 2016 NBA draft. He was supposed to be the next LeBron: he could do pretty much everything but shoot. The problem is, he never did learn that. Things reached a head when his fear of shooting rendered him a nonentity in a playoff series. After the Sixers lost, Simmons's teammates and coach politely criticized his passivity. Simmons demanded a trade, refusing to play another game for the Sixers. Before being traded to the Brooklyn Nets, he racked up $20 million in fines sitting out the season.[42] The moment Simmons started accruing those fines, he tried to wriggle out of them by claiming he couldn't play because of mental health problems. His agent was exploiting a loophole in the collective bargaining agreement saying teams couldn't fine a player if they were unable to play due to mental health issues.[43] That excuse worked for a while until the Sixers got tired of it.

Here's the thing: Simmons probably did have legitimate mental health issues, ones that went beyond basketball. He wasn't just taking advantage of people with mental illnesses. Earlier that year, his sister had publicly accused their half-brother of sexually abusing her when they were children. A judge ordered her to pay him $550,000 after she failed to show up to defend her claims in court.[44] The problem with Simmons's actions wasn't that he was faking mental health issues; it was that he was cold-bloodedly using his own mental struggle as a tool to get whatever he wanted. He let it be known that the mental health problems that barred him from playing another minute for the Sixers would cease to prevent him from playing basketball the moment he was traded to another team. He took his own pain and saw it as a convenient way to skip work and get paid.

That's what Kant is talking about when he says it's wrong to use even your own humanity as a mere means to an end. Simmons cheapened his own suffering when he tried to reduce it to a currency to be exchanged for goods and services. He wasn't just exploiting other people's mental problems; he was exploiting his own. A Kantian would say his greatest sin was that he failed to treat himself with the respect he deserved.

That's the biggest problem with victimhood, from a Kantian perspective: someone who uses their hardships as a shortcut to money and power fails to respect themself. Not only do they overlook their own capabilities, but they commodify their pain. I think people are getting at this Kantian argument when they say that someone's playing the race card, or the victim card, or any identity-based card. Even if they've never heard of the categorical imperative, they're expressing this idea that features of one's own humanity shouldn't be used as mere means to one's practical ends.

Here's a prime example. The most important box to check in college applications these days is "victim." A friend of mine interviews kids in New York City who want to go to Harvard. On a day where she interviewed nine candidates, she says that no fewer than seven of them opened the conversation describing some personal struggle they had encountered, including several stories of abuse by someone in a position of authority with respect to them—teacher, coach, or adult family member. She was particularly struck by the fact that she didn't ask about this, but it was simply the first thing that the candidates chose to share about themselves. Some well-paid college application consultants promising to get the kids into the Ivy League had no doubt advised them all to open with a victimhood statement.

This practice makes young people use their own pain as a mere means to an end. You shouldn't view your feelings about the racism you've experienced or the sexual assault you've survived as a good way to get into college, and you shouldn't be asked to; those things occupy a different plane of value. That's my main critique of victimhood. In many ways, someone who sees themselves as a victim and asks others to see them that way just isn't respecting their own humanity enough.

While the categorical imperative's command to respect your own humanity explains why you shouldn't think of yourself as a victim, its instruction to respect the humanity of others explains why you shouldn't seek superiority over them, either as an individual or a nation. That's what people who wonder if we're Rome are missing: the decline of an empire is nothing to mourn. The decline of a nation is a different matter.

Although Kant claimed to have only one ethical rule, he actually had several different ways of saying it. The one most people are familiar with, the one I've been using, is called the formula of humanity. Another well-known version is the formula of universal law. This is the one that most easily explains why pursuing excellence not only doesn't require dominion over others; it actively opposes it. Kant summed up this take on the categorical imperative with "Act only according to that maxim by which you can at the same time will that it should become a universal law."[45]

That's a bit of a mouthful, but Kant was basically justifying the Golden Rule. "Treat others as you'd want to be treated" is a great principle, and it sounds like common sense, but Kant's genius was that he didn't appeal to intuition or compassion with his more formalized version of the Golden Rule. He argued that sheer rationality compelled one to accept it. To Kant, being nice to people isn't the foundation of ethics. It's a conclusion that falls out of a coldly logical approach to getting what you want.

Imagine you're a member of a community of fishermen. Each of the fishermen is rational and wants to get as many fish as possible, but they've collectively decided to place a limit on the number each can catch in order to prevent overfishing from decimating the stock. The question is, why not cheat? Why not find one way or another to snag a few extra?

Kant would respond with this: you're considering following the plan "I'll break the rule and catch some extra fish so I can end up with more than I'd otherwise have." But, he would say, there's something not just immoral, but fundamentally irrational about pursuing this course of action. You are making an assumption you ought to know is false.

What is that assumption? Well, we began with the stipulation that all the fishermen are rational, not just you. This is where universalization comes in, the ability to imagine what would happen if other people universally behaved the same way as you. If you think following the plan of overfishing is the rational move for you, you ought to conclude that your fellow fishermen will recognize its rationality as well. So when you imagine the consequences of overfishing, you can't just imagine the world where you catch extra fish and everyone else sticks to the rule—to fully respect the rationality of the other fishermen, you have to imagine that they've reached the same conclusion as you and caught extra fish as well. That means that in a world where rational fishermen like yourself all overfished, the population of fish would be devastated and you'd actually end up with less fish. Your plan of overfishing wouldn't achieve its own goal if everyone like you followed it.

In other words, when you follow a plan that won't work if all rational people in your situation follow it, you're making a logical error. Your plan rests on the assumption that other rational people in the same situation as you will somehow reason in a different way than you.

When Kant talks about respecting humanity, it actually strikes me as a bit of a joke, because it's not nearly as lofty a principle as it sounds. What he means is that we need to respect everyone's *rationality*, the defining feature of humanity, the thing that separates us from beasts. The joke a Kantian understands is that respecting people's rationality isn't meant to be a matter of being nice at all; it's more like wearing an oven mitt to respect the heat of a pan. A rational agent must respect the rationality of others, the humanity of others, in order to make plans that effectively achieve his goals; he has to adequately respect the fact of his own rationality as well. When Kant talks about respecting humanity and rationality, just imagine poker players narrowing their eyes at each other across the table, all thinking, *Yeah, I'll respect you all right.*

The problem with conceiving excellence in terms of superiority over others is that it's by definition not universalizable, either for individuals or nations. If your goal is dominance over others, you necessarily must use them as mere means to your end. If everyone reasons that way, we get locked into the trap of hierarchical thinking, and are doomed to make others our victims to avoid becoming theirs.

Carthage and Rome found that out the hard way. Their imperial ambitions ensured that they got locked into an existential struggle not only for dominance, but for survival. Carthage could've thrived for hundreds of years longer, maybe thousands, if it hadn't tried to gain revenge for the First Punic War and grind Rome into the dirt. As for Rome, things may have worked out for it in the end, but history could've easily gone the other way—what if Carthage had simply built more ships in the First Punic War? What if it had simply sent reinforcements to aid Hannibal's invasion of Italy in the Second? Their mutual quest for hegemony guaranteed that one of these giants had to die. That's a lesson China and America both need to keep in mind in the coming years. The question is not who gets to be Rome and who gets to be Carthage; it's how both nations can avoid their fate.

Maybe instead of idolizing Rome, more nations should aspire to be Greece, whose culture loomed so large in Roman thought that it even copied the Greek gods. Carthage contended with Rome for dominance and was utterly destroyed, its people enslaved and its fields salted so nothing would grow. Greece lost its empire when it fell to the Romans in 146 BCE, but it never really faded. When we remember Greece, we hardly even remember that it was once an empire. Greece made its mark on history through its high culture, not armies or territorial control.

That's America's real strength, too. It's our culture of freedom and individuality and all the artistic and scientific innovation that enables. What we ought to fear is not the decline of our empire, but the decline of our nation. Our culture of excellence is being replaced by one of victimhood, one where we fall into the old trap of dividing the world into hierarchies of power and arguing over who gets to be on top. I wish we could find a way to think of ourselves as Kantian fishermen. Our only enemy is the sea.

Chapter Seven

HOW VICTIMHOOD LEADS TO NATIONAL DECLINE

Bread and Circuses

Bread and circuses. That's all the Roman people wanted, according to Juvenal, a poet speaking in the early second century, at the height of the empire.

It was toward the end of the Pax Romana, the Roman peace, two hundred years of relative peace and prosperity, when the empire stretched to its furthest extent. Juvenal was critiquing the politicians' strategy of keeping public approval by offering free grain and games instead of attempting to instill some civic virtue, some shared sense of purpose. He said, "Already long ago, from when we sold our vote to no man, the People have abdicated our duties; for the People who once upon a time handed out military command, high civil office, legions—everything, now restrains itself and anxiously hopes for just two things: bread and circuses."[1]

At the same time, to pay for its growing bills for military, administrative, and social projects, Rome had been debasing the silver in the denarius to mint more money for centuries. This was in some ways Hannibal's revenge, his most lasting legacy for Rome. The Romans had gone broke during their long war against Hannibal, and so that was when they first answered the siren call of minting money to fund public projects, diluting their bronze currency. Printing money was a drug that grew addictive, as many civilizations since have found.

Rome's currency eventually became worthless, but it saved itself through plunder: around 212 BCE, its armies brought back vast wealth from Spain and Sicily.[2] It used that silver to create a new currency, the denarius. But eventually, it decided to try minting more denarii to fund all its projects, which it did by reducing the silver in them.

By the time of Marcus Aurelius, the emperor and Stoic philosopher who reigned just after Juvenal's time, the silver content of the denarius had dropped to about 80 percent. Though that seemed manageable, over the empire's long life the debasement of the denarius steadily compounded.[3] Creating so much money for so long had never been a good idea. Inevitably, inflation rose and eventually became hyperinflation; the government had to raise taxes higher and higher to truly fund its projects, even as it minted more denarii. By 265 CE, there was almost no silver in the denarius at all, only 0.5 percent. Prices rose 1,000 percent per year. Gold was reserved for paying barbarian mercenaries.[4]

By the end of the third century Roman currency was worthless again, and unlike the last time, it couldn't plunder new precious metals to replenish its treasury. Its economy was strangled, as no one was willing to trade for its worthless coins, and trade became local, limited to whatever could be accomplished with primitive forms of barter. The fall wasn't far.

Like Romans, we Americans crave bread and circuses, and we print lots of money to pay for them. We have recreated the bargain between Rome's politicians and its citizenry at the beginning of its decline: the leaders offer bribes to the populace to keep it fat and happy, funding them with money the government doesn't really have, and in return the people allow them to stay in power. The citizens think only of the material goods they want the government to give them, the politicians think only of how to outbid each other to offer those, and no one thinks of the long-term good of the nation.

That's the essence of Juvenal's bread and circuses critique. It's still valid today. He was describing what happens when a nation of underdogs becomes a nation of victims. When a nation peaks—especially when an empire does—its focus shifts from producing wealth to arguing over how to distribute it. This fixation on arguing over how to split the pie goes hand in hand with victimhood complexes: arguing that you're more oppressed than someone else is a powerful way to claim you deserve government largesse more than they do. Victimhood focuses on how to divvy up the economic pie, rather than how to make it bigger. In so doing, it actually makes the pie smaller.

This process of decline has actually been going on for decades. Charlie Sykes identified it almost thirty years ago in his well-titled *A Nation of Victims*, which I only learned about midway through writing this book. In Sykes's version of the tale, the peak of America's happiness occurred in the postwar economic boom of the 1950s.[5] But, he adds, "As it turned out, happiness proved surprisingly elusive for modern man. Expectation proved to be inseparable from anxiety, while the reliance on self often cut off man from his neighbors and left him a prisoner of his own sense of entitlement."[6] In other words, national success is a double-edged sword. National achievement breeds national entitlement. Once the underdog tastes victory, they only want more, and that creates constant anxiety, a gnawing fear of loss. From there, Sykes presents a detailed account of how that diffuse anxiety was sharpened and entrenched by a professional class of therapists who profited from treating it. After that, clinical diagnoses of different forms of victimhood flourished like weeds.[7]

Sykes and I share a similar starting point. We agree that national success sows the seeds in which victimhood takes root. But while Sykes focuses on anxiety as the psychological response to success that enables victimhood, I think there's another important character trait that operates alongside it: laziness. It is the combination of the two that turns underdogs into victims. After all, underdogs experience a kind of anxiety too, but that drives them to overcome the obstacles they face. It's the addition of laziness to the equation that makes underdogs demand that others overcome their anxieties for them.

The Pro-Laziness Movement

Government policies have created a culture of laziness in recent years—mostly in ways that you'd expect, but some you wouldn't.

First the COVID-19 pandemic opened up the spigot of government aid. Initially that aid went to families that, in many cases, genuinely needed it because of government-mandated business closures that prevented people from working. Yet as those lockdowns loosened, the benefits provided to people who stayed home remained intact. The government never turned off the tap.

Notably, this public policy was supported not only by most Democrats, but also by prominent Republican legislators like

Senator Josh Hawley and President Trump, who refused to sign an aid package into law unless it contained a higher threshold ($2,000 vs. $1,600) of government aid to families. This may have been a populist policy to aid his reelection bid, but in any case it's notable that Trump, Hawley, Bernie Sanders, and Kamala Harris, for example, were all on the same side of this issue. It's part of the age-old promise of bread and circuses: it's legal to bribe citizens to reelect you as long as you do it with the government's money. Of course, you're ultimately bribing them with their own money, and diluting its value through inflation too.

Bluntly, this cornucopia of free money has contributed to a culture of laziness that has resulted in the greatest labor shortage in the United States in over a generation. People simply became accustomed to not working—and quite liked it. White-collar employees enjoyed "working" from home with a measurable downtick in how much they were actually completing work, in my experience. So far, we're still early in the process of formally studying it, and the existing evidence is mixed.[8]

Many employees certainly feel more productive when working from home, largely because they get to skip their commutes, but they're also less able to have spontaneous conversations with coworkers and receive career mentoring. And, as organizational psychologist Anthony Klotz points out, the trend toward remote work may be a double-edged sword for American workers because it accelerates outsourcing: "In the United States, employees tend to be paid higher wages than people in many other countries. If you're a remote organization, you can recruit workers from all over the world who can do the same job for a cheaper rate."[9]

While white-collar workers opted to work remotely, other employees who worked in restaurants and stores simply chose not to go back when lockdown ended but generous unemployment aid continued. It was part of a phenomenon that came to be known as the Great Resignation, a term coined by Klotz. In some ways this was by design: the Biden administration explicitly pointed to its desire to make employers "compete" in order to pay higher wages. Yet even as places like Burger King and Walmart offered the highest pay packages in their history for new employees, the new employees didn't show up. As I write, the ratio of job openings to job seekers is at an all-time high.[10] A recent analysis in the *Wall Street Journal* suggests that the US's more generous unemployment benefits than other countries' contributed both to its lower labor-force participation rate and, because of fewer workers to help meet demand, higher inflation.[11]

You would predict that people start going back to work when the unemployment benefits stop. But we're not seeing that happen—at least not yet, as of this writing. Why? Because people got accustomed to the idea of not working and enjoyed it enough to stop working for longer than they could afford.

Nowhere was the new laziness movement better epitomized than the subreddit r/antiwork, which became the place for supporters of the Great Resignation to unite. Its user population exploded during the pandemic, going from 180,000 in October 2020 to more than 1.6 million by January 2022. As the *New York Post* summed it up, the forum is a place where "People post epic text and e-mail screenshots of quitting their jobs, but the real heroes are so-called 'idlers'—those who stay in jobs doing the absolute minimum to get by while still collecting a paycheck."[12] Examples include a user who bragged about getting paid $80,000 a year to answer one or two phone calls and an IT professional who created a simple script to perform their entire job and received $90,000 per year.

The Post interviewed the subreddit's moderator, Doreen Ford, a thirty-year-old part-time dogwalker who identifies as nonbinary and transgender. She said the antiwork movement's goal "is to reduce the coercive element of labor as much as possible by subverting capitalism." A noble sentiment. "What we call laziness is actually people reaching their limits for very good reasons that are outside of their control," Ford explained, adding "Well, some of us are lazy and we just don't want to work."[13] The movement suffered a setback when Ford gave a disastrous interview on Fox News, showing up unwashed and disheveled in a dirty room, opining "I think laziness is a virtue in a society where people constantly want you to be productive 24/7, and it's good to have rest."[14] After the interview, old Facebook posts from Ford surfaced where she admitted to having inappropriate sexual encounters on more than one occasion, blaming some of her actions on her unmet sexual needs.[15] Doreen Ford was in one sense a very poor representative of the antiwork movement and, in another, perhaps the perfect one, a caricature who turned out to be real.

The pro-laziness movement launched by the pandemic dovetailed nicely with a growing clamor for the government to forgive student loan debt; repaying debts is hard work, after all. Once again, the federal government began by offering a moratorium on student loan repayments under President Trump,[16] and once again, people expected that temporary aid to become permanent. The moratorium was repeatedly extended under President Biden, and more and more activists and lawmakers called for it to become an outright cancellation of debt.

Progressive "Squad" politicians such as Representatives Alexandria Ocasio-Cortez, Rashida Tlaib, Ilhan Omar, and Jamaal Bowman began framing student debt cancellation as a matter of progressive racial justice, even as all of them owed tens of thousands of dollars or, in some cases, hundreds of thousands.[17] Somehow, they were perfectly able to understand the idea of conflicts of interest when they demanded a ban on lawmakers trading stock, yet unable to grasp the concept while simultaneously demanding their student loans be forgiven.[18] It brings to mind another of Juvenal's famous critiques: who watches the watchmen?[19]

When the Biden administration was slow to respond, Ocasio-Cortez made the subtext of the old bread-and-circuses bargain explicit: if you want people to vote for you, cancel their debt. She tweeted that Democratic politicians were "delusional" for not realizing they had to make that deal in order to stay in power.[20] She was, as the saying goes, saying the quiet part out loud.

Meanwhile, according to government estimates, even the *pause* on student debt repayment has cost taxpayers more than $100 billion, losing another $4–5 billion in interest payments each month until the moratorium is lifted.[21] Yet somehow, American culture now maintains that it is right and good for students to purchase expensive educations and require others to foot the bill. The notion of *paying back money you borrowed* is now considered outdated, perhaps even systemically racist. An analysis from the Brookings Institute, for instance, argued that the existence of a racial wealth divide necessitates the full cancellation of student debt.[22]

Victimhood fits laziness like a glove. Note that even when antiwork superstars like Doreen Ford explicitly defend laziness as a virtue, they have to justify it by saying indolence is an appropriate response to capitalism's exploitation—stealing from your employers can't be *just* laziness or greed; it has to be part of a grand fight for justice. In the same way, when progressive politicians and activists argue that taxpayers ought to cover their student loans, to avoid the charge that it's just laziness they need a victimhood narrative like systemic racism to give them cover. A good victimhood narrative dresses up naked self-interest until it looks like nobility. It allows you to pretend to fight for others as you fight for nothing but yourself.

Here's the thing about the new culture of laziness in America: it's not limited to the workers. It's spread to corporations, especially those that enjoy monopolies, as many of today's big tech companies do.

How can that be? Google in the 1990s actually had to compete with other firms in order to make a profit. It had to hire the best and brightest to develop algorithms that eventually outcompeted Yahoo, AOL, and others. But today, it doesn't much matter if the engineers at Google do a good or bad job writing an incremental piece of code. It'll still print the same billions in monopoly profit from its search and ad businesses either way. That creates a culture where it doesn't matter if people show up to work or not, or how productive they are.

If you're a manager at Google, you care more about the diversity of gender identities on your engineering team than the quality of the products you build. Google's monopoly ensures that no one can compete with it on its core products, but other major companies *can* compete over diversity, equity, and inclusion rankings, so that's the new arena it has to focus on. If government aid is the bread that keeps us satiated, identity politics is the American circus, the coliseum where we compete with each other to find purpose and status.

Conventional wisdom holds that startup companies might be a disciplining force in the marketplace because they have their back against the wall and are struggling for survival. But this too is no longer the case in an economy overflowing with liquidity. Today a well-written business plan on a piece of paper can command pre-money valuations in the tens of millions. Normally, an entrepreneur wouldn't want to raise more capital than needed, because it would result in unnecessary early dilution—but if they're able to command a high valuation justified only by a business plan written up on a piece of paper, they figure they might as well. So that takes the same culture of excess to startups too. Now they can afford to hire not only the best engineers, but a few diversity hires too, and a proper DEI department—all before they know whether they have a product people can actually use.

These increases in asset valuations accrue to the rich and never trickle down to the poor because they're fueled by an open-handed Fed instead of increases to productivity. As the market's regulators prop it up through loose monetary policy, the assets of the rich become worth more while cash, the asset of the middle class and poor, becomes worth less. In this way, too, we mirror Rome. When asked to describe the arc of the Roman Empire succinctly, historian Ramsay MacMullen simply said, "Fewer had more."[23]

The End of Easy Money

A market crash serves as a much-needed shock to the new culture of laziness that has permeated the American economy—from workers who grew accustomed to staying home to investors who grew accustomed to stocks only going up to monopolies who grew accustomed to printing profits no matter how they performed to young founders who grew accustomed to plentiful capital. I think a market crash is the medicine that we need, and against the right cultural circumstances, could help recreate a national identity built around excellence rather than entitlement.

In the face of now persistent (not "transient") inflation, we need a more cautious fiscal and monetary policy that spends less and tightens monetary supply. As I write, the Federal Reserve is finally embarking on this course, tightening monetary policy in ways it hasn't for over a decade. Some argued that this would create a greater risk of a short-term market crash. They were correct. My view is that the market crash of 2022 will ultimately be a good thing for the country—not just to fight inflation, but to combat the cultural lethargy that the days of easy money have brought.

The last time the United States faced hyperinflation was in the late 1970s. In the early 1980s, Paul Volcker did what he needed to do by rapidly raising interest rates to curb the problem. Yes, this had a deflationary effect on asset prices. Normally, that sounds like a bad thing, but under Volcker that was actually the intended effect; the alternative of unchecked hyperinflation would've been far worse.

But there's one crucial difference between then and now: Volcker's policies were paired with the otherwise business-friendly, deregulatory policy atmosphere set by President Ronald Reagan, which allowed fundamental economic growth to offset the deflationary impact of rising interest rates. By contrast, as the Fed faces the need to raise interest rates in 2022 and 2023, it does so against the backdrop of President Biden's interventionist policies: greater regulations, the prospect of higher taxes, and historically large spending bills. These tactics create an even higher risk of an economic crash when paired with tighter monetary policy to stave off hyperinflation. This is part of the reason I believe an economic crash—including but not limited to the stock market crash—is even likelier today than in Volcker's time, if inflation grows so out of control we're forced to adopt his draconian measures.

There's another difference too. Reagan inspired a greater sense of cultural confidence in the idea of the United States itself than Biden does, both within and beyond America's shores. That confidence in the American spirit translates directly into confidence in American currency.

Both in the 1980s and today, the US dollar was backed by nothing more than the full faith and credit of the United States government. The value of that promise in an uncertain world made our dollar the world's reserve currency—something that values the dollar more richly in global currency markets than would otherwise be the case. As I explained in chapter 5, this is a precious status that we can't afford to squander.

But the cultural circumstances that allowed the dollar to thrive as the reserve currency under Reagan no longer exist today: Americans at home and foreigners abroad have simply lost confidence in America itself. There's no other way to say it. America's citizens doubt its stability; other countries doubt its word, as they watch us stagger from one regime to the exact opposite every couple years. And that may deal the biggest economic blow of all—one whose consequences have been covered up in the short run by a soaring stock market, a speculative ESG bubble, and government handouts. But once the Federal Reserve adopts tighter monetary policy this time around, America may find itself with less cultural confidence in the nation. Our nation's cultural decline threatens to become a vicious cycle where the perception of decline itself creates heavy economic costs.

There's no guarantee that the dollar will ever return to its status as the world's reserve currency. The International Monetary Fund now accepts the Chinese yuan as a reserve currency alongside the US dollar. America's debt load continues to rise as we spend money we don't have. Most important of all, however, is an image problem—both in the eyes of America's observers abroad and our own citizens at home—of a nation that is in decline. Cultural and psychological attitudes aren't the stuff of classical macroeconomic analysis, but they form the backdrop against which an economy ultimately thrives.

Speaking as one such American, I think the loss of confidence is warranted—for all of the reasons that I lay out in this book. A nation of victims is unlikely to navigate turbulent geopolitical waters. The nation that defeated the Soviet Union during the Cold War wasn't one that thought of itself as a victim on the global stage, nor one whose own citizens viewed themselves as each other's victims.

But there's an optimistic note to all of this: the cultural revival that I call for in this book will have economic benefits too. And ironically I think that it may take an economic crash that ends the American era of bread and circuses, the days of easy money. When hard times come, we'll either sink or become strong. I think that crash has begun. I'm optimistic that we'll rise to meet the challenge.

How Victimhood Makes Inequality Worse

So the main way victimhood causes national decline is by making the economic pie smaller as everyone focuses on grabbing as much of it as they can instead of growing it. American national success breeds laziness through the abundant flow of easy money, and that laziness in turn breeds victimhood as the idle argue that they deserve to receive money without working for it. As citizens squabble over who most deserves government beneficence, the nation declines culturally through division, and economically through lack of productivity. Then at a certain point when both types of decline become noticeable, the nation's fall becomes a self-fulfilling prophecy as everyone loses confidence in it. As the rest of the world doubts our stability, we lose our economic advantages.

But there's a natural counterargument to this line of thinking: So what if victimhood lowers the GDP? So what if it makes the economic pie smaller? Maybe that's not the metric that matters most. If arguing over the fairest way to split the proceeds of American success results in a more just distribution, or even one that's perceived to be more just, maybe it will make the happiness pie grow even as it makes the economic one shrink.

Well, when victimhood is the tool people use to justify getting a greater share of the economic pie, their happiness probably suffers; it can't make people happy being in a constant state of grievance. But it is true that human happiness is greatly affected by perceptions of fairness in distribution of goods, not just by the absolute level of material goods people have. In fact, plenty of experimental evidence indicates notions of fairness are so fundamental, they're actually a feature not only of humans, but primates in general and some other animals. The seminal article on this is Sarah Brosnan and Frans de Waal's "Monkeys Reject Unequal Pay," which reports on the researchers' discovery that capuchin monkeys would refuse to participate in an experiment once they saw other monkeys receive greater rewards for performing the same tasks.[24]

There's a funny viral YouTube video where Brosnan and de Waal show a short clip from the original experiment. A monkey gives the researcher a rock, is rewarded with a slice of cucumber, and is perfectly content to eat it. Then she witnesses the monkey next to her give a rock and be rewarded with a much more desirable grape. She gives another rock to the researcher, and when she receives cucumber again, she throws it back at the scientist and rages at him, reaching for the grapes and shaking the walls of her cage. He repeats the procedure, giving another grape to the other monkey, and when he returns to the first one she tests her rock before giving it to him. You can practically see her thinking—"I'm doing the same thing, right?" Then she once again throws the cucumber slice she receives back with great disdain and shakes her cage in fury.[25] No doubt the antiwork crowd would take it as a perfect representation of capitalism.

After that 2003 article, experiments revealed similar aversion to inequality in dogs, wolves, rats, crows, and ravens, although small sample sizes and confounding factors sometimes delivered mixed results. The moral of the story seems to be that the more a species has evolved to succeed through cooperation, the more its happiness is affected by the perception of unfair inequality. Notably, in all of these experiments there seemed to be wide variation between individuals. Even in animals that care about fairness, some care a lot more than others.

There is a rich field attempting to study the same phenomenon in humans using survey data to deduce the relationship between national income inequality and individual and national happiness. Not coincidentally, this work was launched at the same time as inquiry into animal conceptions of fairness—starting in 2003, economists Thomas Piketty and Emmanuel Saez began drawing intense scrutiny toward income inequality in the United States, using detailed analysis of tax return data to argue that over the last few decades gains in income have overwhelmingly gone to the ultra-rich.[26] According to their most recent analysis, the top 1 percent of earners' post-tax share of national income rose from 9.1 percent in 1979 to 15.7 percent in 2014.[27]

Their focus on the very top earners, the one percent, was the animating force behind both the Occupy Wall Street movement and the growing academic focus on income inequality. That academic literature generally agrees that a country's net happiness tends to be lower as income inequality is higher, although there's robust debate about whether that's because the poor are so unhappy that they drag the average down, or whether everyone is less happy. A 2022 study attempting to resolve this dispute found that there are elements of truth to both theories: when income inequality is high, every group except the very rich is less happy, and the poorer someone is, the less happy they tend to be.[28]

This evidence suggests that it isn't simply an absolute lack of material goods that makes those with less unhappy, since even those with plenty tend to be less happy when inequality is higher— like the capuchins and other cooperative social animals, human happiness seems to be tightly tied to perceptions of relative wealth.

Interestingly, some chimpanzees, bonobos, and capuchins even objected to experiments when they received better rewards than their partners, not worse ones, a much rarer phenomenon. That was actually what launched the whole field of inquiry. Brosnan first wondered about animal conceptions of fairness when she was distributing peanuts to a bunch of low-status capuchins, and a high-ranking male monkey traded her a prized orange to be given a mere peanut as well, a startling display of capuchin noblesse oblige. That trend suggests that humans, the most intelligent, most cooperative primates of all, might display an even stronger aversion to unfair inequality, sometimes even when it favors them. That theory is consistent with the evidence human happiness studies have yielded so far.

There are, however, a couple of difficulties with reaching the conclusion that inequality makes most humans less happy. First, as with animal studies, the study of how inequality affects human happiness is still a young field, plagued by confounding variables; assessing different countries with different economic systems in different time periods can yield different conclusions. But even more significantly, there is a theoretical mismatch between the questions the animal studies and human ones tend to focus on: the animal experiments show that cooperative animals reject unfair inequality, while most human studies simply look at the question of how inequality itself correlates with happiness. This may be in part because social scientists can't easily take up the question of how fair the economic systems they assess are.

A paper called "Income Inequality and Happiness" from University of Virginia professor Shigehiro Oishi and others addresses both of these difficulties.[29] It's also particularly useful for my purposes because the authors focus specifically on America, using survey data from 1972 to 2008 to track the relationship between Americans' happiness and national income inequality. They concluded that all but the richest Americans were happier in times of lower income inequality and, importantly, that the relationship was explained by considerations of fairness: "Americans perceived others to be less fair and trustworthy in the years with greater income disparity, and this perception in turn explained why Americans reported lower levels of happiness in those years."[30]

The authors suggest that these results help answer the question of why Americans haven't become happier since the 1960s as national wealth has skyrocketed, even as massive economic growth in European countries did correlate with increased happiness.[31] In short, it seems Americans are made unhappy by inequality because we attribute it to unfairness, activating our deep-seated biological aversion to unfair inequities.

That may be because capitalist systems have a natural tendency to concentrate wealth, especially the American one. The shift from discussing income inequality toward wealth inequality really took off with Thomas Piketty's 2014 book *Capital in the Twenty-First Century*, which argued that unchecked capitalism tends to produce wealth inequality so vast that it outweighs whatever's happening with income.

Essentially, Piketty argues that when the rate of return on invested capital exceeds the rate of a society's economic growth, wealth from investments will accrue faster than wealth from labor, which steadily widens the gap between rich and poor. He assembles detailed empirical evidence to argue that in most capitalist societies during the last two centuries, the rate of return on invested capital hovers around 5 percent, while GDP growth is substantially less. That means growing wealth inequality is the default state of affairs, only disrupted by exceptional events like world wars and the Great Depression. That growing wealth gap is perpetuated by inheritance, Piketty argues, which results in an informal oligarchy. The two main forces that can resist this trend to inequality are deliberate government redistribution of wealth and high economic growth.[32]

Liberals often take Piketty's work to justify a wealth tax, and that is one of the main policies he himself argues for at the end of his book. But he also argues for hefty inheritance taxes, which would short-circuit the capitalist path to oligarchy that he fears. Later in this book, I'll argue for the superiority of inheritance taxes over wealth taxes as part of our return to a merit-based culture of excellence. Another alternative to a wealth tax is to simply do a better job guaranteeing equality of opportunity. Remember, human and animal studies demonstrate that it's not inequality itself that we object to, it's *unfair* inequality, and ensuring citizens have equal opportunities to succeed would rightly create a perception of fairness, even in the presence of wealth inequality. That's actually a core part of John Rawls's theory of justice, which was the dominant liberal conception of fairness before Piketty changed the conversation. I'll return to the Rawlsian argument later as well.

My point for now is that the era of easy money and the culture of laziness it enabled both supercharged Piketty's problem. When discussing the rise of wealth inequality in the United States over the last couple decades, Piketty correctly points out that returns on capital accelerated even as economic growth slowed, but he fails to explain why that happened. My answer is that a combination of loose monetary policy in the late 1990s and post-2008 era and overly generous fiscal policy like government loans to buy houses in the 2000s both contributed heavily to the phenomenon of high returns on capital alongside low economic growth. Loose monetary policy artificially inflates the assets of the rich without genuinely increasing productivity, which exacerbates wealth inequality both through inflation (which decreases the value of the assets of the poor) and by leading to the imbalance between investment and labor returns that Piketty identifies.

When laziness and victimhood enter the equation and people compete to receive government handouts instead of working, economic growth suffers even more. By squabbling over how to split the economic pie instead of growing it, then, we may actually be making wealth inequality worse. Even if we did manage to achieve some more just distribution in the short term, by Piketty's reasoning, if we did it in a way that slowed growth more than returns on invested capital, we would only be changing who the haves and have-nots are, and creating more have-nots.

Reducing both economic factors to the same level might solve the inequality problem, but at the cost of leaving everyone worse off. That's the solution to inequality Kurt Vonnegut satirized in "Harrison Bergeron." He imagined a version of America so obsessed with equality that it constitutionally mandated it in every respect, dragging everyone down to the lowest common denominator by forcing the beautiful to wear ugly masks, the strong to wear heavy weights, and the smart to listen to thought-disrupting radios.[33] One wonders if some modern progressives might think Vonnegut was describing a utopia. We should not infer from Piketty's theory of inequality that the grand solution is to carefully adjust returns on capital and economic growth downward to the same level. The solution to inequality can't be to have everyone stand in breadlines; that's been tried before, and no one liked it. Boris Yeltsin despaired for the Soviet Union when he visited an American supermarket.[34] That tour played a major role in his capitalist reforms once he rose to power.

Piketty's theory gives us insight into a condition any realistic strategy for achieving greater wealth equality must meet: if it sacrifices too much economic growth, it's probably just a way of changing peoples' positions on the ladder of wealth. Switching which monkey gets the cucumber and which gets the grape doesn't actually solve much.

How Victimhood Stifles National Dialogue

A victimhood narrative isn't just a story a person tells about themself. It spreads and dictates what the entire culture can say. For a prime example of this, consider a case where American victimhood has made us resurrect the legacy of a Roman emperor and redefine it. Let's talk about Septimius Severus, whom the narrative of black victimhood has recently decided to dub "the black emperor."

That wasn't the Romans' title for him; it's one contemporary society seems to be bestowing. You can read about him in books like *Severus: The Black Caesar*,[35] or if you have a more academic bent, you can read articles like "Rediscovering the Lost Roman Caesar: Septimius Severus, the African and Eurocentric Historiography," in the *Journal of Black Studies*.[36] Or maybe you'd learn about him in school in Black History Month.[37] If you want, you could just watch the adventure TV version of *The Black Caesar* "The first black man to set foot on British soil came not as a slave, but as Emperor," the synopsis breathlessly declares.[38]

Quite an accomplishment. It's almost enough to make you forget that Septimius was a ruthless general who often sold his defeated enemies into slavery, as he did when he conquered Parthia and enslaved one hundred thousand women and children.[39] In fact, I think that in today's America, the fact that Septimius Severus had slightly darker skin than the average Roman (maybe one shade, not three) really *is* enough to make it irrelevant that he enslaved people. We will make him some symbol of blackness rising above slavery, and we won't teach that he enslaved a lot of people because that doesn't fit the narrative. The black emperor is the hero we need.

Plenty of Americans wouldn't even have seen Septimius Severus as black, by the way—he had Italian Roman ancestry on his mother's side and descended from Punics on his father's. Out of curiosity, reading about the debate over Septimius Severus's race made me wonder why Hannibal, himself fully Punic, isn't known as the black general who led an African empire. I then found that there is indeed a longstanding effort to declare Hannibal a hero of black history.[40] There was an uproar when a History Channel documentary portrayed him as black.[41] When the question came up in an ancient history classroom at the University of Pennsylvania, Professor William C. McDermott quipped, "Yes, Hannibal was as black as King David."[42] Carthaginians were Phoenicians, who had Semitic ancestry and spoke a language similar to Hebrew. So maybe we can call Hannibal a great Jewish general and Septimius Severus the Jewish emperor, if we must translate ancient Carthaginian ancestry into the language of modern identity politics. Representation matters, after all.

Romans just didn't see race through the strange lens America uses. They documented Hannibal and Septimius Severus's characters, but didn't think to mention their skin colors. None of Septimius Severus's contemporaries would've thought of him as black; they didn't see anyone that way. Although it's hard for the American mind to understand this, though the Romans were of course able to see that some people had darker skin than others, to them that was a fact little different from some people having darker eyes or hair than others. Just as we don't divide the world into green-eyed people, brown-eyed ones, and so on, the Romans didn't think skin color had much value in explaining who people were or how they behaved. Where an American would see a person by their skin color, a Roman would see them by their nationality. While if we traveled through time we might look at Septimius Severus and see him as black or brown, the Romans would have looked at his clothes, heard his speech, and seen him only as Roman.[43]

It reminds me of something a guy once told a college friend of mine while he was visiting South Africa. "You call black people in your country African-Americans and 'people of color' and all these other names," he said. "You know what we call them here? Americans."

The great irony in remembering Septimius Severus for being the first black emperor is that the narrative that compels us to remember him requires us to forget his deeds. We remember him for a superficial feature of his identity instead of any of the things he would've wanted to be remembered for, just as we often see each other for our skin color instead of any of the things we want to be seen for. He would've wanted to be remembered for being a soldier and a general, a conqueror and a reformer of the military. The fact that his conquest often involved slavery would make his preferred narrative conflict with our uses for him. To substantially increase military pay and throw games to keep the populace happy, he—you'll be shocked to hear this—massively diluted the silver purity of the denarius, reducing it to 50 percent.

The black emperor is the emperor we need, but the emperor we deserve to learn about is the general who kept the empire together but continued the debasement of the denarius to fund his wars and appease the public. Not a black emperor or a white one; just Roman like all the others.

In 211 CE, Septimius Severus died of illness in Eboracum, a Roman province on an island at the northern edge of the empire. The people of that island still remember him through sardonic Hogwarts professor Severus Snape. Some fans present intriguing evidence that J. K. Rowling hints that Snape may even be a descendant of his namesake. For instance, Eboracum, renamed North Yorkshire after Vikings conquered it, holds a village called Snape, which has the ruins of a Roman villa thought by some to be Septimius Severus's.[44]

Reading Septimius Severus as black reminds me of queer readings of characters, where a consumer of a work of art creates their own narrative about a character's sexual orientation irrespective of what the author intends. It gets to the whole death-of-the-author debate. Perhaps there's something similar going on when Harry Potter fans read one of their favorite characters as the descendant of Roman royalty. But it's one thing to read Severus Snape as a descendant of Septimius Severus, and another to read Septimius Severus as black. Whether the author is dead to the reader is an interesting theoretical question about the bargain behind fiction, and about the bargain behind constitutional law, for that matter. But history has no author.

Victimhood has become so entrenched in American culture that it even determines the way we talk to each other and the things we can say. It determines which historical figures we remember and how we remember them. It determines who gets to talk first, or who gets to talk at all.[45] It determines how we address each other, which often means that when we disagree on pronouns, we simply don't talk to each other or about each other. I've noticed that the frequent conservative uncertainty over which pronouns to use for transgender people sometimes leads them to simply avoid talking about them, especially in mixed political company, to avoid charges of bigoted language.

When we Americans do talk to each other, victimhood increasingly determines what we're allowed to say. We all know there's a new category of *things you just can't say*. That's even what we call them. What we mean by this label is that you just can't say some ideas no matter how much evidence you provide for them or how politely you state your position. You can't share some opinions no matter how well you warrant their truth, because the reasons you can't share them have nothing to do with whether they're true or not. Even the reason we can't say some things—that they oppose favored progressive victimhood narratives—is something you just can't say, which is why this category is presented as a primitive, a fundamental fact with no further justification.

Many things you just can't say fall into the broad category of wondering if different groups might have innately different traits in some ways. As Larry Summers found out when he was fired as president of Harvard, you just can't say that there's greater variability among men's scientific ability than women's; you certainly can't say that men naturally tend to be better or more interested in science. As a conservative who talks to liberals, I occasionally listen to them talk to me privately, in hushed tones, preface their comment with how good a liberal they are, then quietly confess that they suspect there might be some biological differences in the mental traits of sexes or even races. They always swear me to secrecy, as if they're relieved to have a friend they can confess these forbidden thoughts to, someone to whom they can finally say the things you just can't say. It makes me feel like a priest. Personally, I'm skeptical that there'd be much natural variation in the intellectual abilities of races defined by skin color, since, unlike skin color, there are hundreds, possibly thousands of genes that affect the many traits we associate with intelligence. That point convinces some people. If the topic weren't forbidden, they could've been convinced sooner.

The category of things you just can't say grows as America's victimhood complexes do. I believe, for example, that you now cannot say that women have vaginas, or that mothers are women. This linguistic update came to public attention when Representative Cori Bush described mothers as "birthing people."[46] When people objected, progressives said that it was an isolated incident from a single politician; a month later, the Biden administration replaced the word "mothers" with "birthing people" in its 2022 budget.[47] Language changes very quickly these days, because the moment we see a new progressive term, most of us adopt it, reasoning that it's far better to be ahead of the trend than behind it. This principle of "better safe than sorry" is even truer for organizations than individuals, since they face more scrutiny and risk. Organizations playing it safe then pass new rules about what you can say down to individuals who play it safe.

This stuff would almost be funny if the consequences for the nation weren't so serious. The inevitable consequence of the growing category of things you just can't say is that you don't voice your true views in public, leading to national policies that a majority don't actually believe in, but everyone must be seen to believe in. You can't, for instance, point out the hypocrisy between saying sexual orientation is immutably inherited (despite the total absence of a gay gene), while saying that gender is completely fluid over one's life (despite the existence of X and Y chromosomes). So we will create public policies founded on contradictory beliefs, which can only lead to new injustice. A just-published paper argues, for instance, that the growing use of "birthing people" in the medical profession will have harmful health consequences for women by obscuring their unique biological needs.[48] Meanwhile, in private, we increasingly associate only with people who think like us because they're the only ones we can speak freely to. Then our beliefs are reinforced. All the while, resentment grows.

America's victim complexes continue to proliferate as we desperately use them to grab pieces of a shrinking pie of resources. We compete with each other for higher rank on the ladder of victimization, we talk to each other less and less honestly for fear of offending ever-changing rules, we associate only with those who share our beliefs, and our grievances against each other fester and grow. Where will this lead? Nowhere good, of course, but what exact shape will our decline take? On its current trajectory, will our nation fizzle, or go out with a bang?

I see more and more Americans discussing the possibility of a second civil war, both publicly and privately. As I write, two books on the subject have just come out, Stephen Marche's *The Next Civil War* and Barbara F. Walter's *How Civil Wars Start*. Walter's book has been especially influential, since she's a leading expert on civil war who's studied it for over thirty years. Walter argues that the three factors of growing distrust in democracy, increasing factionalism, and rising racial resentment all bode very poorly for the US. She sums it up with "Where is the United States today? We are a factionalized [autocratic democracy] that is quickly approaching the open insurrection stage, which means we are closer to civil war than any of us would like to believe."

Other scholars of civil war disagree, and there's a robust and growing debate on the topic. I won't take a stand on the question, because that's a book-length issue in its own right, but what I do know is that the more we speak of civil war, the more likely it becomes. There are even growing accelerationist movements in America trying to hasten our descent into civil war. The most prominent of them calls itself the "Boogaloo Bois." In true

American fashion, it uses the term "bois" instead of "boys" to make clear that it's gender neutral.[49]

The group is a loose collection of white supremacists, militia members, anti-police activists, and others, united only by their desire to bring about a second American civil war—the boogaloo, jokingly named after the obscure sequel movie *Breakin' 2: Electric Boogaloo.* The movement uses memes and inside jokes to avoid being taken seriously (its favored uniform is a Hawaiian shirt), but in recent years, the group has finally worked up enough nerve to become violent. At around the same time, one member killed a security contractor and a police officer in California,[50] others were involved in a plot to kidnap Michigan governor Gretchen Whitmer,[51] and others set fire to a police precinct in Minneapolis in a successful effort to make the George Floyd riots more violent.[52]

An *Atlantic* interview of JJ McNab, a fellow with the Program on Extremism at George Washington University who has studied antigovernment extremists for more than twenty years, closed by asking her why the movement wanted to bring about violent revolution. "They want Rome to fall," she responded. "They want chaos to bring it down." Movements like the Boogaloo Bois are an effort to make war speak itself into existence. I write this book in the hope that peace can work the same way.

I was talking to a friend about Rome once, as one does, and he pointed out that the common folk of Europe in the Middle Ages must have known that they lived in the ruins of a much greater civilization. "It's all the empty granaries," he said. His point was that by simply looking out into the fields and seeing all the ancient, unused granaries everywhere, it must've been obvious to people that long ago their lands were far more populated. And like the Old English poet marveling at the ruins of Bath, they would've known that some ancient power once built towers far beyond their modern capabilities. The work of giants.

We tell a narrative of human history where it's always progressing, where we humans are always improving, becoming more knowledgeable, more civilized. We tell ourselves that the arc of our species bends toward progress. It's easy for us to tell ourselves that narrative because, in our day, technology really does seem to inevitably progress. Just as it's hard for us Americans to imagine how the Romans truly didn't see race, it's hard for us to imagine the post-Roman period where the people living in Rome's ruins would've seen the arc of human history as one of decline, as one where knowledge and skill were inevitably lost.

Are we Rome? When I look at America sometimes, I can't help but remember what Dio Cassius said, the rare person to recognize his own empire's decline: "Our history now descends from a kingdom of gold to one of iron and rust." This was a kingdom of gold, once, and now it's becoming rust and iron. It's not our buildings that have decayed, but our freedoms, and our identities too, reduced from complex wholes to primitive parts. But we can look at our history and see that something has been lost.

It's hard to see an empire's decline while it's happening, when it's been going on for decades or centuries and it's all you've ever known. But then you look one day and you find yourself out on open fields, surrounded by ruins and empty granaries. Things no longer work, and there are fewer people who know how to repair them.

It's easy to despair, once you see the ruins around you, and to begin to think that you belong to a narrative of inevitable decline. But those farmers would've been wrong if they'd concluded humanity had declined. The poet who wrote "The Ruin" was wrong when he thought the Romans had died out a hundred generations earlier. Rome was still flourishing even then, though it was far from Britain.

Rome's decline began in earnest when its age of merit ended and ushered in nepotism, cronyism, corruption, and spectacle— bread and circuses. After Septimius Severus and his family's brief dynasty held the empire together for a while longer through military might, Rome fell into the Crisis of the Third Century, a wartorn period where the empire nearly collapsed, fifty years with twenty-six emperors. Even this wasn't the end for Rome. Aurelian reunited the empire, and it limped along for another two hundred years before falling to barbarians.

The Western Roman Empire fell, at least. In 285 CE, Aurelian's successor, Diocletian, had divided the empire into eastern and western halves because it had grown too large to be manageable. And so when the western empire fell late in the fifth century CE, Rome lived on. We sometimes miss this story because just as we impose the narrative that Septimius Severus was black, our label "Byzantine Empire," a categorization we create to understand the world, makes us see it incorrectly. The people we label Byzantines just saw themselves as Roman.

The Eastern Roman Empire lasted another thousand years before falling to the Ottomans in 1453 CE. So, you see, whether Rome lasted hundreds of years or thousands is simply a matter of definition. Maybe America will be the same way.

Chapter Eight

THE NEED TO FORGIVE

Kantian Victims

"Christ was a victim."

Peter Thiel summed up his objection to this book like he was a lawyer making his closing argument. We were having a drink at his home in Southern California a couple of weeks before Christmas last year. He'd come out of his bedroom into the living room, emerging from what appeared to be a deeply contemplative evening of reflection. We talked about *Woke, Inc.*, my last book, for a bit, and our conversation quickly turned to the upcoming one that I had begun to write—about victimhood and excellence.

"If you think excellence is the solution to wokeness, you're wrong," Peter said. Instead, he argued that the solution was simple, and that there was only one: Christianity.

The founder of PayPal and other companies characterized wokeness as Christianity without forgiveness. He didn't like valorizing "excellence" because he thought that either the word meant some kind of artificial, bureaucratic meritocracy, or it would be subjectively defined by each person for themselves, rendering it too vague to serve as a guiding principle for a culture. The right answer to victimhood culture isn't to deny victimhood status, he claimed, but to recognize that *everyone* is a victim. Even Christ himself.

If we all recognize that everyone is a victim and everyone is an oppressor, Peter's thinking goes, no one will be able to use victimhood to claim the moral high ground, so everyone will have to give up their arms and forgive each other. I think of his theory as the social version of mutually assured destruction, where claims of victimization are the social equivalent of nukes. An eye for an eye makes the whole world blind. If we all show that we have victim cards and threaten to play them, no one will.

This reasoning is actually a Kantian argument that using victimhood as a tool to gain power isn't universalizable—it's irrational because it doesn't work if everyone does it. If you have a good victim card and consider using it to gain social status, you have to imagine what will happen if everyone else who has a victim card plays theirs too. They're rational people just like you are, so whatever you decide to do, you should assume they'll do too. But here's the thing: everyone else *does* in fact have their own victim card. If everyone plays theirs, victimhood will no longer be a special status that confers advantages to those who claim it. So if we just skip to the part where we recognize that everyone is a victim, we rob victimhood claims of their power.

I don't think Peter is wrong. Recognizing that everyone has valid claims to victimhood is the first and perhaps most important step in our nation's path out of its current morass. That's one reason why in the first half of this book I laid out all the valid claims to victimhood different groups of Americans can make— black people, white people, liberals, conservatives, you name it. But there's a counterargument that this approach must overcome.

One could argue that society is already trying things his way, and it's not working. We've already arrived at a world where everyone claims to be a victim. It's the natural consequence of making claims of oppression a path to social status. Everyone grabs whatever well-established victimhood identity they can avail themselves of, and as many as possible. Wielding a good victim card is the twenty-first-century equivalent of making sure you're armed in the Wild West: don't leave home without it. When skin color or gender alone won't do the trick, we find ways to casually signal our victim identities in conversation, like cowboys flashing their guns. In conversations that touch on social justice, just watch the white guys waiting patiently for the opportune moment to drop the fact that they're gay, or Hispanic, or Jewish. We're already a nation of victims.

But here's what Peter's argument missed: not all claims of victimhood are equally powerful. We'll never get this mutually assured social destruction that makes everyone refuse to play their victim card, one could argue, because some people are carrying six-shooters and others have cannons. Instead of giving up our arms, we compete to outgun each other.

Sure, maybe we can recognize that a gay black woman, a straight Chinese woman, and a gay white man—and sure, even a straight white man who drives a truck—all have socially valid claims to victimhood. We already recognize that. But there's obviously a hierarchy that makes some victim identities more powerful than others. The gay black woman is clearly at the top of the intersectional ladder. And in social settings with all four present, the straight Chinese woman and gay white man would subtly compete with each other to win her validation as the second-most oppressed. If the gay white man is conversationally framed as a white man by the two nonwhite people, at some point he'll redirect the discussion toward his gayness. If the Chinese woman is then the oppressor because she's one of the straight ones, she'll highlight her womanhood. If the straight white man points to the fact that he lost his manufacturing job, he's told to shut up and check his privilege.

These are just the rules of the game, the law of the intersectional jungle. There's a hierarchy that gives some victims greater status than others, so the simple recognition that everyone's a victim is not by itself enough to compel everyone to give up their grievances.

Let me put this objection in Kantian terms: Peter and I are making an argument that using victimhood as a shortcut to power and status isn't universalizable—an eye for an eye makes the whole world blind, so let's all set our weapons aside and forgive each other our trespasses. But this gets to a complication in Kantian reasoning: the gay black woman, straight Chinese woman, and gay white man can all make valid claims to victimhood, but they are not in fact in the same situation when we look closely, with a fine enough grain. The gay black woman benefits much more from a world where victimhood claims are a path to power, and she stands to lose more if all four agree to set all their claims aside, so why should rationality command her to do so?

At first glance, it might seem foolish for everyone to forgive each other when some have greater grievances than others. "An eye for an eye makes the whole world blind" sounds good, but it's not a compelling argument when one party starts out with a lot more power than the other—it's just the desperate plea the weaker one makes to save their skin. To put this point in terms of my fisherman example from chapter 6, the Kantian argument against overfishing no longer works as well if you're in a different situation from the other rational fishermen because you start out with far more ability to overfish than they do. If you have greater ability to cheat because you have much larger nets than everyone else, for instance, you can break the rule without fearing that everyone else will.

But this concern is actually a better objection to the Kantian argument for sustainable fishing than the one for national forgiveness. There's a key difference between the two situations: it's a well-known feature of the American system that power often changes hands. The gay black woman may be at the top of the food chain right now, the apex victim, but she ought to reason that someday soon, the shoe will be on the other foot. If all the Kantian fishermen periodically exchange which one gets to use the largest nets, the argument against overfishing suddenly returns in full force: if you catch too many fish when it's your turn, you ought to reason that the next guy will when it's his. So deciding to break the rule once again leads to a world where everyone breaks it and everyone has less.

That's actually the situation the American nation of victims is in today. At the moment I write these words, Democrats control both houses of Congress and the presidency, along with most of the levers of cultural power, like universities, news outlets, and media. It is this particular favorable national environment that allows the gay black woman to extract maximum advantage from pressing each of her victimhood claims. She's the one with the largest net, for the moment. But in the American system, that privileged status is temporary and contingent, not inherent.

By the time you read this, things may have changed dramatically. The first domino to fall may be liberal political control, from the local to national level. The congressional midterm elections are coming up in November 2022, and it's no secret that all signs are pointing to a red wave of Republican victories. The party in power always faces an uphill battle in midterm elections to begin with, and Democrats are burdened by President Biden's plummeting approval ratings, down from 55 percent when he entered office to around 42 percent today.[1] This parallels a sharp reversal in party affiliation. A Gallup poll found that at the start of 2021, 49 percent of respondents leaned toward the Democratic party compared to 40 percent toward the Republican party, while by the end of the year, the tables had turned and Republicans led 47 percent to 42 percent.[2] It was one of the largest swings ever recorded. Democratic congressmen are fleeing like rats from a sinking ship. So far, thirty House Democrats have announced their retirement, an exodus the likes of which hasn't been seen in three decades.[3]

Analysts are conducting autopsies of the impending Democratic wipeout before it even occurs. An op-ed from Christopher Caldwell in the *New York Times* gave a particularly astute pre-mortem assessment:

> How did Democrats get into so much trouble so quick? Inherited trends, including Covid-19, deficits and geo-strategic overreach, are partly to blame. So is poor policy-making on issues like the economic stimulus. But the heart of the problem lies elsewhere. Democrats are telling a story about America—about the depth and pervasiveness of racism, and about the existential dangers of Mr. Trump—that a great many Americans, even a great many would-be Democrats, do not buy.[4]

Famed Democratic analyst James Carville once memorably said "It's the economy, stupid," to explain what the 1992 presidential election came down to. Today, the carnage Democrats face in the voting booth could be summed up with "It's wokeness, stupid." No one likes it. I sometimes read the comments on *New York Times* articles, and these days it seems half of them begin with the author's obligatory disclaimer that they're a lifelong Democrat, then end with a long rant about how much they hate and fear the Spanish Inquisition–style wokeness that's overtaken their party. Carville himself cracked open the door for Democrats to publicly acknowledge the issue in a widely discussed interview with *Vox*, saying "Wokeness is a problem and everyone knows it. It's hard to talk to anybody today—and I talk to lots of people in the Democratic Party—who doesn't say this. But they don't want to say it out loud." When asked why that was so, he answered "Because they'll get clobbered or canceled."[5]

Carville's interview made waves not because he'd been uniquely insightful, but because he'd been one of the first on the left to publicly observe that the emperor had no clothes. In the 2022 election, we will see what happens once the entire crowd feels free to say the same, first from the privacy of the voting booth, then publicly once they see that others agree their emperor is naked. The progressive left appears to have confused the ability to control what people say with the power to dictate how they vote.

While today the gay black woman possesses the greatest ability to profit from a world where victimhood claims are an easy path to power and wealth, by the time you read this, straight white conservative men may be the ones eagerly seeking compensation for all their own built-up grievances. In other words, the fishermen are about to trade nets. But in our nation of victims, when one group of American fishermen gains control of the largest net, it catches as many fish as it can in the limited time it has, concerned only with matching the haul of the previous owner. We can either collectively relinquish our many victimhood claims or press them to the fullest whenever we take our turn controlling the levers of power and watch the nation's resources dwindle as each new apex victim raids it.

So we all have reason to forgive each other our grievances even though some groups can benefit more from victimhood claims than others: as we exchange political control, we rotate *which* groups are best able to press their claims. A regime where victimhood is a path to power then inevitably becomes a race to the bottom. But there's another reason we all have incentive to give up our arms, too.

Political control tends to be a pendulum in the American system, swinging from one party to another, but there are some arenas in American life that operate differently. Universities and news and entertainment media, for instance, seem firmly entrenched in the far left's worldview. Even if there is a brewing political backlash toward progressive identity politics, it may take years or even decades to reach these cultural institutions. One could argue, then, that the gay black woman and others currently at the top of the victim hierarchy have a strong incentive not to embrace national forgiveness because they still stand to lose more from it, since their status in cultural institutions is firmly rooted.

But there's still a brewing backlash against wokeness, and when it can't voice itself in one outlet, it will simply find another. Consider liberal dominance of universities, for instance. Conservatives know they can't challenge that from within the university system. But this fact simply makes them vent their frustration in the systems they can control. The Florida House of Representatives, for instance, just passed two controversial bills aimed at trying to alter the hierarchy of victimhood in the educational arena.[6]

One of them, HB 7, inspired by Governor Ron DeSantis's "Stop WOKE" agenda, attempts to prevent teachers and employers from indoctrinating those under their power with CRT-inspired theories. It expands Florida's civil rights law to make it discrimination to make students and employees feel guilt, anguish, or other forms of psychological distress on the basis of their race, color, sex, or national origin. It also prohibits training or instruction involving other tenets of CRT, such as the insistence that virtues like merit and excellence are the products of white supremacy.[7] The other bill, HB 1557, is dubbed the "Don't Say Gay" bill by critics. It forbids instruction on sexual orientation or gender identity in kindergarten through third grade, and requires that discussions of those topics in other grade levels be age appropriate.[8]

Personally, I think bills like these tread into dangerous waters. I'm not a fan of the wave of CRT bans and book bans sweeping the country. I default to the view that the answer to speech is more speech. Voltaire had the right of things. No matter how noble the intentions behind these bills are, the inherent vagueness in any ban on speech tends to have a chilling effect that makes the law silence more speech than it's meant to. My purpose in mentioning these bills is not to argue for or against them, but to point out that laws like these are the inevitable consequence of making victimhood claims a path to power and enshrining the liberal hierarchy of victimhood in cultural institutions. If the ones at the bottom of the ladder can't express their backlash in universities or media, they'll simply relocate their frustrations to whichever institutions they *can* control, then voice them even louder.

Like their liberal opponents, conservatives embrace the principle that since it's hard to hit any target perfectly, justice requires you to overshoot. This mutual pattern of excessive backlash creates a nation destined to spiral. When everyone embraces the ideology of victimhood, we're gradually led to mutually assured destruction—not the theory (which is about avoiding destruction, after all), but the destruction itself. With nuclear weapons, the threat of mutually assured destruction is obvious and happens all at once, and is therefore avoided by all. But social weapons work more subtly. The logic of victimhood draws us into our mutual demise slowly but surely, like the grip of a black hole, each step toward ruin seeming rational and necessary as we take it. The fact that the path to destruction is gradual rather than sudden is what makes it possible to actually get there.

My favorite part of the story about the emperor's new clothes is the ending, a small detail most don't remember. When the people in the crowd all start exclaiming that the emperor has no clothes, he himself finally recognizes the truth. But it's too late for him to turn back. All he can do is keep walking, so he does so even more proudly than before.

America is trapped too, locked in a grievance-fueled race to the bottom propelled by two major forces: cyclical control of the political levers of power and unrestrained backlash to the entrenched cultural ones. The only way to break free of this vicious cycle is to find a way to forgive each other instead of trying to win at the game of playing the victim. Otherwise all we'll be able to do is walk proudly toward our bitter end as it finally comes into view.

How Forgiveness Enables Excellence

I've said a lot about the various forms of American victimhood so far in this book. But ultimately I want to look to the future, not the past; toward excellence, not grievance. To do that, I owe you an account of what excellence really is. So far I've defined it in negative terms. I've told you that victimhood shrinks the economic pie, that it makes people resentful and unhappy, that it divides us, even that excellence can't consist in being superior to anyone. But there is more to being an excellent person or nation than having wealth or even happiness, more to it even than respecting others as equals. I owe you a positive account of what it means to pursue excellence.

I have a somewhat unconventional conception of excellence, one inspired by my faith. It's best if I begin with a concrete example of someone who rejected victimhood to embrace excellence and, by doing so, helped his would-be enemies do the same.

Daryl Davis is an accomplished black musician who plays R&B and the blues. He's played with musical icons like B.B. King and Chuck Berry, the father of rock and roll. He even played with Bill Clinton. But he's more famous for his unusual hobby: befriending Ku Klux Klan members.

Davis became fascinated with the phenomenon of racism when he was ten years old and experienced it for the first time. He was the son of an American diplomat, so he'd spent his childhood traveling the world, attending racially diverse schools. After his family moved to Massachusetts, he joined an all-white Cub Scout pack. One day while he was marching in a parade with the other boys and carrying the American flag, members of the crowd started hurling bottles and rocks at him. He concluded they had an inexplicable hatred of Cub Scouts until he realized he was the only one being targeted. Later that day, his parents sat him down and explained that it had been about the color of his skin. Davis says he found that explanation so absurd that "I literally thought they were lying to me."[9]

That incident sparked a lifelong obsession with uncovering the roots of racism. As a young man who'd recently graduated from college, he stumbled on the beginnings of an answer when he played piano at an all-white Maryland bar frequented by white supremacists. A shared love of excellence happened to be the catalyst.

After Davis's set was done, a man came up and complimented his skills, saying he'd never heard a black man play like Jerry Lee Lewis. Davis said Lewis was a friend of his and he knew for a fact that black men had taught him how to play.[10] Skeptical but fascinated, the other man bought him a drink. They had a great conversation about music, and he mentioned that never in his life had he had a drink or even a conversation with a black man.

"Why is that?" Davis asked.

"I'm a member of the Ku Klux Klan," he said.[11] Now it was Davis's turn to be skeptical. The other guy showed him his Klan membership card, gave him his number, and asked him to call next time he was doing a gig in town so he could come watch. The two men became friends; years later, the man left the KKK.[12]

That first friendship led to many more. Davis convinced his new friend to put him in touch with Roger Kelly, the grand dragon of the Maryland KKK. Davis set up an interview with him without letting him know he was black. At the end, Kelly gave him his business card and asked him to stay in touch. He did—he invited Kelly to his gigs and then his home, where Davis would bring over black people and Jews to chat with him. A couple years later, Kelly became imperial wizard, the national leader of the KKK. He began inviting Davis to his own home.[13]

Davis started attending Klan rallies, making it clear to the members that he disagreed with them but shaking hands, taking pictures, and having polite intellectual conversations about their differences. Kelly eventually left the KKK and handed Davis his robe and hood. Davis befriended the next two leaders of the Maryland KKK and they left it too; he claims to have effectively ended the Maryland Klan.[14]

Over the last few decades, he says he's directly convinced more than two hundred white supremacists to abandon the KKK and similar groups. Many of them hand him their robe and hood when they leave. One of those, former Tennessee grand dragon Scott Shepherd, now calls himself a reformed racist and fights against white supremacy.[15] "Daryl saved my life," he said. "Daryl extended his hand and actually just extended his heart, too, and we became brothers."[16]

Predictably, many black people and antiracists say that Davis is committing a grave sin by attending Klan meetings and befriending white supremacists. They often call him an Oreo (black on the outside, white inside) or an Uncle Tom. There's that ugly phrase again, the one slur against dark-skinned people anti-racism not only allows, but requires. Davis doesn't let it faze him. He says that when he shows his critics his vast trove of robes and hoods and asks them how many white supremacists they've convinced to give up their racism, they usually shut up.[17]

Daryl Davis didn't exactly shed the identity of black victim-hood; it's more like he shrugged it off as others tried to place it on him. Forgiveness came very easily to him because he never allowed himself to feel harmed. He's been so successful at persuading white supremacists to abandon their racism through the simple power of *being himself* around them, unencumbered by the false identities they or anyone else would impose on him.

Excellence is an easy concept to appeal to but a hard one to define. As Justice Potter Stewart once said when attempting to define pornography, "I know it when I see it."[18] In most contexts, an intuitive understanding of excellence is enough. But as Peter Thiel pointed out to me, if we're going to exchange our national fixation on victimhood for one centered on excellence, we have to have at least some idea of what it means. He argued that we face the dilemma of either over defining excellence, leading to a rigid bureaucratic focus on raising artificial measures like GDP or standardized test scores, or under defining it, leading to the vague pursuit of whatever people want. The dilemma is that a conception of excellence must be either artificially objective or hopelessly subjective.

I lean toward the subjective side of things, but I aim to convince you that the pursuit of excellence doesn't have to be *hopelessly* subjective. I do have an account of what it means to be excellent, and people like Daryl Davis exemplify it. My understanding is shaped by principles from my Hindu faith. To put it concisely, to be excellent is to actualize one's true inner self.

Most people probably know little more of Hindus than that we believe in a cycle of reincarnation. This is true, to a point, but it misses the goal of the process. Unlike Christians, we have no notion of heaven or hell; there is life after death, but it takes place in the same world we're in now. To us, the ultimate goal is *moksa*, the end of the cycle of reincarnation, which one can only reach by achieving perfect self-knowledge. Our essential selves are not attached to particular features of our identities like skin color or sex, and our true selves continue even when we are reborn and those features change.

This gets pretty deep into theology, but the Hindu belief is that at our core, we are all just the matter of the universe given fleeting form in life. That life might take the form of a tree, or a bird, or a human; if it's human, it might take the shape of a man or a woman; if a man, maybe a father. But each of these identities is a contingent, temporary form imposed on the matter of the universe, easily shed when one life ends and the soul begins another. Our true selves are like water taken from a vast ocean, temporarily taking on the shape of whatever vessel they're poured into. If you see water in a pot, it takes one shape, but pour it into a cup, and it takes an entirely different one; spill the cup to the ground and the water becomes a puddle, a form far different from the first two, with much different characteristics. But the water itself is unchanged.

The cycle of death and rebirth isn't endless, but a process aimed at shedding our contingent identities and thereby gradually coming to understand our true natures, our true selves. The purpose of the cycle of reincarnation is to teach us what we really are, that our true selves aren't attached to any of the particular vessels we happen to find ourselves in during any given lifetime. To a Hindu, pursuing excellence amounts to successfully abandoning our attachment to the layers of artificial identities that prevent us from seeing our true selves, illusions upon illusions. Some identities, of course, are much easier to lose than others. It is far easier for me to cast off the man-made identity of CEO than father, for instance, or American.

We have to achieve self-knowledge gradually, removing the identities furthest from our cores first. But in the end, if the water has been in a pot, then a cup, then a puddle, then a cloud, then a raindrop, it may eventually realize that it is none of those things. And then it is no loss to lose its form completely and once again become part of the sea. Once we truly understand what our essential selves are, the death that ends the cycle of rebirth is really nothing more than, after a long and difficult journey, finally finding our way home.

From my perspective, then, when I gave you the account of what excellence isn't, I was simultaneously telling you what it is. Victimhood, like superiority, is one of the artificial identities furthest from our cores, one of the first that must be cast aside to become our true selves. When we see ourselves and others as true equals, we become excellent by taking an important step toward seeing everyone as they really are.

Through this lens, forgiving someone else's prejudice is not some grand act of self-sacrifice, but the simple realization that neither you nor they are defined by the wrong they have done you. Forgiving someone's bigotry involves not giving up a grievance you have a right to, but understanding that what they did to you was the least and smallest part of who they are, that they merely mistook you for the least and smallest part of who you are.

That's what I find so appealing in the life and works of Daryl Davis. He's a living example of someone who embodies these ideals. Because he spent the formative years of his childhood in other countries, away from the racial lens America imposes on the world, he never defined himself by his race. And when he came to America and others defined him by his skin color, instead of seeing himself as a victim, he rightly saw them as confused. Where an American inculcated in victimhood would've seen it as unwise and dangerous to talk to white supremacists, Davis instinctively understood that they simply hadn't seen his true self, and that if he merely showed them who he was, they would have no choice but to change.

The question that launched Davis's quixotic quest to befriend white supremacists, the question he asks them to their faces, is "How can you hate me when you don't even know me?" When they see him as nothing more than a black man, he shows them a musician, a citizen, a friend, knowing their racism cannot easily survive.

This way of thinking is completely alien to the American mindset. Our nation of victims thinks racism must be confronted because it's the product of evil oppressors. Because we think of prejudiced people as innately evil and punish anyone who denies that, we think that it would be the height of foolishness to simply talk to them. But Davis understands that prejudice is merely the byproduct of ignorance of one's true self, and it therefore has to be not confronted, but dissolved.

Like the cycle of reincarnation, although the cycle of victimhood may seem endless, it can be broken simply by seeing yourself and others for what you really are. When you free yourself from the illusion that you're a mere victim, you simultaneously free yourself from seeing others as mere oppressors. They will see your excellence and want the same thing for themselves; when you show others your true self, you help them become theirs. The way I see it, when all those KKK members gave up their robes and hoods, they were just shedding the artificial identity that was furthest from their core. Superiority and inferiority are the greatest illusions of all.

At the beginning of an interlude where he meditates on forgiveness, Douglas Murray raises the case of Quinn Norton, who was hired by *The New York Times* and then just as quickly unhired once it emerged that a few years earlier she had used crude words like "fag" and the N-word as she argued in the cesspools of the internet. Murray's presentation of the aftermath stuck with me:

> In a subsequent piece in *The Atlantic* Norton explained what she thought had happened. She acknowledged that many things she had written and tweeted in the past had been ignorant and embarrassing. She also explained what it felt like to, in her words, have a "doppleganger" version of herself swiftly emerge online. In common with other people who had been the subject of online shaming this version of herself that people were railing against was not "who she was" but a simplified, out-of-context version of tiny parts of herself.[19]

"What is a fair way to describe somebody?" Murray asks. "Norton, for instance, might henceforth be summed up as 'the racist, homophobic tech journalist fired by *The New York Times*.' She might think a fairer version of her life could be 'Writer and mother'...So who gets to call it?"[20]

"That's not who I am" sounds like the flimsiest excuse of all, and that's how I took it at the time Norton said it. As Murray points out, isn't that just when everyone says when they have no excuse left to appeal to, when their own words condemn them? Anyone who utters it seems to be arguing with their past self and losing.

I'm no exception. I'm not particularly proud of when I vaguely intimated that we wanted to bring in some third party to resolve a lawn-mowing dispute with my aunt's black neighbor, and he'd ranted about my skin color and threatened my life. That memory returned to me as I was writing this chapter on forgiveness, because I'm still in the process of figuring out how to forgive him and myself for the events of that day.

I'd planned on talking about that experience with the neighbor in *Woke, Inc.*, but everyone told me to take it out. They said it reflected poorly on me. "What exactly did you mean when you threatened to bring in a third party?" they asked me. "The police? Lawyers? All over the way a guy mows his lawn?"

That's not who I am, I thought. It felt not like an excuse, but a truth I knew deep down, but could not get them to see. That's how it must feel to everyone who says it. I'm willing to bet that guy thinks the same thing to himself when he remembers sounding off against Indian people and talking about shooting me.

The things that man and I said to each other that morning weren't who we were at all. Yes, we said them, and so they must reflect a small part of us. But only the parts of us farthest from our cores. Just illusions piled on top of illusions.

I'm not some kind of expert on forgiveness; most of us aren't. But we need to figure out a way to start doing it. You know, I think what Daryl Davis does is very admirable, talking to white supremacists and befriending them and all. But everyone can't be a Daryl Davis. I doubt I could. I hope to have dinner with my aunt's neighbor one day, but I haven't even talked to him again. He couldn't bring himself to apologize to us, either. That's why his wife came over to do it. So I get it when people say it's far too much to ask to expect black people to talk to KKK members, or gay people to talk to homophobes. Maybe sometimes it's even too much to ask for Democrats and Republicans to talk to each other: the gravitational pull of grievance is just too strong today.

But there are many steps before sainthood. You don't have to befriend your enemy; you don't have to fully forgive them; you don't even have to talk to them. We might just start with understanding that they could be worthy of these things. That you may have only seen the smallest and least part of them, and they must've only seen the smallest and least part of you.

These grievances we hold and the way they make us treat each other are not who we are. They're just temporary forms our true selves have been molded by, easily abandoned once we release these shapes and find our next lives. Who knows? Maybe I'll be the black man next time; for all I know, I was before. The water all makes it back to sea in the end.

Chapter Nine

A THEORY OF DUTY

The Paradox of Meritocracy

I remember when I came home from Evendale Elementary School in first grade in 1992, and I had received a certificate at school that day. It was a piece of paper, but thicker than the kind I was accustomed to writing on.

My teacher had awarded it to me because I had written a first grader's summary of Alex Haley's book *Roots*. I hadn't actually read the book, but my parents were particular about watching the TV adaptation, and I'd ended up watching it with them. In retrospect, I'm pretty sure the level of violence that you see in that TV series was something that most American parents would say you're not supposed to show a six-year-old. But call it part of being the kid of immigrants who didn't operate according to those same norms. As long as it wasn't sexual, they were pretty much fine with it.

The certificate had two prominent words at the top, in elaborate cursive that signified to me that it was something important: "Merit Award." I didn't know what that word was, but I accepted the certificate and brought it home anyway.

My aunt Brindha from Fort Wayne was visiting our house at the time. She looked at the certificate, and her face lit up when she saw that it said "Merit" at the top. I still remember her explaining to me that merit was a very big deal, even as I struggled to understand exactly what it meant.

What exactly is merit? And why is it worth preserving?

Merit is the idea of rewarding someone in a manner that accords with the achievement of excellence in a particular sphere of life. Merit norms are sphere-specific—that is, they are generally not transferable from one sphere of life to another.

There are very practical reasons for a nation to want to create and preserve a meritocracy. The spheres of national life that operate according to principles of merit tend to be better than those that don't. For example, a National Basketball Association that selects the best basketball players tends to produce the highest-quality basketball for viewing—and the rewards that accrue to the best basketball players tend to accrue in proportion to how good at basketball they are (the amount of fame they receive, the amount of money they are paid by the league, and so forth). If those same rewards start to accrue to players who don't necessarily play the best basketball but instead generate the greatest level of attention for their antics off the court, then the overall quality of basketball suffers. That'll happen whenever rewards select for player attributes that have less to do with basketball and more to do with something else.

Funnily enough, there's actually an American tradition of using NBA stars as paragons of merit in arguments about distributive justice. In chapter 7, I discussed Thomas Piketty's theory that capitalism naturally tends toward increasing wealth inequality and mentioned John Rawls's theory of justice as fairness as an alternative to Thomas Piketty's recommendations. The most famous objection to Rawls's theory revolves around the idea that NBA superstars obviously deserve to be rich. It also turns out to raise a Piketty-style paradox that strikes at the heart of meritocracy itself. But before we talk about the notorious Wilt Chamberlain argument, let's talk about Rawls.

It's impossible to have a serious discussion of inequality and fairness without contending with the work of John Rawls. Ever since he published *A Theory of Justice* in 1971, it has set the standard for thinking about political theory, becoming required reading in classes in many disciplines around the world. His theory both questions the fairness of meritocracy and suggests a way for society to harness the inequality it produces. While Piketty wants to *reduce* inequality, Rawls wants to *use* it to allow everyone to have more.

I've already told you the beginnings of Rawls's theory, because Rawls is, well, just Kant writ large. Remember, the categorical imperative is just a more philosophically grounded version of the Golden Rule. Rawls's theory of justice is basically the Golden Rule on steroids. Instead of applying it to everyday interactions, he scales it up to imagine what an entire society would look like if it were built from the ground up so that each person treated others as they would want to be treated. That's why he calls it a theory of justice as fairness.

To imagine this perfectly fair society, Rawls asks us to think of what kind of system we'd all agree to if we negotiated about it from scratch. But there's a catch: he asks us to imagine the social contract we'd all agree to from a fair bargaining position. That means we have to conduct the hypothetical negotiation from behind what he calls the "veil of ignorance," blind to particular features of our identities that might bias us, such as our race, class, gender, appearance, sexuality, and talents. That blindness to our distinctive identities is what allows others to know the principles we endorse aren't just efforts to give our particular tribes advantages over theirs. In Hindu terminology, Rawls is saying fair bargaining about the structure of society requires that we all negotiate as our true selves.

What social contract would we all agree to from this fair bargaining position? Rawls suggests two principles of justice. First and most fundamentally, everyone has to have equal basic rights, including things like the right to vote and hold office, freedom of speech and association, freedom from physical harm, and the right to own property.[1] But Rawls is really remembered for his second principle, where he describes the fair way to allow goods beyond basic rights to be *unequal*: social and economic inequalities are to be arranged so that they are both attached to positions open to all under fair equality of opportunity, and to the greatest benefit of the least advantaged.[2]

That last part, called the Difference Principle, has become one of Rawls's most influential proposals. The heart of the idea is that we would all approve of a society with some inequality if—and only if—that relative inequality allowed everyone to have more in *absolute* terms. From behind the veil of ignorance, not knowing whether we'll be the richest or poorest members of society when we remove our veils, after ensuring that we'll have equal rights and equality of opportunity, we'll want to make sure that if we're the worst off, we'll still be doing as well as possible. Instead of embracing perfect equality at the cost of having everyone spending hours each day standing in line at barren supermarkets,[3] we'll choose the world where even the worst off have full bellies, air-conditioning, and smartphones, even if the best off have yachts. And who knows? If the society truly has fair equality of opportunity, we can all dream of owning yachts too, one day, and a few really will.

It's important to remember that Rawls wasn't writing in a vacuum. He was theorizing not from an armchair, but during the height of the Cold War, when it still seemed entirely possible the Soviet Union would win the battle of ideas. He knew that the great debate of his era was between the equality of communism and economic growth of capitalism. His theory was actually intended to outline a defense of an idealized, liberal version of capitalism, one that reaped its economic benefits but mitigated the unfairness of the inequality it naturally produces. We'd all want to keep the incentives capitalism offers people to innovate and work hard, Rawls was implying just beneath his abstract language, but we would agree *only* to a version of capitalism that ensured everyone got to share in its rewards. From behind our veils, not knowing whether we'd end up rich or poor in the society we agreed to, we'd vote to make the economic pie larger, but only if we were sure we'd get an extra piece.

Rawls was America's best soldier in the intellectual theater of the Cold War. That's why President Clinton awarded him the National Medal of Arts in 1999, saying, "Almost single-handedly John Rawls revived the disciplines of political and ethical philosophy with his argument that a society in which the most fortunate help the least fortunate is not only a moral society but a logical one. Just as impressively, he has helped a whole generation of learned Americans revive their faith in democracy itself."[4] Although Clinton said "democracy," that was really his polite way of saying "capitalism." We'd all choose to sail out into the rising tide of capitalism, Rawls argued, but only if everyone is guaranteed a seaworthy boat.

Historian Adrian Wooldridge has recently produced one of the most extensively researched accounts of meritocracy ever in *The Aristocracy of Talent*, tracing its development all the way from Plato and Confucius to the modern era. Although he ultimately defends meritocracy, arguing that it's necessary for the West to keep up with China, he gives Rawls due credit for providing one of the strongest arguments against it:

> Rawls argued that...[p]eople no more deserved their success because they were blessed with high IQs than they did because they have rich parents. Differences in talent are as morally arbitrary as differences in class...Rawls's strictures applied as much to effort as IQ: hard work did not make you any more deserving of superior reward, because the propensity to work hard was also inherited... The difference principle represented an agreement to regard the distribution of natural talents as a national asset—a nationalized industry, as it were—and to share in the benefits of this distribution whatever it turned out to be. Those who had been favored by nature, whoever they were, could gain from their good fortune only on terms that improved the situation of those who lost out.[5]

Rawls's genius was that he managed to navigate the debate between capitalism and communism in a way no one saw coming. He took the anti-capitalist premise that even hard work and talent don't entitle some to possess more than others and used it to justify a liberal capitalist system where the best off shared the fruits of their labors with the worst off. In his system, capitalism's winners don't use its losers as mere means to an end because inequality is only permissible when it allows those with the least to have more. Rawls found a way to reject meritocracy while embracing its benefits, an ideological way to have his cake and eat it too.

The Rawlsian vision of a fair capitalist system was dominant in the West during the Cold War and for the two decades after. But as the fear of communism receded and the inequality of capitalism compounded, Piketty's focus on the growing *gap* between rich and poor steadily replaced Rawls's emphasis on raising the *absolute* wealth of the poor. Having defeated our common enemy and satisfied our basic material needs, our enmity turned inward. We began to resent the fact that some people had much more than others. Rawls may have missed the fact that human happiness is affected by relative wealth just as surely as absolute wealth—once they all have enough food, some monkeys will throw away their cucumbers in righteous anger as they watch others eat grapes.

With the benefit of hindsight and empirical data, Piketty's theory raises a powerful critique of Rawls: the inequality enabled by capitalism will naturally tend to widen, outpacing the redistribution from rich to poor that Rawls's fair system relies on. When the one percent become too rich and sheer wealth begins to allow them to rewrite the political and social rules in their favor, the natural inequality produced by capitalism may even allow its winners to undermine basic equal rights and fair equality of opportunity.

This kind of critique that capitalism's tendency toward inequality overpowers government redistribution was actually raised decades earlier by Robert Nozick, the philosophical father of libertarianism, though he inferred much different conclusions than Piketty would. Piketty would say the government has to try even harder to redistribute wealth through progressive measures such as a global wealth tax. Nozick said that trying to fight inequality in a free market system would be like trying to hold back the tide, because merit will always upset whatever pattern of equality you try to impose. This is the point of his famous Wilt Chamberlain objection to Rawls.

The argument is simple yet powerful. Consider Wilt Chamberlain: 7'1", 275 pounds, holder of the probably unbreakable record of scoring one hundred points in a game. The man who, after being criticized as selfish when he led the NBA in points and rebounds, decided to lead it in assists the next season. Imagine we gave everyone in the nation an equal amount of money, or imposed whatever pattern of distribution Rawls would recommend. Everyone would still rush to hand their money over to Wilt so they could watch him play and he would very quickly become much richer than everyone else, no matter how you taxed him. Whether he deserves his athletic gifts or not, says Nozick, the fact is that Wilt Chamberlain's sheer talent will quickly upset whatever pattern of equality you try to impose on the world. There's nothing unjust about it, because everyone has a right to decide how to spend their money.[6]

The problem Nozick raised gets even worse when we consider Wilt Chamberlain's son. Wilt, who died in 1999, claimed to have slept with twenty thousand women and had no children.[7] But let us suppose that Wilt Chamberlain had a son and decided to leave his vast fortune to him. Now we have generational wealth that wasn't earned through merit, free to continue compounding through investment, disrupting whatever kind of equality the government tried to create, and all done through legitimate voluntary transfers of wealth: first from basketball fans to Wilt, next from Wilt to his son. The moral of the story is that your society can have equality or freedom, but not both.

Not only that, but as long as people are free to reward merit with money and the wealthy are free to give their assets to their children, a meritocratic capitalist system is doomed to recreate hereditary aristocracy, just as Piketty fears it has been doing for the last few decades. If the Chamberlain family has a good financial advisor, Wilt's talentless grandson will be the richest of them all. Instead of working, he'll hire lobbyists to rewrite the rules to protect his wealth and make sure he and his descendants stay on top.

That's the paradoxical thing about meritocracy: it contains the seeds of its own demise. The free transfer of wealth in a meritocratic system will create inequality. That inequality will widen and become entrenched as parents pass their wealth to their less-deserving children. And the resulting hereditary aristocracy will undermine the equality of opportunity necessary for meritocracy.

Wooldridge points out that these are very ancient problems inherent to meritocracy. Early in his book, he says, "All thinking about meritocracy is a series of footnotes to Plato," referencing a similar claim about all of Western philosophy.[8] The ideal government Plato described in *The Republic* was meant to be a meritocracy ruled by philosopher kings. Wooldridge notes that meritocracies throughout the ages have explicitly attempted to model themselves after Plato's recommendations. In one example I found amusing, Harvard University was founded by a group of would-be Platonic guardians who called themselves the Boston Brahmins[9]—a strange name, given Harvard's reluctance to admit Brahmins today.

In Plato's ideal system, unlike those of his imitators, being a philosopher king came with a heavy price, in order to bypass the problems of inequality and aristocracy exemplified by Wilt Chamberlain and his hypothetical son: "The ruling class must forgo the pleasures of family life and owning property. Anything less will lead to corruption."[10] India's ancient caste system—at least the pre-British form of it—contains a similar vision.

Judging by Harvard's record-breaking $53.2 billion endowment[11] and its 2022 class of 36 percent legacy students,[12] these Platonic ideals didn't find much purchase in the institution built by the Boston Brahmins. Wooldridge writes that they always "gave people with the right names the benefit of the doubt," a proud tradition that continues to this day.[13] Plato didn't envision legacy admission into the ruling class; nor did he imagine the guardians of the republic boasting of their 33.6 percent annual return.[14] And he'd probably admit a lot more Asians.

As Wooldridge mentions, Marcus Aurelius was another who tried to be a philosopher king in the Platonic tradition. He embodied the ideal more fully than the Boston Brahmins and their descendants, embracing an ascetic lifestyle and ruling the Roman empire with Stoic wisdom and restraint.[15] But even he fell short. Surprisingly for such a thorough historian, Wooldridge passes up the opportunity to observe that Marcus Aurelius himself illustrates the way meritocracy almost invariably defeats itself eventually through nepotism.

He was the last of the Five Good Emperors, who were named so by no less an authority than Niccolò Machiavelli.[16] Each of the first four had adopted his heir to choose the best ruler for the empire. That system of merit was what had allowed Rome to enjoy the latter half of the Pax Romana during their near-hundred-year reign. When Dio Cassius said that Rome's history went from a kingdom of gold to one of rust and iron, he was describing the transition from Marcus Aurelius to his biological son Commodus.

Commodus was the first Roman emperor to be born during the reign of his father—born in the purple. He was as cruel and foolish as his father had been wise. He immediately devalued the denarius to fund lavish games where he often fought and killed humans and animals. Commodus once threw an attendant into an oven after he found his bathwater lukewarm. In the arena, although he would spare gladiators because they always submitted to him, he would bind together amputees and club them to death, pretending they were giants. Americans even made a movie about his reign, although in our version Russell Crowe kills him to save Rome.[17]

Commodus was actually strangled in his bath by his wrestling partner Narcissus after the Senate grew tired of him. Afterward came the Year of the Five Emperors, a year of bitter civil war which saw Septimius Severus survive and take power; you may remember him as the black emperor, in spite of my efforts. But with Commodus, Rome's age of merit had ended for good and it entered its long decline.

Marcus Aurelius did everything right except one: he could deny himself, but not his son. He trusted Commodus too much and gave him too much, and with that one decision Rome began to die. History's most successful meritocracy was inevitably undone, as Plato had foretold, by a father's love for his son.

Preserving a Stable Meritocracy through Inheritance Taxes

"For all his extremism," writes Wooldridge, "Plato remains as relevant as ever. He identified the most profound problem with meritocracy: the tension between the natural instinct to look after your children and the meritocratic imperative to provide equality of opportunity." But, he adds, "Plato's own solution to this problem—state-sponsored orgies and communal child-rearing—was clearly far-fetched."[18] As was often the case, Plato's questions were better than his answers.

Meritocracy has many virtues, but to preserve it as a stable system undistorted by widening inequality and nepotism requires some kind of extreme measure. Piketty's preferred solution is a punishing global wealth tax. He was advocating a one-time global 90 percent wealth tax on all assets over $1 billion back in 2014, years before Bernie Sanders or Elizabeth Warren favored any kind of wealth tax.[19]

A decade later, Piketty's thinking has won the day on the left, though it's still catching up to the extreme degree of his recommendation. A wealth tax is quickly becoming the drumbeat progressives rally behind. In his platform during the 2020 Democratic primary, Sanders advocated an annual progressive wealth tax starting at 1 percent on married couples with net worth above $32 million, rising to 8 percent on wealth over $10 billion.[20] In March 2021, Warren and progressive House Democrats Pramila Jayapal and Brendan Boyle proposed a 2 percent annual tax on households with net worth between $50 million and $1 billion, with an additional 1 percent for those with more than $1 billion. The details constantly change, but it's clear the left is increasingly rallying around a wealth tax as the main solution to inequality.

At first glance, the idea makes perfect sense: if widening wealth inequality is the problem, a wealth tax must be the solution. It sounds good, but in my opinion it would undoubtedly cause a market crash, one that would cost the middle class and poor far more than the wealthy.

Here's what progressives miss: *every multimillionaire subject to the wealth tax would have a statutorily mandated incentive to write down the value of his or her assets.* While today we often seen multimillionaires overstate the value of their assets (to receive a mention on the Forbes 400 list or whatever), the exact opposite is destined to occur if the government were to assess a significant annual tax on absolute wealth. Every wealthy individual with a net worth above $50 million (using Elizabeth Warren's proposal as an example) would have an irresistible incentive to artificially deflate the value of any illiquid asset they hold—say, investments in private companies, investment funds, real estate, art, and so forth.

What is a piece of art worth? What's a private company worth? What is land really worth? Value is often a very subjective question, and with a wealth tax, everyone who owns these hard-to-value assets would suddenly say they were all worth much less.

Why is that a bad thing? Because when everyone devalues their assets at the same time, we have the recipe for a financial crisis, just like we did in 2008. The initial devaluation of assets would be bad enough: if all investors in private companies had an incentive to say those private companies were suddenly worth less, then those companies would *be* worth less. That's because their value is defined by the willingness of those same investors to buy more shares in those companies. This in turn would reduce the ability for those companies to raise money, which in turn affects the number of people they hire.

As if that weren't bad enough, this initial devaluation would also trigger a domino effect that follows from another practical reality: debt that is tied to those same assets whose value would be written down. As it turns out, wealthy people do the same thing with their homes and other assets that everyone else does: they borrow against what they own. As the value of all those assets suddenly plummeted, they would need to sell more of those very assets in order to repay debt borrowed against them—what experts would call a deleveraging cycle. Soon enough, everyone's selling all their assets to pay their debts as the banks come calling. This is the anatomy of a market crash of the kind we saw in 2008 and in 1932, especially from the starting point of a market near all-time highs today.

So it's no mystery that the stock market winces and drops as a knee-jerk reaction each time candidates on the far left start speaking publicly about the wealth tax or other policies like it. They pretend that only the very wealthy buy stock or participate in financial markets. But they like it too, along with everyone who has a retirement account or pension plan, which includes most Americans. A 2021 Gallup poll found that 56 percent of all American adults owned stock, whether through shares in individual companies, mutual funds, or retirement accounts. Stock ownership wasn't just a game for the wealthy: 63 percent of Americans with incomes between $40,000 and $100,000 had exposure to the stock market.[21]

So if we had a wealth tax, the stock market would crash, and everyone with a retirement account or pension would suddenly be a lot poorer. But it wouldn't just be the elderly and the middle-aged. College students who trade on Robinhood to avoid commissions would go on Reddit to console each other with memes about their portfolios getting cut in half.

My own life would remain mostly the same if the market crashed. But my friends' and family's wouldn't. Ironically, the people who wouldn't be fine are the very people who the wealth tax was designed to help in the first place: the retirees who thought they'd saved enough to get by but now wonder how they'll survive without the same investment income, the workers fired by companies whose access to capital disappears in a market crash, the would-be homeowner who no longer has the same easy access to a mortgage.

The far left's Manichean worldview doesn't allow it to see that the real world is more complex than it is convenient. Everything must be good or evil, and since wealthy people must be bad, taxing what makes them bad must be good. People on the far left sometimes seem to derive their facts from their values instead of other facts. This approach often makes their ideals sound more reasonable than their prescriptions.

Preserving meritocracy and preventing wealth inequality from creating aristocracy requires some radical measure, but Plato's recommendations of denying elites property and requiring communal child-rearing are nonstarters, while the modern focus on a wealth tax hurts those it's intended to help. Sky-high progressive income taxes like those recommended by Alexandria Ocasio-Cortez would be even worse.

Ocasio-Cortez has pushed for raising the top marginal tax rate to 70 percent on incomes over $10 million, but any kind of income tax would leave the wealthiest Americans entirely unscathed and prevent others from joining their ranks. Raising income taxes would increase tax evasion, decrease social mobility, and widen wealth inequality, as even Bill Gates has observed.[22] Income taxes prevent the middle class from accumulating wealth, tying a heavy anchor to it while leaving the richest untouched. They also give people incentive to take it easy instead of working hard, since they know they'll just hand a hefty chunk of the fruits of their labor over to the government anyway. That incentive to be lazy reduces economic productivity, ultimately dragging everyone down. As Piketty argues, when economic growth slows but return on capital stays constant, wealth inequality widens.

The way to save meritocracy from degenerating into aristocracy is to give inheritance and estate taxes real teeth, while cutting the progressive income taxes that penalize those who work hard and create value while they're still alive. Tax someone's wealth heavily, sure. But wait until they die. You can't take it with you, after all. Neither should your kid.

This approach is both efficient and fair. Unlike an income tax, it encourages spending money rather than uselessly hoarding it, because most people would rather spend their money while they're alive than have it taxed heavily when they die. Unlike a wealth tax, it gives no incentive for wealthy people to simultaneously deflate the value of all their assets, avoiding a market crash. And, most importantly, a hefty inheritance tax with no gaping loopholes gives us the best of meritocracy while avoiding the worst: people have an incentive to work hard and innovate during their lifetimes, but their children must start fresh, without getting to ride on their parents' coattails.

That's not only good for everyone else; it's also good for would-be trust-fund kids themselves. There's nothing that ruins character as much as having everything in life handed to you on a silver platter. I'm fine with Wilt Chamberlain becoming rich, but if his hypothetical son is no basketball superstar, there's no need for him to get that NBA wealth. He can work for a living, and he and everyone else will be better off for it. I want my son to work for a living. I want him to build things, not be handed them. That's part of what it means to be a citizen: to contribute to the nation instead of feeding off it.

Although Piketty is known more for his suggestion of a global wealth tax, he's a supporter of high inheritance taxes too. Remember, according to him, capitalism naturally produces wealth inequality because returns on investment tend to outpace economic growth, and therefore outweigh returns on labor. Once capital is free to compound over generations, this advantage of invested wealth over earned income leads capitalism to harden into aristocracy. If Piketty's right, then the path to capitalist nobility can be short-circuited simply by cutting off the transfer of wealth from parents to their children.

Piketty and Emmanuel Saez have written a paper called "A Theory of Optimal Inheritance Taxation." It's quite rigorous and thorough, though I cannot recommend it; only an economist could love it. One thing that's striking about it is that beneath all the economic jargon and pages of equations, Piketty proposes a compromise between his solution to inequality and Rawls's.

You see, when deciding the question of how high inheritance taxes should be, it turns out a lot depends on whose interests you care about. If you care about the preferences of the wealthiest people along with everyone else, it turns out that some academic work suggests the best inheritance tax rate is *zero*.[23] Piketty and Saez end up making their theory revolve around a Rawlsian argument that we should choose the inheritance tax rate that's best for the worst off, defining the worst off as *those who don't receive inheritances at all*:

One normatively appealing concept is that individuals should be compensated for inequality they are not responsible for—such as [inheritance] bequests received—but not for inequality they are responsible for—such as labor income. This amounts to [setting aside the interests of people who receive inheritances] and [caring only about what's best for] zero-bequest receivers. About half the population in France or the Unites States receives negligible bequests. Hence, this "Meritocratic Rawlsian" [approach] has broader appeal than the standard Rawlsian case.[24]

Just as Rawls was defending capitalism against communism beneath all his jargon, Piketty and Saez are having a furious debate with Rawls beneath theirs. They're saying that Rawls is going too far when he claims that people don't deserve to profit from the talents they're born with, that they don't even deserve to profit from the work ethic they're born with or taught. He's giving too much ground to the communists. People *do* deserve to make more than others through talent and hard work, Piketty and Saez are saying, so allow inequalities that stem from income. That's just the beauty of the free market. Let Wilt Chamberlain become as rich as he can; his height is not a national asset. Only a communist would think so. But don't let his son become rich riding the coattails of his father, because he's done nothing to deserve it.

Who are the worst off? That's a question I raised in *Woke, Inc.* as an objection to Rawls.[25] Should we be making the gay black woman or the disabled white truck driver as well-off as possible? I have no idea. Even worse, a Rawlsian approach makes the two yell at each other as they compete to be the biggest victim. Because almost every little intersectional group can make a plausible claim to be the worst off, in the nation Rawls helped make, we all end up competing over who's the biggest victim. Who are the worst off? No one really knows, but everyone suspects it's themselves.

But Piketty and Saez are proposing a dry yet elegant answer to the question, one that both tells us who the worst off are and helps us prevent Wilt Chamberlain's talentless grandchildren from ruling the world. The worst off in a capitalist meritocracy, they're saying, are the 50 percent of us who inherit nothing. This is also an elegant solution, they suggest, because that's an answer at least half of us could get behind.

Once you plug in those who inherit nothing as the worst off and choose the inheritance tax that makes them as well-off as possible, Piketty and Saez's equations spit out the answer that the optimal inheritance tax rate in the United States is 59 percent.[26] That's neat.

Why is the optimal inheritance tax rate from the perspective of those who inherit nothing not 100 percent? After all, that would cost them nothing in inheritance money. Well, you have to factor in stuff like the fact that if the inheritance tax *was* 100 percent, every rich person would be hell-bent on spending all their money during their lifetime, so the 100 percent tax would actually collect about $0. You also have to factor in social mobility—some of the 50 percent who inherit nothing expect to become rich, so they don't want a 100 percent inheritance tax either. Factors like these are why Piketty and Saez have so many equations.

Let's not take that 59 percent inheritance tax rate as gospel; there are a lot of assumptions behind it, as the authors observe. The point is that the inheritance tax rate should be very high. If anything, I'd take the figure Piketty and Saez arrive at as a minimum. We shouldn't allow people to become billionaires just by having rich parents.

Redistributing Duty

Nozick would cry out that preventing this amounts to a major imposition on freedom—after all, your wealth is your property, and you can give your property to whoever you want. One could also argue that a very high inheritance tax would also remove an incentive for value creation. Some people spend their lives building empires precisely so they can pass them down to their children; they want to build dynasties that will outlive them.

My response is that we should think of high inheritance taxes not just as a way of redistributing wealth, but a way of redistributing *duty*. Yes, by definition preventing parents from creating dynasties is a restriction on their liberty. Civilization itself amounts to a collective agreement for each individual to give up some liberties so that the group can prosper. The purpose of a high inheritance tax is to preserve the meritocratic system that allows wealth to be built in the first place—including the flat (and low) income tax regime that I would favor for everyone while they're still alive. If a talented person benefits from that system and becomes rich, they owe it to everyone else to preserve meritocracy so others have the chance to do the same. The goal of creating a hereditary dynasty is an illegitimate one in a meritocracy. It's the duty of a successful citizen to preserve the way of life that allowed them to succeed.

With great power comes great responsibility. That's a very American idea. Those citizens who have the power to destroy our meritocratic system have the duty to accept restrictions preventing them from doing so. They are still free to create business empires, companies that last hundreds of years after their deaths; it's not as if all their works will crumble when they die. They should also be free to make sure their children won't starve or be homeless after they're gone. They should be free to accumulate wealth and spend their money as they see fit under a system of minimal taxation for as long as they're alive. But what a citizen in a meritocracy is not free to do is create hereditary dynasties that undermine the very equality of opportunity that allowed them to thrive.

A high inheritance tax isn't just about making parents better citizens; it's also about doing the same for their children. Toward the end of *Woke, Inc.* I argued that teenagers should do national service during summers as part of their high school education.[27] The main goal of that wasn't for the nation to get free labor—the labor of teenagers is often not terribly valuable. The purpose of national service is to better those who serve, to make them conceive of themselves as citizens working together to build a nation. In the same way, a high inheritance tax would remind the wealthiest children that they're citizens embarked on a common project with everyone else. It would remind them that they're no better or worse than anyone else. It would remind them that we're bound by our shared pursuit of excellence under conditions of equal opportunity.

Making their own way in the world, on their own merit, not only makes children better citizens; it makes them better *people*. A high inheritance tax is as much for the sake of those who would inherit as anyone else. People should be given the chance to stand on their own and find out who they are. They should have the opportunity to be underdogs instead of incumbents, to fight against long odds and win. The underdog who claws their way to the top understands things the lifelong favorite will never know.

Nobody cries for rich kids, but in a way, they're necessarily deprived. They're deprived of the chance to define themselves outside the shadow of their parents' wealth. Rich or poor, everyone deserves the opportunity to find out what they're made of instead of having their parents' bank accounts decide it for them. Being born in the lap of luxury is just another powerful illusion wrapped around someone from birth, always distorting their view of the world and themselves.

That's what happened to Commodus. Being born heir to the empire warped his worldview from an early age, poisoning his character. He grew up in the grip of the illusion that the world revolved around him, that there was something fundamentally better about him than everyone else, and so he came to believe that the empire was meant to serve him instead of the other way around. Dio Cassius wrote that he was "not naturally wicked but, on the contrary, as guileless as any man that ever lived. His great simplicity, however, together with his cowardice, made him the slave of his companions, and it was through them that he at first, out of ignorance, missed the better life and then was led on into lustful and cruel habits, which soon became second nature."[28] Being denied his grand inheritance wouldn't have been bad for Commodus at all; on the contrary, it would've given him the chance to become a decent man.

The biggest downside to my proposal of a high inheritance tax is actually that it would end up *benefiting* the children of the wealthy. This relates to that idea from Piketty and Saez—the higher the tax is, the harder the wealthy will try to spend their money during their lifetimes. That's not necessarily a bad thing, since that increased consumption will generate economic activity. But it's an inevitable consequence of my proposal that parents will try to give their money to their children before they die, and they'll likely do it in the form of giving them the best educations money can buy.

The children of the wealthy will still end up forming a kind of aristocracy, but one that comes not directly from inheriting wealth, but from having developed their knowledge and talent.

This is the main objection Daniel Markovits makes to meritocracy. Markovits argues that the real source of inequality is not a wealth gap, but an education gap that turns into an income gap that perpetuates itself:

> Elaborate elite education produces superordinate workers, who possess a powerful work ethic and exceptional skills. These workers then induce a transformation in the labor market that favors their own elite skills, and at the same time dominate the lucrative new jobs that the transformation creates. Together these two transformations idle mid-skilled workers and engage the new elite, making it both enormously productive and extravagantly paid. The spoils of victory grow in tandem with the intensity of meritocratic competition. Indeed, the top 1% of earners, and even the top one-tenth of 1%, today owe perhaps two-thirds or even three-quarters of their total incomes to their labor and therefore substantially to their education. The new elite then invests its income in yet more elaborate education for its children. And the cycle continues.[29]

Although he's a proponent of meritocracy, Wooldridge identifies the same problem Markovits does, expressing it concisely: "And from the 1980s onwards the [meritocratic] revolution began to consume itself as merit made money and money purchased education."[30]

This is a serious problem, although it's not one caused by a high inheritance tax, but simply one that might be exacerbated by it. In our present world, the very richest already send their children to $50,000-per-year preschools. What a high inheritance tax would change is that it would give others who are not quite as rich incentive to do the same.

In some ways, this is a good problem to have—we have at least made significant progress if the rich perpetuate their advantage by training their children to be skilled and hardworking instead of simply giving them all their wealth. If this path still leads to a form of aristocracy, at least these aristocrats will have character and ability, which is good both for them and the nation. But there is still more that can be done to address this merit-based path toward aristocracy. As Wooldridge puts it, "The answer to [this problem] is more meritocracy: we need to redouble our efforts to remove formal advantages for the rich while also developing better ways to distinguish between innate ability and mere learning."[31]

Wooldridge suggests that a system of standardized testing focusing on innate ability and fully funded national scholarships would help level the educational playing field. He points out that the SAT, for instance, measures innate academic ability more than people often think: "A 2006 analysis of a large collection of studies found that coaching for the SAT produced an improvement of 50 points on a scale of 1600; a more recent study found a 20-point improvement. Neither of these numbers is insignificant, but they are both small compared with other affluence-related advantages and much smaller than on tests of knowledge rather than reasoning."[32]

In another intriguing solution to the problem of educational advantages, Wooldridge proposes that "National merit scholars might also be given free university educations in exchange for agreeing to spend a certain number of years in the public sector. This would address the public sector's growing problem with recruiting high-flyers...It would also repair the fraying link between public service and intellectual excellence."[33] He notes that this kind of bargain was proposed by Thomas Jefferson when he designed the University of Virginia, and that Singapore, one of the world's most successful meritocracies, "obliges scholarship winners to pay off their debt by working for the state. It is worth reintroducing the idea more widely in a West where public service is going out of fashion."[34]

I find Wooldridge's solution to the problem of education appealing. The answer to inequality produced by education is not to deprive the rich of good educations, but to provide them to the poor. And by giving generous scholarships in exchange for public service, we would find yet another way to instill civic virtue while maintaining meritocracy. Through the combination of high inheritance taxes and scholarships given for service, we would remind both rich and poor that excellence and citizenship are two sides of the same coin. Today's Republican Party would do well to consider it: a theory of justice as duty might just be our missing shade of red.

REINCARNATE

My dad named me after a Hindu sage named Vivekananda. He wasn't like the other Hindu saint figures we learned about as kids: the other ones lived so long ago that the passage of time somehow made the mystical stories about them more believable, yet distant. But Vivekananda walked the earth during the same century that I was born. He'd attended Chicago's World Fair, familiar to any kid who grew up in the Midwest who's visited one of its many museums on a school field trip. He'd delivered lectures about Hinduism at Harvard in the same classrooms where I'd go on to take western philosophy classes.

He'd made a prophecy earlier in his life that he would die before the age of forty. And indeed he did. On July 4, 1902—exactly seventy-six years after the day when John Adams and Thomas Jefferson died, 126 years after the United States was born—thirty-nine-year-old Vivekananda awoke at dawn and meditated for three hours at his monastery. He taught his pupils like he did every day, and then at 7:00 p.m. went to his room and asked not to be disturbed. He died at 9:20 p.m. that day while meditating, achieving what his disciples call *mahasamadhi*. That's the state when a yogi experiences their oneness and unity with their true self, or God, since in Hindu theology those are one and the same. The doctors who conducted his autopsy reported that the rupture of a blood vessel in his brain was the likely cause of death. I'm no doctor, but I don't think the American Medical Association has yet issued a consensus on the pathophysiology of *mahasamadhi*, so I'm not sure the autopsy proves anything one way or the other.

I started to think that my dad was trying to make a point when my parents named my little brother Shankar after the great Shankaracharya, another Hindu sage, who lived around the year 700 CE. Like Vivekananda, Shankaracharya died young, at the age of thirty-two. Like Vivekananda, he made the choice to achieve *mahasamadhi* on his own terms: texts say that he was last seen by his disciples behind the Kedarnath Temple, walking up the Himalayan mountains until he could no longer be traced. I was almost thirty-two years old when I visited Kedarnath myself some years later.

This was how Hindu sages were to conclude their lives. Once they grew old and had fully achieved life's purpose, they would leave their homes, say goodbye to their families, and wander off alone into the woods. They would take no food with them, no water. The journey didn't require those things; in fact, they would have led them astray.

The old wise men would get lost in the woods somewhere, and then they'd stop to fast and pray. As they meditated on what they really were, they would gradually shed all of their intellectual attachments to the world, all the false identities they'd accumulated throughout their lives. They'd give up identifying with whatever work they'd done for decades. There are no fish to catch in the woods, so they couldn't be fishermen anymore; no homes to build, so they couldn't be builders. No more fields to till.

They'd give up their affection for their friends, their hatred of their enemies, even their love for their families. None of these things were with them in the woods. One by one, the old sages would give up all the intellectual commitments they'd imposed on the matter of the universe during their life, all the things tying their minds to the world, gradually and methodically shedding those illusions like a snake freeing itself from its worn-out skin.

That's how they'd spend their final days, searching for their true selves in the wilderness as their bodies wasted away. As their intellectual attachment to the world faded, so did their physical one, until finally there was nothing left of either.

What happened next? The stories didn't say. Perhaps the wisest of the sages escaped the cycle of life and death, casting off the illusions binding together their matter so completely that it never came back together. As for the rest, my great-aunt Perishammal would often tell me, "When a baby's just been born, sometimes it will smile, a fleeting memory from its last life." She was lost in a fire, not the woods. But wherever she is now, I hope she's more herself than ever before.

Those stories about how the sages met their ends made an impression on my young mind. Their attitude toward death made a kind of sense that I couldn't explain. At times I imagined myself going out into the woods one day once I was old and weary, ready to let life's burdens go.

I don't expect you to share my beliefs, whether religious or political. The idea that people are reborn over and over until they're able to completely give up their intellectual attachment to their physical form is a tough pill to swallow.

But consider the reincarnation of a *nation*. Perhaps we Americans aren't part of a nation that's dying, but part of one that's merely lost in the woods, searching for its true self, waiting to be reborn.

There's a rich history of using individuals and nations to understand each other. That's what most of this book is about, actually. When Plato wrote about the ideal republic almost two and a half millennia ago, his true purpose was to figure out what the ideal person would be like. He thought the question of what a just nation would look like was much easier, so he started there, on the hope that understanding the just nation would give him insight into the just man.

His answer was ultimately that both nation and man must keep the different parts of their souls in harmony, allowing neither appetite, reason, nor ego to overpower the others. You can see echoes of Plato today in Sigmund Freud's theory of the mind or the American system of checks and balances between three branches of government.

It's ironic that so many kings, emperors, and other would-be philosopher-kings throughout the ages have modeled themselves and their countries after Plato's ideal republic. It's ironic that serious historians like Wooldridge complain that Plato's recommendations of ruling-class orgies, communal child-rearing, and noble lies to enable it all aren't realistic. Maybe they'd sound more plausible if we translated them into proposals for how people could balance the different parts of their soul in harmony—the more Plato extended his analogy, the more outlandish it had to become. For much of humanity's civilized history, we have been taking Plato's elaborate allegory about the nature of justice and acting as if he were speaking literally. But his goal was always to start with a metaphor about nations to deduce something of the reality of individuals.

Plato may not have gotten all the way there, but the way I think of it, he left it to posterity to start from the other side and work its way to the middle where he left off. So let's begin with a metaphor about the rebirth of individuals to deduce the reality of the rebirth of nations.

The Hindu belief system about how people are reincarnated isn't for everyone, but it may seem much truer to you when it's applied to nations. Unlike individuals, it's often not clear when a nation comes into being or when it departs. When was Rome born, and when did it die? Was it created when a wolf brought Romulus a scrap of meat, when some villagers on a few hills chose a king, when their king was replaced by a senate, when the senate's authority was replaced by an emperor's? When did Rome die? When Julius Caesar crossed the Rubicon with his army, when Marcus Aurelius gave way to Commodus, when Diocletian split East from West, when barbarians sacked Rome, when Ottomans sacked Constantinople a thousand years later? When my middle school stopped teaching Latin?

It's inaccurate to call any of these moments births or deaths; they can only be understood as both. They were all moments where Rome released its grip on one form and its soul migrated into another. Maybe it's still not entirely gone. In *The Sopranos*, when a Jewish man wonders where the Romans are now, Tony snarls "You're looking at them, asshole."[1] Maybe he's right, in a way. Maybe Rome's just finally given up its physical form for good and become embedded in the fabric of the universe. Or maybe it didn't quite escape the cycle. Maybe it was reborn in 1776.

Thomas Jefferson thought every American leader ought to study the fall of Rome in order to avoid its mistakes.[2] He and America's other founders saw themselves as modern Romans, consciously trying to recreate the best parts of its life as a republic. They would scrutinize the lives and deeds of Rome's leaders the way we pore over the Founding Fathers' lives today, trying to figure out whether they were good men or bad ones, where they went right and wrong.[3] The United States of America was always supposed to be one of Rome's next lives, but a better version of it, a more perfect union. What happened to the Romans? You're looking at them. Once more, they decline.

What happened to the Americans? Where did that strange people go? When was their nation born, and when did it begin to die? Was America born in 1619, when captive Africans arrived in Virginia? A year later, when the *Mayflower*'s pilgrims set foot onto Massachusetts's shores? Was America born when their descendants declared independence from Britain in 1776, when they ratified the Articles of Confederation in 1777, when they replaced those with the Constitution in 1788? Was America born when North and South split, when Lee gave up his sword at Appomattox, when the Reconstruction amendments declared citizens' rights, when the civil rights movement won them?

You fear that your nation is dying, but you cannot even say when it was born. That's because it was always only a metaphor to think that nations live and die at all, only an illusion that helps them hold their matter together for a time. Nations don't die the way people do; they're constantly reborn as something else.

We Americans have been lost in the woods before, lost in a fire now, wondering who we really are. It's not an easy process. We hunger for a justice we cannot describe and thirst for vengeance against villains long dead, and so we take what revenge we can on their memories and call it justice, though it does not sate us. The pangs of guilt and resentment wrack us. Are we a racist nation, we wonder? Have we always been? Were we exceptional, once, even partly? When did that stop? Who bears the fault for it all? We feel some kind of death approaching, and our nation's life flashes before its eyes.

But unlike the great sages, we haven't given up our intellectual attachments, so the American mind can think only of its hunger and thirst, of all the good things we're losing and the ones we never had. A great experiment draws to a disappointing end, its bold hypothesis disproven. All that seems to remain is the question of blame. The American nation begins to eat itself in its hunger; its flesh wastes away. And its mind, still clinging desperately to all the illusions and false identities that have held it together, can think of nothing but the pain. Though America hates what it is, it fears becoming nothing.

We're not a nation that tells itself Horatio Alger stories anymore. Those stories held us together, gave us something to aspire to. Instead we hurl competing tales of victimhood at each other, trying desperately to grab as much as we can before the nation's body falls apart, not caring that our grievances are what make it fall apart. Sometimes I cynically wonder if I can help get Horatio Alger stories back in schools by telling everyone he was gay: *You see, you've been erasing a prominent gay author from American history, and representation matters . . .* Well, it's worth a shot. Horatio Alger was gay. That is why we must read his underdog stories.

Victimhood identities have become like magic words. Invoke the right ones and you get into college, get a good job, get respect and status, get heard. It reminds me of a Ted Chiang short story called "Understand." The protagonist and antagonist take brain-enhancing drugs to become super-intelligent, so smart that they can create and destroy other people's identities simply by saying powerful words to them, words that force them to see the world differently. The story ends with the antagonist lifting a finger and saying the word "understand," and simply hearing that word forces the protagonist to connect all the dots and see how all the earlier events in the story fit together, and his new understanding of the world forces him to give up. Sometimes we Americans seem to be playing the same kind of game, except it's the victims that have all the magic words, the ones that end debate and change the world the moment they're uttered.

I worry that this book has all been in vain, that I will have written seventy thousand words and the people I most wanted to hear them will just chant their favorite spells to defeat me. *He's just spouting conservative talking points. He's just an Uncle Tom.* Let me tell you something funny about being a racial minority in America: by admitting I dislike being called an Uncle Tom, I've guaranteed that it will happen more often.

Call me an Uncle Tom if you must. I won't let it define either of us. Call me a racist, a homophobe, a sexist, a bigot of all kinds. I still won't let it define either of us. But I wish I could find a magic word to recreate your identity the way you use them to create mine.

Reincarnate. Understand. It's time to be reborn; we Americans aren't ready to become nothing. We're not ready to take our place at Rome's side as an idea in the fabric of human thought. So let go of these attachments that cause you such pain, these false identities. Let go of your false inferiority; let go of your false superiority. Let go of the grievances that give you a false purpose, a thing to hold on to. Let go of the tribal identities that give you comfort as the world grows dark. See the missing shade of red. You can still reincarnate. Here is a truth about magic words that America needs to learn: call a man good, and more often than not, he will be.

You know, Plato actually believed in reincarnation too. He thought that all learning amounted to remembering things we once knew in a past life, when we were one with the universe, perhaps one that we remembered when we smiled as a baby. Maybe that's why I've tried so hard to remind you in this book of things the nation once knew, but has forgotten somewhere in the violent cycle of rebirth. Americans often speak of privilege and accuse each other of having it. My education was a great privilege. It was a great privilege to learn about Longstreet and Hume, about Plato and Kant and Rome, and a great privilege to share those things with you.

I can imagine what Hume would say to you, if you were allowed to not only learn about him, but grow fond of him: if you think my racist footnote is problematic, just wait until you hear about induction. You fear what comes next, because your nation's present and past seem so bleak. But the future does not have to resemble the past, no matter how many times it has before. For all we know, one day we'll sleep to war and wake up to peace. I may be a bad man today, Hume might tell you, but who knows who I'll be tomorrow?

Sometimes I remember the stories I read as a young boy and I see America as the old man in the woods, tired and hungry, on his last legs.

He imagines the final death. *Mahasamadhi. Moksa.*

What's it like to lose your form completely? What will it be like to be nothing?

It's nothing to fear, he realizes eventually. You're just going back to the place you were before you were first born, the place you see just behind your eyes.

But not yet. There's still so much to learn. Perfection awaits, he can glimpse it, but it's still far away. The pursuit goes on.

He smiles and begins again.

ACKNOWLEDGMENTS

I would like to specially recognize Chris Nicholson, without whose brilliant support I would not have published this book. He was instrumental in turning my vision for this book into reality, and I am deeply grateful for his partnership.

I would like to thank Alex Pappas, Daisy Hutton, Patsy Jones, Katie Robison, Rudy Kish, and the entire Center Street team for publishing this book, and Keith Urbahn, Megan Stencel, Frank Schembari, and the entire Javelin team for serving as my agent—and for taking a bet on me as a first-time author two years ago when few others were willing to.

Finally, thanks to my family, who supports me in pursuing my dreams every day. I am grateful to my wife, Apoorva, for being my harshest critic: when she says she likes something, I know she means it! And I thank my parents every day for giving me the education that I enjoyed, the greatest gift I ever received.

NOTES

INTRODUCTION: HISTORY OF THE NACIREMA

1. Horace Miner, "Body Ritual among the Nacirema," *American Anthropologist* 58, no. 3 (1956): 503–507, https://doi.org/10.1525/aa.1956.58.3.02a00080.

2. Jacey Fortin, "California Tries to Close the Gap in Math, but Sets off a Backlash," *New York Times*, November 4, 2021, https://www.nytimes.com/2021/11/04/us/california-math-curriculum-guidelines.html.

3. Bobby Caina Calvan, "Schools Debate: Gifted and Talented, or Racist and Elitist?" Associated Press, October 28, 2021, https://apnews.com/article/new-york-education-new-york-city-united-states-race-and-ethnicity-f8cbdb50edba9802fe9ad503cfe7d467.

4. David French, "New College Student Survey: Yes, Speech Can Be Violence," *National Review*, October 11, 2017, https://www.nationalreview.com/2017/10/college-students-speech-can-be-violence/.

5. Ursula K. LeGuin, *Wizard of Earthsea: The First Book of Earthsea* (Gollancz, 2019).

6. John McWhorter, "'Woke' Went the Way of 'P.C.' and 'Liberal,'" *New York Times*, November 16, 2021, https://www.nytimes.com/2021/11/16/opinion/woke-progressive-liberal.html.

7. Matt Lewis, "AOC's 'Woke' Whine Is Why the Dems Can't Stop Losing," *Daily Beast*, November 9, 2021, https://www.thedailybeast.com/alexandria-ocasio-cortezs-woke-whine-is-why-the-dems-cant-stop-losing.

8. James George Frazer and Robert Fraser, *The Golden Bough: A Study in Magic and Religion* (Folio Society, 2018).

9. Helen Pluckrose, "Demystifying Critical Race Theory So We Can Get to the Point," *Counterweight*, July 5, 2021, https://counterweightsupport.com/2021/07/02/demystifying-critical-race-theory-so-we-can-get-to-the-point/.

10. Women's March, "We apologize deeply for the email that was sent today. $14.92 was our average donation amount this week. It was an oversight on our part to not make the connection to a year of colonization, conquest, and genocide for Indigenous people, especially before Thanksgiving,"

Twitter, November 23, 2021, https://twitter.com/womensmarch/status/1463229266976464912.

11. Jared M. Diamond, *Guns, Germs and Steel: A Short History of Everybody for the Last 13,000 Years* (Vintage, 2005).

12. Vivek Ramaswamy, *Woke, Inc.: Inside Corporate America's Social Justice Scam* (Center Street, 2021), chap. 15.

13. "We Respond to the Historians Who Critiqued the 1619 Project," *New York Times*, December 20, 2019, https://www.nytimes.com/2019/12/20/magazine/we-respond-to-the-historians-who-critiqued-the-1619-project.html.

14. Bret Stephens, "The 1619 Chronicles," *New York Times*, October 10, 2020, https://www.nytimes.com/2020/10/09/opinion/nyt-1619-project-criticisms.html.

15. Constance Grady, "Thomas Jefferson Spent Years Raping His Slave Sally Hemings. A New Novel Treats Their Relationship as a Love Story," *Vox*, April 8, 2016, https://www.vox.com/2016/4/8/11389556/thomas-jefferson-sally-hemings-book.

16. "Sally Hemings: Life of Sally Hemings," *Monticello.org*, https://www.monticello.org/sallyhemings/.

17. Frank25. "Happy Uncle Tom day, Dinesh!!!" Twitter, October 11, 2021, https://twitter.com/Frank2536600063/status/1447694442949906432.

18. Frank25. "Why is it that Fox puts that skin lightening make-up on you? Do you like it? Does it make you feel white?" Twitter, October 14, 2021, https://twitter.com/Frank2536600063/status/1448467953914159106.

19. Warner Davis, "The Racial Stereotype behind Attacks on Tim Scott," *Wall Street Journal*, May 17, 2021, https://www.wsj.com/articles/the-racial-stereotype-behind-attacks-on-tim-scott-11621276995.

20. Harriet Beecher Stowe and Elizabeth Ammons, *Uncle Tom's Cabin: Authoritative Text, Backgrounds and Contexts, Criticism* (W. W. Norton & Company, 2018).

CHAPTER ONE: NATION OF UNDERDOGS

1. Ellin Stein, "What's Fact and What's Fiction in King Richard," *Slate*, November 20, 2021, https://slate.com/culture/2021/11/king-richard-movie-accuracy-will-smith-richard-williams.html.

2. Eoghan Macguire and Don Riddell, "Richard Williams: 'Close to Being Killed So Many Times,'" *CNN*, December 16, 2015, https://edition.cnn.com/2015/12/16/tennis/richard-williams-venus-serena-tennis/index.html.

3. Roger Rosenblatt, "The Proudest Papa," *Time*, September 20, 1999, http://content.time.com/time/subscriber/article/0,33009,992014,00.html.

4. "Ram Trucks TV Spot, 'Underdog' [t1]," ISpot.tv, https://www.ispot.tv/ad/qexG/ram-trucks-underdog-t1.

5. "Michael Jordan (Ft. Chicago Bulls & Washington Wizards)—NBA Hall of Fame Enshrinement Speech," *Genius*, https://genius.com/Michael-jordan-nba-hall-of-fame-enshrinement-speech-annotated.

6. "Jussie Smollett Charges Dropped; 'His Record Has Been Wiped Clean,'" *CBS News Chicago*, March 27, 2019, https://chicago.cbslocal.com/2019/03/26/jussie-smollett-charges-dropped/.

7. Ray Sanchez, "Michelle Obama's Ex-Top Aide Texted the Jussie Smollett Prosecutor Early in the Case. Some Want That Investigated," *CNN*, March 30, 2019, https://www.cnn.com/2019/03/30/us/jussie-smollett-tina-tchen/index.html.

8. *Illinois Prosecutors Bar Association—IPBA Statement on Jussie Smollett Case Dismissal*, http://www.ilpba.org/announcements/7249825.

9. Gabrielle Fonrouge, "Jussie Smollett's Lawyers Claim Judge 'Lunged' at One of Them, Ask for a Mistrial," *New York Post*, December 3, 2021, https://nypost.com/2021/12/02/jussie-smolletts-lawyers-claim-judge-lunged-at-one-of-them/.

10. "Only Black Juror in Jussie Smollett Case Couldn't Get Past Ex-'Empire' Actor's Reaction to Noose," *USA Today*, December 14, 2021, https://www.usatoday.com/story/entertainment/2021/12/14/jussie-smollett-case-black-juror-confused-reaction-noose/8894592002/.

11. John Adams, Letter from John Adams to Abigail Adams, post May 12, 1780. 2 pages. Original manuscript from the Adams Family Papers, Massachusetts Historical Society.

12. "John Adams to Thomas Jefferson, February–3 March 1814," *Founders Online*, National Archives, https://founders.archives.gov/documents/Jefferson/03-07-02-0140.

13. "Dubai Sheikh's Words Lost in Translation with Viral Quote," *Australian Associated Press*, October 27, 2021, https://www.aap.com.au/factcheck/dubai-sheikhs-words-lost-in-translation-with-viral-quote/.

14. Mark J. Perry, "International Evidence: Life Expectancy and GDP," American Enterprise Institute, June 3, 2010, https://www.aei.org/carpe-diem/international-evidence-life-expectancy-and-gdp/.

15. Robert Rector, "How Poor, Really, Are America's Poor?" *Heritage Foundation*, March 5, 2020, https://www.heritage.org/poverty-and-inequality/commentary/how-poor-really-are-americas-poor.

16. Daniel Markovits, *The Meritocracy Trap*, Kindle ebook ed. (Penguin Books, 2019).

17. In chapter 9, I defend a version of meritocracy that can accommodate his criticisms and discourage Americans from seeing themselves as victims.

18. Christopher Clarey, "Naomi Osaka Brought to Tears by Heckler at Indian Wells," *New York Times*, March 13, 2022, https://www.nytimes.com/2022/03/13/sports/tennis/naomi-osaka-indian-wells.html.

19. William Saletan, "Rachel Dolezal's Most Disturbing Claims Are over Her Own Victimization," *Slate*, June 16, 2015, https://slate.com/news-and-politics/2015/06/rachel-dolezal-claims-to-be-the-target-of-hate-crimes-the-former-naacp-officials-most-disturbing-statements-are-about-her-victimization.html.

20. Storms Reback and Rachel Dolezal, *In Full Color: Finding My Place in a Black and White World* (Benbella Books, 2017).

21. Colleen Flaherty, "Prominent Scholar Outs Herself as White Just as She Faced Exposure for Claiming to Be Black," *Inside Higher Ed*, September 4, 2020, https://www.insidehighered.com/news/2020/09/04/prominent-scholar-outs-herself-white-just-she-faced-exposure-claiming-be-black.

22. Colleen Flaherty, "MeTooSTEM Leader Admits to Faking Identity," *Inside Higher Ed*, August 5, 2020, https://www.insidehighered.com/quicktakes/2020/08/05/metoostem-leader-admits-faking-identity.

23. "Indiana Racial Justice Activist Lied about Being Black," Associated Press, September 20, 2020, https://apnews.com/article/indiana-race-and-ethnicity-5b056dd481696537f65c1d5af7eabeed.

24. Colleen Flaherty, "Unmasking Another White Professor Allegedly Posing as a Person of Color," *Inside Higher Ed*, October 9, 2020, https://www.insidehighered.com/news/2020/10/29/unmasking-another-white-professor-allegedly-posing-person-color.

25. Helen Lewis, "The Identity Hoaxers," *The Atlantic*, January 12, 2022, https://www.theatlantic.com/international/archive/2021/03/krug-carrillo-dolezal-social-munchausen-syndrome/618289/.

26. United States Supreme Court. *Gutter v. Bollinger*, June 23, 2003, Legal Information Institute, Cornell Law School, https://www.law.cornell.edu/supct/html/02-241.ZO.html.

27. Adam Liptak and Anemona Hartocollis, "Supreme Court Will Hear Challenge to Affirmative Action at Harvard and U.N.C.," *New York Times*, January 24, 2022, https://www.nytimes.com/2022/01/24/us/politics/supreme-court-affirmative-action-harvard-unc.html.

28. Scott Jaschik, "The Numbers and Arguments on Asian Admissions," *Inside Higher Ed*, August 7, 2017, https://www.insidehighered.com/admissions/article/2017/08/07/look-data-and-arguments-about-asian-americans-and-admissions-elite.

29. Anemona Hartocollis, "Harvard Rated Asian-American Applicants Lower on Personality Traits, Suit Says," *New York Times*, June 15, 2018, https://www.nytimes.com/2018/06/15/us/harvard-asian-enrollment-applicants.html.

30. Hartocollis, "Harvard Rated Asian-American Applicants."

31. Mark J. Drozdowski, "The Historical Parallel between Asian American and Jewish Students," BestColleges.com, February 8, 2022, https://www.bestcolleges.com/news/analysis/2021/08/09/historical-parallel-between-asian-american-and-jewish-students/.

32. Jonathan Chait, "The Left Is Gaslighting Asian Americans about College Admissions," *The Intelligencer*, February 8, 2022, https://nymag.com/intelligencer/2022/02/the-left-is-gaslighting-asian-americans-on-school-admissions.html.

33. John B. Judis and Ruy Teixeira. "New York's Race-Based Preferential Covid Treatments," *Wall Street Journal*, January 7, 2022, https://www.wsj.com/articles/new-york-race-based-covid-treatment-white-hispanic-inequity-monoclonal-antibodies-antiviral-pfizer-omicron-11641573991.

34. Katy Grimes, "Oakland Mayor Announces Basic Income Program, but Not for Poor White Families," *California Globe*, March 26, 2021, https://californiaglobe.com/articles/oakland-mayor-announces-basic-income-program-but-not-for-poor-white-families/.

35. Editorial Board. "The Radical Potential of Guaranteed Income Based on Race," *Daily Californian*, April 17, 2021, https://www.dailycal.org/2021/04/16/the-radical-potential-of-guaranteed-income-based-on-race/.

36. Mark Calvey, "Oakland's Basic Income Plan Could Face Legal Challenges," American City Business Journals, https://www.bizjournals.com/sanfrancisco/news/2021/04/01/oakland-s-basic-income-plan-could-face-legal-chall.html.

37. Guy Marzorati, "Oakland Guaranteed Income Program Now Says It's Not Exclusively for People of Color," KQED, April 2, 2021, https://www.kqed.org/news/11867881/oakland-guaranteed-income-program-now-says-its-not-exclusively-for-people-of-color.

CHAPTER TWO: THE CIVIL WAR

1. Joseph Callaway, "The Confederacy's "Hardest Hitter": Reevaluating James Longstreet's Civil War Record on the Tactical Offensive," thesis, Georgia State University, 2018, https://scholarworks.gsu.edu/history_theses/119. I drew many details about Longstreet's maneuvers from here.

2. James Longstreet, *From Manassas to Appomattox: Memoirs of the Civil War in America* (J. B. Lippincott, 1896), 386–387.

3. Jeffry D. Wert, *Gettysburg: Day Three* (Simon & Schuster, 2001), 283.

4. William Faulkner, *Intruder in the Dust*, Kindle ed. (HarperPerennial Classics, 2013).

5. Roy Blount Jr., "Making Sense of Robert E. Lee," *Smithsonian Magazine*, July 1, 2003, https://www.smithsonianmag.com/history/making-sense-of-robert-e-lee-85017563/.

6. Gary W. Gallagher, "Blue and Gray: How Lee's 'Old War Horse' Gained a New Following," HistoryNet, September 21, 2017, https://www.historynet.com/blue-gray-lees-old-war-horse-gained-new-following/.

7. Kenneth Weisbrode, "An Unlikely Friendship," *New York Times*, June 9, 2014, https://opinionator.blogs.nytimes.com/2014/06/09/an-unlikely-friendship/.

8. Weisbrode, "An Unlikely Friendship."

9. Ron Chernow, *Grant* (Penguin Press, 2017), 857.

10. Jubal Anderson Early, *Memoirs of General Jubal Early* (Roy P Jensen Inc Remainders, 1996).

11. Douglas Southall Freeman, *R.E. Lee: A Biography* (Charles Scribner's Sons, 1936).

12. "Confederate Brigadier General James Longstreet: (1821–1904)," *History on the Net*, March 17, 2022, https://www.historyonthenet.com/confederate-brigadier-general-james-longstreet-1821-1904.

13. Longstreet, *From Manassas to Appomattox*.

14. Jeffry D. Wert, *General James Longstreet, The Confederacy's Most Controversial Soldier: A Biography* (Simon & Schuster, 1993).

15. Steven E. Woodworth, "Film Review: Gods and Generals," *TeachingHistory.org*, 2011, https://teachinghistory.org/nhec-blog/25077.

16. Janet McConnaughey and Rebecca Santana, "Robert E. Lee Statue Is Last Confederate Monument Removed in New Orleans," *Chicago Tribune*, August 22, 2019, https://www.chicagotribune.com/nation-world/ct-new-orleans-general-lee-statue-20170518-story.html.

17. David Hume, *Dialogues Concerning Natural Religion* (Antiquarius, 2021).

18. William B. Huntley, "David Hume and Charles Darwin," *Journal of the History of Ideas* 33, no. 3 (1972): 457, https://doi.org/10.2307/2709046.

19. Matias Slavov, "No Absolute Time," *Aeon*, August 21, 2019, https://aeon.co/essays/what-albert-einstein-owes-to-david-humes-notion-of-time.

20. David Rutledge, "What We (Maybe) Get Wrong about David Hume," *ABC Religion & Ethics,* June 15, 2021, https://www.abc.net.au/religion/what-we-maybe-get-wrong-about-david-hume/13385708.

21. John Immerwahr, "Hume's Revised Racism," *Journal of the History of Ideas* 53, no. 3, (1992): 481–486, https://doi-org.proxy.lib.umich.edu/10.2307/2709889.

22. Immerwhar, "Hume's Revised Racism," 482.

23. Jonathan A. Knee, "Review: The Scandalous Friendship That Shaped Adam Smith," *New York Times*, September 21, 2017, https://www.nytimes.

com/2017/09/21/business/dealbook/infidel-professor-adam-smith-david-hume.html.

24. Patrick Young, "Gen. Longstreet's Infamous Letter: On Joining the Republicans and 'Betraying' the Confederates 1867," The Reconstruction Era, November 11, 2019, https://thereconstructionera.com/gen-longstreets-infamous-letter-on-joining-the-republicans-betraying-the-confederates-1867/.

25. Stephen A. Holmes, "Where Are the Monuments to Confederate Gen. James Longstreet?" *CNN*, August 23, 2017, https://www.cnn.com/2017/08/23/opinions/where-are-monuments-to-confederate-general-longstreet-opinion-holmes/index.html; Charles Lane, "The Forgotten Confederate General Who Deserves a Monument," *Washington Post*, January 27, 2016, https://www.washingtonpost.com/opinions/the-forgotten-confederate-general-who-would-make-a-better-subject-for-monuments/2016/01/27/f09bad42-c536-11e5-8965-0607e0e265ce_story.html.

26. Justin Weinberg, "Should We Continue to Honor Hume with Buildings and Statues?" *Daily Nous*, July 3, 2020, https://dailynous.com/2020/07/03/honor-hume-buildings-statues/.

27. William Faulkner, *Requiem for a Nun* (Vintage, 2015); Barack Obama, "A More Perfect Union," March 18, 2008, Constitution Center, Philadelphia. Speech.

28. Amy Sokolow, "Harvard Poll: 52% of Young Americans Think Democracy Is 'in Trouble' or 'Failing,'" *Boston Herald*, December 1, 2021, https://www.bostonherald.com/2021/12/01/harvard-poll-52-of-young-americans-think-democracy-is-in-trouble-or-failing/.

29. William G. Gale and Darrell M. West, "Is the US Headed for Another Civil War?" Brookings Institution, September 16, 2021, https://www.brookings.edu/blog/fixgov/2021/09/16/is-the-us-headed-for-another-civil-war/.

30. Paul Duggan, "Charge Upgraded to First-Degree Murder for Driver Accused of Ramming Charlottesville Crowd," *Washington Post*, December 14, 2017, https://www.washingtonpost.com/local/crime/driver-accused-of-plowing-into-charlottesville-crowd-killing-heather-heyer-due-in-court/2017/12/13/6cbb4ce8-e029-11e7-89e8-edec16379010_story.html.

31. Hawes Spencer and Michael Levenson, "Charlottesville Removes Robert E. Lee Statue at Center of White Nationalist Rally," *New York Times*, 9 July 2021, https://www.nytimes.com/2021/07/09/us/charlottesville-confederate-monuments-lee.html.

32. "Trump Defends Keeping Fort Bragg Name amid Calls to Rename Bases Named after Confederate Leaders," *ABC11 Raleigh-Durham*, WTVD-TV, July 19, 2020, https://abc11.com/fox-news-sunday-fort-bragg-renaming-history-of/6324657/.

33. "Army Installations: Potential New Names," Naming Commission, March 17, 2022, https://www.thenamingcommission.gov/names.

34. Lois Lowry, *The Giver* (HarperCollins Children's Books, 2022).

CHAPTER THREE: THE CONSTITUTIONAL WAR

1. Akhil Amar, "Substance and Method in the Year 2000," *Pepperdine Law Review* 28, no. 3 (2001): 631n178.

2. Ramaswamy, *Woke, Inc.*, chap. 13.

3. United States Supreme Court, *The Slaughter-House Case*, April 14, 1873, *Legal Information Institute*, Cornell Law School, https://www.law.cornell.edu/supremecourt/text/83/36.

4. United States Supreme Court, *Plessy v. Ferguson*, May 18, 1896. *Legal Information Institute*, Cornell Law School, https://www.law.cornell.edu/supremecourt/text/163/537.

5. For but one example of many, see both his dissent and Chief Justice Roberts's in *Obergefell v. Hodges*. Roberts recounts the standard Scalian argument against substantive due process in a more measured way. United States Supreme Court, *Obergefell v. Hodges*, June 26, 2015, *Legal Information Institute*, Cornell Law School, https://www.law.cornell.edu/supremecourt/text/14-556.

6. I explained the way American culture's obsession with diversity stems from Supreme Court affirmative action law in chapter 9 of *Woke, Inc.*

7. United States Supreme Court, *Dred Scott v. Sandford*, March 6, 1857, *Legal Information Institute*, Cornell Law School, https://www.law.cornell.edu/supremecourt/text/60/393.

8. United States Supreme Court, *Lochner v. New York*, April 17, 1905, *Legal Information Institute*, Cornell Law School, https://www.law.cornell.edu/supremecourt/text/198/45.

9. United States Supreme Court, *Roe v. Wade*, January 22, 1973, *Legal Information Institute*, Cornell Law School, https://www.law.cornell.edu/supremecourt/text/410/113.

10. Joe Carter, "Justice Scalia's Two Most Essential Speeches," *Ethics and Religious Liberty Commission of the Southern Baptist Convention*, February 18, 2016, https://erlc.com/resource-library/articles/justice-scalias-two-most-essential-speeches/.

11. United States Supreme Court, *United States v. Carolene Products Company*, April 25, 1938, *Legal Information Institute*, Cornell Law School, https://www.law.cornell.edu/supremecourt/text/304/144.

12. Bruce A. Ackerman, "Beyond 'Carolene Products,'" *Harvard Law Review* 98, no. 4 (1985): 713, https://doi.org/10.2307/1340988.

13. Jed Rubenfeld, "Affirmative Action," *Yale Law Journal*, 107, no. 2 (1997): 427, https://doi.org/10.2307/797261.

14. United States Supreme Court, *Bowers v. Hardwick*, June 30, 1986. Legal Information Institute, Cornell Law School, https://www.law.cornell.edu/supremecourt/text/478/186%26gt.

15. William N. Eskridge Jr., "Is Political Powerlessness a Requirement for Heightened Equal Protection Scrutiny?" *Washburn Law Journal* 50, no. 1 (2010): 1.

16. Douglas Murray, *The Madness of Crowds: Gender, Race and Identity*, ebook (Bloomsbury Continuum, 2019), 34.

17. Ramaswamy, *Woke, Inc.*, chap. 9.

18. Marcy Strauss, "Re-evaluating Suspect Classifications," *Seattle University Law Review* 35 (2011): 135–174.

19. Susannah W. Pollvogt, "Beyond Suspect Classifications," *Journal of Constitutional Law* 16, no. 3 (2013–2014): 739–803, at 797.

20. United States Supreme Court, *City of Cleburne v. Cleburne Living Center, Inc.*, April 23, 1985, Legal Information Institute, Cornell Law School, https://www.law.cornell.edu/supremecourt/text/473/432.

21. Pollvogt, "Beyond Suspect Classifications," 800.

22. Charlie Savage, "'Court Packing' Issue Divides Commission Appointed by Biden," *New York Times*, December 8, 2021, https://www.nytimes.com/2021/12/07/us/politics/supreme-court-packing-expansion.html.

CHAPTER FOUR: RACE THEORY

1. "States That Have Banned Critical Race Theory 2022," World Population Review, https://worldpopulationreview.com/state-rankings/states-that-have-banned-critical-race-theory.

2. Plato, *Republic* 338c, http://www.perseus.tufts.edu/hopper/text?doc=Perseus%3Atext%3A1999.01.0168%3Abook%3D1#note94.

3. "Basic Tenets of Critical Race Theory," *Encyclopedia Britannica*, https://www.britannica.com/topic/critical-race-theory/Basic-tenets-of-critical-race-theory.

4. Chris Cillizza, "Analysis: Nancy Pelosi's Stunningly Tone-Deaf Quote on George Floyd," *CNN*, April 21, 2021, https://www.cnn.com/2021/04/21/politics/george-floyd-nancy-pelosi-derek-chauvin/index.html.

5. Luis Andres Henao et al., "For George Floyd, a Complicated Life and a Notorious Death," Associated Press, June 10, 2020, https://apnews.com/article/virus-outbreak-us-news-ap-top-news-hip-hop-and-rap-houston-a55d2662f200ead0da4fed9e923b60a7.

6. Jemima McEvoy, "Sales of 'White Fragility'—and Other Anti-Racism Books—Jumped over 2000% after Protests Began," *Forbes*, July 22, 2020,

https://www.forbes.com/sites/jemimamcevoy/2020/07/22/sales-of-white-fragility-and-other-anti-racism-books-jumped-over-2000-after-protests-began/?sh=57a68ea0303d.

7. Helen Pluckrose, "Demystifying Critical Race Theory So We Can Get to the Point," *Counterweight*, July 5, 2021, https://counterweightsupport.com/2021/07/02/demystifying-critical-race-theory-so-we-can-get-to-the-point/.

8. Pluckrose, "Demystifying Critical Race Theory."

9. Michelle Alexander, *The New Jim Crow*, Kindle ebook ed. (New Press, 2020), 36.

10. Alan Greenblatt, "The Racial History of the 'Grandfather Clause,'" NPR, October 22, 2013, https://www.npr.org/sections/codeswitch/2013/10/21/239081586/the-racial-history-of-the-grandfather-clause.

11. Alexander argues that segregation laws were proposed as part of a deliberate effort to drive a wedge between poor white and black people to prevent them from uniting politically. Alexander, *The New Jim Crow*, 42.

12. United States Supreme Court, *Brown v. Board of Education*, May 17, 1954, *Legal Information Institute*, Cornell Law School, https://www.law.cornell.edu/supremecourt/text/347/483%26gt.

13. Alexander, *The New Jim Crow*, 51.

14. Alexander, *The New Jim Crow*, 55.

15. Alexander, *The New Jim Crow*, 4.

16. Alexander, *The New Jim Crow*, 7.

17. Patricia A. Langan, "The Racial Disparity in U.S. Drug Arrests," *US Department of Justice*, October 1, 1995, https://bjs.ojp.gov/content/pub/pdf/rdusda.pdf.

18. Alexander, *The New Jim Crow*, 77.

19. Alexander, *The New Jim Crow*, 80.

20. Alexander, *The New Jim Crow*, 94–98.

21. Alexander, *The New Jim Crow*, 99.

22. Dave McMenamin, "Lebron James Explains Why He Deleted Tweet on Police Shooting of Ma'khia Bryant," ESPN, April 22, 2021, https://www.espn.com/nba/story/_/id/31306343/lebron-james-explains-why-deleted-tweet-police-shooting-makhia-bryant.

23. Morgan Chalfant, "White House Says Fatal Shooting of Black Teen in Columbus 'Tragic,'" *The Hill*, April 21, 2021, https://thehill.com/homenews/administration/549519-white-house-says-fatal-police-shooting-of-black-teen-in-columbus.

24. Maegan Vazquez and Kate Sullivan, "Biden Calls Georgia Law 'Jim Crow in the 21st Century' and Says Justice Department Is 'Taking a Look,'"

CNN, March 26, 2021, https://www.cnn.com/2021/03/26/politics/
joe-biden-georgia-voting-rights-bill/index.html.

25. James Forman Jr., "Racial Critiques of Mass Incarceration: Beyond the
New Jim Crow," *NYU Law Review* 87, no. 1 (2012): 21–69, https://www.
nyulawreview.org/wp-content/uploads/2018/08/NYULawReview-87-1-
Forman_Jr.pdf.

26. Forman, "Racial Critiques of Mass Incarceration," 35.

27. Forman, "Racial Critiques of Mass Incarceration," 35.

28. Alexander, *The New Jim Crow*; Forman, "Racial Critiques of Mass
Incarceration," 51.

29. Forman, "Racial Critiques of Mass Incarceration," 36.

30. "Minnesota Poll Results: Minneapolis Policing and Public Safety Charter
Amendment," *Star Tribune*, September 18, 2021, https://www.startribune.
com/minnesota-poll-public-safety-minneapolis-police-crime-charter-
amendment ballot question/600097989/.

31. Art Swift, "Blacks Divided on Whether Police Treat Minorities Fairly,"
Gallup, August 10, 2021, https://news.gallup.com/poll/184511/blacks-
divided-whether-police-treat-minorities-fairly.aspx.

32. Forman, "Racial Critiques of Mass Incarceration," 46.

33. Rachel E. Morgan, "Race and Hispanic Origin of Victims and Offenders,
2012–15," *US Department of Justice*, October 2017, https://bjs.ojp.gov/
content/pub/pdf/rhovo1215.pdf.

34. It's worth noting that although Pfaff and other critics rightly point out
that far more of the current prison population is composed of violent
offenders than nonviolent drug offenders, this gap is partly explained by
the fact that violent offenders tend to have longer sentences. Drug crimes
are responsible for more new admissions to the prison system, although
violent offenders stay there longer. This important difference is called the
"stock versus flow" distinction. Jonathan Rothwell, "Drug Offenders in
American Prisons: The Critical Distinction between Stock and Flow,"
Brookings, July 29, 2016, https://www.brookings.edu/blog/social-mobility-
memos/2015/11/25/drug-offenders-in-american-prisons-the-critical-
distinction-between-stock-and-flow/.

35. German Lopez, "The First Step Act, Explained," *Vox*, December 19, 2018,
https://www.vox.com/future-perfect/2018/12/18/18140973/state-of-the-
union-trump-first-step-act-criminal-justice-reform.

36. German Lopez, "Why You Can't Blame Mass Incarceration on the War on
Drugs," *Vox*, May 30, 2017, https://www.vox.com/policy-and-
politics/2017/5/30/15591700/mass-incarceration-john-pfaff-locked-in.

37. I discuss these in chapter 9.

38. Adam B. Coleman, *Black Victim to Black Victor: Identifying the Ideologies, Behavioral Patterns, and Cultural Norms That Encourage a Victimhood Complex*, Kindle ebook ed. (Wrong Speak Publishing, 2021).

39. Coleman, *Black Victim to Black Victor*, 50.

40. Kevin Smithwick, "Children and Youth," Rochester Area Community Foundation, https://www.actrochester.org/children-youth/single-parent-families-by-race-ethnicity.

41. Coleman, *Black Victim to Black Victor*, 26.

42. Coleman, *Black Victim to Black Victor*, 50.

43. Coleman, *Black Victim to Black Victor*, 51.

44. Coleman, *Black Victim to Black Victor*, 59.

45. Anthony Leonardi, "Black Lives Matter 'What We Believe' Page That Includes Disrupting 'Nuclear Family Structure' Removed from Website," *Washington Examiner*, September 21, 2020, https://www.washingtonexaminer.com/news/black-lives-matter-what-we-believe-page-that-includes-disrupting-nuclear-family-structure-removed-from-website.

CHAPTER FIVE: CONSERVATIVE VICTIMHOOD

1. Gregory Krieg, "Stacey Abrams Says 'Democracy Failed' Georgia as She Ends Bid for Governor," *CNN*, November 17, 2018, https://www.cnn.com/2018/11/16/politics/stacey-abrams-concession/index.html.

2. "Why Stacey Abrams Is Still Saying She Won," *New York Times*, April 29, 2019, https://www.nytimes.com/interactive/2019/04/28/magazine/stacey-abrams-election-georgia.html.

3. Ben Nadler, "Voting Rights Become a Flashpoint in Georgia Governor's Race," Associated Press, October 9, 2018, https://apnews.com/article/fb011f39af3b40518b572c8cce6e906c.

4. Mark Niesse, "What You Need to Know about Georgia's 53,000 Pending Voters," *Atlanta Journal-Constitution*, October 15, 2018, https://www.ajc.com/news/state--regional-govt--politics/what-you-need-know-about-georgia-000-pending-voters/0aulxJgIulIpKgMmpexBmK/.

5. Alan Judd, "Georgia's Strict Laws Lead to Large Purge of Voters," *Atlanta Journal-Constitution*, October 27, 2018, https://www.ajc.com/news/state--regional-govt--politics/voter-purge-begs-question-what-the-matter-with-georgia/YAFvuk3Bu95kJIMaDiDFqJ/.

6. William Cummings et al., "By the Numbers: President Donald Trump's Failed Efforts to Overturn the Election," *USA Today*, January 6, 2021, https://www.usatoday.com/in-depth/news/politics/elections/2021/01/06/trumps-failed-efforts-overturn-election-numbers/4130307001/.

7. Nick Corasaniti et al., "The Times Called Officials in Every State: No Evidence of Voter Fraud," *New York Times*, November 11, 2020, https://www.nytimes.com/2020/11/10/us/politics/voting-fraud.html.

8. "Joint Statement from Elections Infrastructure Government Coordinating Council and the Election Infrastructure Sector Coordinating Executive Committees," Cybersecurity and Infrastructure Security Agency, November 12, 2020, https://www.cisa.gov/news/2020/11/12/joint-statement-elections-infrastructure-government-coordinating-council-election.

9. Alana Wise, "Trump Fires Election Security Director Who Corrected Voter Fraud Disinformation," NPR, November 18, 2020, https://www.npr.org/2020/11/17/936003057/cisa-director-chris-krebs-fired-after-trying-to-correct-voter-fraud-disinformati.

10. "Read the Full Transcript and Listen to Trump's Audio Call with Georgia Secretary of State," *CNN*, January 4, 2021, https://www.cnn.com/2021/01/03/politics/trump-brad-raffensperger-phone-call-transcript/index.html.

11. Maggie Haberman and Annie Karni, "Pence Said to Have Told Trump He Lacks Power to Change Election Result," *New York Times*, January 6, 2021, https://www.nytimes.com/2021/01/05/us/politics/pence-trump-election-results.html.

12. David Cohen, "Gop Senator Says Trump's Election Allegations Are Unfounded," *Politico*, January 10, 2022, https://www.politico.com/news/2022/01/09/mike-rounds-trump-election-republicans-526806.

13. *2000 Mules*, Dinesh D'Souza, Salem Media Group, 2022.

14. "United States House of Representatives Elections, 2020," Ballotpedia, https://ballotpedia.org/United_States_House_of_Representatives_elections,_2020.

15. Mabinty Quarshie, "Rep. Madison Cawthorn Calls Jan. 6 Rioters 'Political Prisoners,' Warns of 'Bloodshed' at GOP Event," *USA Today*, August 31, 2021, https://www.usatoday.com/story/news/politics/2021/08/31/madison-cawthorn-warns-bloodshed-pushing-election-fraud-claims/5662711001/.

16. Nick Gass, "Trump Accuses Cruz of 'Fraud,' Calls for New Iowa Election," *Politico*, February 3, 2016, https://www.politico.com/story/2016/02/trump-cruz-stole-iowa-tweet-deleted-218674.

17. Jake Thomas, "Trump's Laying Groundwork to Defend Dr. Oz if He Loses Pennsylvania Primary," *Newsweek*, May 19, 2022, https://www.newsweek.com/trumps-laying-groundwork-defend-dr-oz-if-he-loses-pennsylvania-primary-1708400.

18. Michael Waldman et al., "Voting Laws Roundup: October 2021," *Brennan Center for Justice*, July 22, 2021, https://www.brennancenter.org/our-work/research-reports/voting-laws-roundup-october-2021.

19. Alexandra Jaffe and Colleen Long, "Biden Challenges Senate on Voting: 'Tired of Being Quiet!'" Associated Press, January 12, 2022, https://apnews.com/article/voting-rights-joe-biden-georgia-voting-martin-luther-king-jr-dc4544c23622f35fc95d63afe512554d.

20. Andrew E. Busch, "'Jim Crow 2.0' Is Imaginary—and Divisive," *RealClear Politics*, August 20, 2021, https://www.realclearpolitics.com/articles/2021/08/20/jim_crow_20_is_imaginary__and_divisive_146276.html.

21. David Litt, "The Senate Filibuster Is Another Monument to White Supremacy," *The Atlantic*, June 27, 2020, https://www.theatlantic.com/ideas/archive/2020/06/senate-filibuster-monument-white-supremacy/613579/.

22. Stevie Rosignol-Cortez, "Fact Brief: Did Democrats Make Record Use of the Filibuster in the Last Congress?" Repustar, June 27, 2021, https://repustar.com/fact-briefs/do-both-political-parties-have-a-history-of-using-filibusters.

23. Alexa Corse, "Biden Draws Criticism after Raising Prospect of Illegitimate 2022 Election," *Wall Street Journal*, January 20, 2022, https://www.wsj.com/articles/biden-draws-criticism-after-raising-prospect-of-illegitimate-2022-election-11642704627.

24. George Orwell, *Animal Farm* (Penguin Group, 1945).

25. Bill Grueskin, "How the New York Times Editorial Page Got Sued by Sarah Palin," *Columbia Journalism Review*, September 10, 2020, https://www.cjr.org/opinion/how-the-new-york-times-editorial-page-got-sued-by-sarah-palin.php.

26. United States Supreme Court, *New York Times Co. v. Sullivan*, March 9, 1964, *Legal Information Institute*, Cornell Law School, https://www.law.cornell.edu/supremecourt/text/376/254.

27. Deanna Paul, "Jurors in Sarah Palin's Defamation Suit against New York Times Knew Judge Planned to Dismiss Her Claims," *Wall Street Journal*, February 16, 2022, https://www.wsj.com/articles/jurors-in-sarah-palins-defamation-suit-against-new-york-times-knew-judge-planned-to-dismiss-her-claims-11645051450.

28. JackHunter, "The View's Blatant Conspiracy Theory Hypocrisy Isn't Going to Get Called Out," *The Week*, January 5, 2022, https://theweek.com/talking-points/1008621/left-wing-conspiracism-is-bad-too.

29. Ken Bensinger et al., "These Reports Allege Trump Has Deep Ties to Russia," *BuzzFeed News*, March 5, 2019, https://www.buzzfeednews.com/article/kenbensinger/these-reports-allege-trump-has-deep-ties-to-russia.

30. Kimberley A. Strassel, "Durham and the Clinton Dossier," *Wall Street Journal*, November 4, 2021, https://www.wsj.com/articles/durham-and-the-clinton-dossier-trump-russia-collusion-justice-11636064837.

31. Strassel, "Durham and the Clinton Dossier."

32. Jerry Dunleavy, "Declassified Recorded Talk with Carter Page Shows Denials Concealed from FISA Court," *Washington Examiner*, January 28, 2021, https://www.washingtonexaminer.com/news/stefan-halper-fbi-carter-page-trump-steele-fisa.

33. Office of the Inspector General. "Review of Four FISA Applications and Other Aspects of the FBI's Crossfire Hurricane Investigation," *United States Department of Justice*, December 2019, https://www.justice.gov/storage/120919-examination.pdf.

34. David Shortell and Evan Perez, "Two of Four FISA Warrants against Carter Page Declared Invalid," *CNN*, January 24, 2020, https://www.cnn.com/2020/01/23/politics/fisa-carter-page-warrants/index.html.

35. Catherine Herridge et al., "Justice Department Watchdog Releases Report on Origins of Russia Investigation," *CBS News*, December 9, 2019, https://www.cbsnews.com/news/ig-report-release-justice-department-watchdog-report-origins-russia-investigation-today-2019-12-09-live-updates/.

36. Robert S. Mueller, "Report on the Investigation Into Russian Interference in the 2016 Presidential Election," *US Department of Justice*, March 2019, https://www.justice.gov/archives/sco/file/1373816/download.

37. Anthony P. Carnevale, "The New 'Good Jobs.'" *Bloomberg*, December 1, 2016, https://www.bloomberg.com/news/articles/2016-12-01/the-new-good-jobs.

38. Jeffrey Selingo, "The False Promises of Worker Retraining," *The Atlantic*, January 8, 2018, https://www.theatlantic.com/education/archive/2018/01/the-false-promises-of-worker-retraining/549398/.

39. Veronique De Rugy, "Policy Disincentives in Maintaining Labor Force Attachment," Mercatus Center at George Mason University, November 20, 2019, https://www.mercatus.org/publications/regulation/policy-disincentives-maintaining-labor-force-attachment.

40. Jonathan Haidt, *The Righteous Mind: Why Good People Are Divided by Politics and Religion* (Pantheon, 2012).

CHAPTER SIX: EMPIRE IN DECLINE

1. "The Ruin," *Old English Poetry Project*, Rutgers University, https://oldenglishpoetry.camden.rutgers.edu/the-ruin/.

2. This view has been popularized by the show *Vikings* on the History Channel.

3. Mike Finger, "Finger: Spurs' Lonnie Walker Earning Degree at 'University of Pop,'" *San Antonio Express-News*, November 1, 2021, https://www.expressnews.com/sports/columnists/mike_finger/article/Finger-Spurs-Lonnie-Walker-earning-degree-at-16577917.php.

4. Jack Holmes, "Gregg Popovich Worries That the U.S. Is Experiencing Its Own Roman Fall," *Esquire*, August 21, 2020, https://www.esquire.com/news-politics/a49371/lessons-from-greg-popovich/.

5. Christopher Ingraham, "Two-Thirds of Southern Republicans Want to Secede," *The Why Axis*, Christopher Ingraham, July 14, 2021, https://thewhyaxis.substack.com/p/two-thirds-of-southern-republicans.

6. Joe Garofoli, "Gavin Newsom Wants California to Be Its Own Nation-State in the Trump Era," *San Francisco Chronicle*, February 13, 2019, https://www.sfchronicle.com/politics/article/Gavin-Newsom-wants-California-to-be-its-own-13611747.php.

7. Alysha Tsuji, "Gregg Popovich Goes on Passionate Tirade in Wake of Trump Election: 'We Are Rome,'" *USA Today*, November 12, 2016, https://ftw.usatoday.com/2016/11/san-antonio-gregg-popovich-trump-election-rant-we-are-rome.

8. Virgil, *Aeneid* (Arcturus Publishing Ltd, 2022).

9. Dwight D. Eisenhower, *Crusade in Europe* (Johns Hopkins University Press, 1997), 325.

10. Livy, *Ab Urbe Condita*, xxii.52.6. Most details we know of the Battle of Cannae are drawn from the accounts of Livy and Polybius.

11. "Cannae and the Elusive Face of Battle," Erenow.net, https://erenow.net/ancient/spqr1stedition/64.php.

12. Graham Tillett Allison, *Destined for War: Can America and China Escape Thucydides's Trap?* (Scribe, 2020).

13. Justin Hodiak and Scott W. Harold, "Can China Become the World Leader in Semiconductors?" *The Diplomat*, September 25, 2020, https://thediplomat.com/2020/09/can-china-become-the-world-leader-in-semiconductors/.

14. Adrian Potoroaca, "Intel's Planned Comeback: 10nm Production Now Surpassing 14nm, 7NM Remains a Work in Progress," *TechSpot*, July 24, 2021, https://www.techspot.com/news/90539-intel-10nm-production-now-surpassing-14nm-7nm-remains.html.

15. Joel Hruska, "Everybody Wants a Piece of TSMC's 3nm Process Node," *ExtremeTech*, August 12, 2021, https://www.extremetech.com/computing/325736-everybody-wants-a-piece-of-tsmcs-3nm-process-node.

16. Debby Wu, "TSMC and Intel Get into a Rare Public Spat over U.S. Chipmaking," *Bloomberg*, December 7, 2021, https://www.bloomberg.com/news/newsletters/2021-12-07/tsmc-intel-trade-barbs-over-u-s-chipmaking-fully-charged.

17. Dan De Luce and Ken Dilanian, "China's Growing Firepower Casts Doubt on Whether U.S. Could Defend Taiwan," *NBCNews.com*, March 27, 2021, https://www.nbcnews.com/politics/national-security/china-s-growing-firepower-casts-doubt-whether-u-s-could-n1262148.

18. Claude Berube, "Is America Still Born to Rule the Seas?" *War on the Rocks*, December 7, 2021, https://warontherocks.com/2021/12/is-america-still-born-to-rule-the-seas/.

19. Thomas Newdick, "The First Littoral Combat Ship Has Been Decommissioned after Just 13 Years of Service (Updated)," *The Drive*, October 1, 2021, https://www.thedrive.com/the-war-zone/42582/the-first-littoral-combat-ship-has-been-decommissioned-after-just-13-years-of-service.

20. "China Racing ahead of US Navy at Breakneck Speed; Building 20 Warships per Year in 17 Shipyards—Top Official," *Eurasian Times*, November 4, 2021, https://eurasiantimes.com/chinas-pla-navy-us-navy-a-breakneck-20-warships-per-year/.

21. GCR Staff, "Senators Call for $25bn Revamp of America's Naval Shipyards," *Global Construction Review*, May 24, 2021, https://www.globalconstructionreview.com/senators-call-25bn-revamp-americas-naval-shipyards/.

22. Konstantin Toropin, "With a Wink and a Nod, Japan Has an Aircraft Carrier Again," *Military.com*, October 27, 2021, https://www.military.com/daily-news/2021/10/27/wink-and-nod-japan-has-aircraft-carrier-again.html.

23. Roger Cohen, "In Submarine Deal with Australia, U.S. Counters China but Enrages France," *New York Times*, September 16, 2021, https://www.nytimes.com/2021/09/16/world/europe/france-australia-uk-us-submarines.html.

24. Bradley Bowman et al., "Don't Assume the US Will Fight China and Russia One at a Time," *Defense One*, October 29, 2021, https://www.defenseone.com/ideas/2021/10/dont-assume-us-will-fight-china-and-russia-one-time/186453/.

25. Claude Berube, "Is America Still Born to Rule the Seas?" *War on the Rocks*, December 7, 2021, https://warontherocks.com/2021/12/is-america-still-born-to-rule-the-seas/.

26. Paul McLeary, "In War, Chinese Shipyards Could Outpace Us in Replacing Losses; Marine Commandant," *Breaking Defense*, June 17, 2020, https://breakingdefense.com/2020/06/in-war-chinese-shipyards-can-outpace-us-in-replacing-losses/.

27. David Axe, "Yes, the Chinese Navy Has More Ships than the U.S. Navy. But It's Got Far Fewer Missiles," *Forbes*, December 10, 2021, https://www.forbes.com/sites/davidaxe/2021/11/10/yes-the-chinese-navy-has-more-ships-than-the-us-navy-but-its-got-far-fewer-missiles/?sh=74b8bfe461b6.

28. John Bradford and Olli Pekka Suorsa, "'Lightning Carriers' Could Be Lightweights in an Asian War," *War on the Rocks*, October 29, 2021,

https://warontherocks.com/2021/10/lightning-carriers-emerge-as-asias-new-capital-ships-strategic-investments-with-varied-operational-value/.

29. H. I. Sutton et al. "China Builds Missile Targets Shaped like U.S. Aircraft Carrier, Destroyers in Remote Desert," *USNI News*, November 7, 2021, https://news.usni.org/2021/11/07/china-builds-missile-targets-shaped-like-u-s-aircraft-carrier-destroyers-in-remote-desert.

30. Brad Lendon, "US Air Force Pulls Bombers from Guam," *CNN*, April 25, 2020, https://www.cnn.com/2020/04/24/asia/guam-us-air-force-bombers-pull-out-intl-hnk/index.html.

31. Arthur Herman, "The U.S. Needs a Hypersonic Capability Now," *Wall Street Journal*, December 6, 2021, https://www.wsj.com/articles/america-needs-a-hypersonic-capability-china-xi-beijing-missile-weapons-attack-defense-budget-11638827597.

32. Joseph Trevithick, "Third Test of the Air Force's Hypersonic Weapon Has Failed like the Ones before It," *The Drive*, December 23, 2021, https://www.thedrive.com/the-war-zone/43575/third-test-of-the-air-forces-hypersonic-weapon-has-failed-like-the-ones-before-it.

33. David E. Sanger and William J. Broad, "China's Weapon Tests Close to a 'Sputnik Moment,' U.S. General Says," *New York Times*, October 27, 2021, https://www.nytimes.com/2021/10/27/us/politics/china-hypersonic-missile.html.

34. Stephen Silver, "Report: Chinese Hypersonic Missile 'Overcame the Constraints of Physics," *National Interest*, November 28, 2021, https://nationalinterest.org/blog/buzz/report-chinese-hypersonic-missile-%E2%80%98overcame-constraints-physics-197041.

35. "Russia to Have Sea-Based Hypersonic Weapons as of 2022—Putin," *TASS*, November 30, 2021, https://tass.com/defense/1368667.

36. "North Korea Says It Fired New 'Hypersonic Missile,'" *BBC News*, September 29, 2021, https://www.bbc.com/news/world-asia-58729701.

37. Kimberlé Crenshaw, "Demarginalizing the Intersection of Race and Sex: A Black Feminist Critique of Antidiscrimination Doctrine, Feminist Theory, and Antiracist Politics [1989]," in *Feminist Legal Theory: Readings in Law and Gender, edited by Katharine T. Bartlett and Rosanne Kennedy* (Routledge, 2018), 57–80, https://doi.org/10.4324/9780429500480-5.

38. Murray, *The Madness of Crowds*, 44.

39. Murray, *The Madness of Crowds*, 84.

40. United States Supreme Court, *Parents Involved in Community Schools v. Seattle School District No 1*, June 28, 2007, *Legal Information Institute*, Cornell Law School, https://www.law.cornell.edu/supct/html/05-908.ZS.html.

41. Immanuel Kant, *Kant: Groundwork of the Metaphysics of Morals* (Renaissance Classics, 2012).

42. Liz Roscher, "Ben Simmons Reportedly Fined $19m by 76ers This Season, Could Lose $12m More," *Yahoo! Sports*, February 1, 2022, https://sports.yahoo.com/nba-ben-simmons-fined-19-million-by-76-ers-this-season-could-lose-12-million-more-184639128.html.

43. Jason Cordner, "Source Sports: 76ers Can't Fine Ben Simmons Anymore Thanks in Part of CBA Loophole," *The Source*, October 27, 2021, https://thesource.com/2021/10/27/source-sports-76ers-cant-fine-ben-simmons-anymore-thanks-in-part-of-cba-loophole/.

44. Natalie Wolfe, "Ben Simmons' Sister Olivia Ordered to Pay $550k to Half-Brother Sean Tribe over Tweets," *Fox Sports*, FOX SPORTS Australia, September 15, 2021, https://www.foxsports.com.au/basketball/nba/ben-simmons-sister-olivia-ordered-to-pay-550k-to-halfbrother-sean-tribe-over-tweets/news-story/8c43646f986bc8c994b419174e970629.

45. Immanuel Kant, *Kant: Groundwork of the Metaphysics of Morals.*

CHAPTER SEVEN: HOW VICTIMHOOD LEADS TO NATIONAL DECLINE

1. Juvenal, *Satire* 10.77–81.

2. Michael Shutterly, "Roman Coins from the War against Hannibal," *CoinWeek*, November 22, 2020, https://coinweek.com/ancient-coins/roman-coins-from-the-war-against-hannibal/.

3. Jeff Desjardins, "Currency and the Collapse of the Roman Empire," *Visual Capitalist*, March 11, 2019, https://www.visualcapitalist.com/currency-and-the-collapse-of-the-roman-empire/.

4. Desjardins, "Currency and the Collapse of the Roman Empire."

5. Charles J. Sykes, *A Nation of Victims: The Decay of the American Character* (St. Martin's Press, 1992), 28.

6. Sykes, *A Nation of Victims,* 32.

7. Sykes, *A Nation of Victims,* 38–39.

8. Rebecca Stropoli, "Are We Really More Productive Working from Home?" *Chicago Booth Review*, August 18, 2021, https://www.chicagobooth.edu/review/are-we-really-more-productive-working-home.

9. Morgan Smith, "Professor Who Predicted 'The Great Resignation' Shares the 3 Trends That Will Dominate Work in 2022," CNBC, January 14, 2022, https://www.cnbc.com/2022/01/14/the-great-resignation-expert-shares-the-biggest-work-trends-of-2022.html.

10. Bryan Mena, "U.S. Job Openings, Quits Remained Elevated at End of Last Year," *Wall Street Journal*, February 1, 2022, https://www.wsj.com/articles/job-openings-us-growth-labor-market-turnover-02-01-2022-11643670099?mod=article_inline.

11. Greg Ip, "An American Labor Market Mystery," *Wall Street Journal*, February 4, 2022, https://www.wsj.com/articles/an-american-labor-market-mystery-11643976005.

12. Alex Mitchell, "'Anti-Work' Threads on Reddit Are Fueling the Great Resignation," *New York Post*, January 17, 2022, https://nypost.com/2022/01/17/anti-work-threads-on-reddit-fueling-the-great-resignation/.

13. Mitchell, "'Anti-Work' Threads on Reddit."

14. Ronny Reyes, "Dog Walker, 30, Who Works 20-Hour Week Goes Viral While Promoting the 'Anti-Work Movement,'" *Daily Mail Online*, January 27, 2022, https://www.dailymail.co.uk/news/article-10448117/Dog-walker-30-works-20-hour-week-goes-viral-promoting-anti-work-movement.html.

15. Graham Linehan, "Another Redditor Predator Makes Himself Known," *Glinner Update*, January 28, 2022, https://grahamlinehan.substack.com/p/another-redditor-predator-makes-himself.

16. Elizabeth Gravier, "Trump Extended Federal Student Loan Relief—Here's What Financial Experts Say You Should Do If You Qualify," CNBC, March 17, 2022, https://www.cnbc.com/select/trump-memorandum-student-loans/.

17. Conor Skelding, "These Woke POLS WANT Student Loans Forgiven—Including Their Own," *New York Post*, January 29, 2022, https://nypost.com/2022/01/29/the-squad-want-student-loans-forgiven-including-theirs/.

18. Erin Fuchs, "AOC: 'No Mystery' Why It's Hard to Ban Lawmaker Stock Trading," Yahoo News, February 3, 2022, https://news.yahoo.com/aoc-congress-stock-trading-153940351.html.

19. Juvenal, *Satire* VI.346–348.

20. Ayelet Sheffey, "AOC Says It's 'Actually Delusional' to Think Democrats Can Get Re-Elected without Acting on Student Debt or Expanding Child Tax Credits," *Business Insider*, December 17, 2021, https://www.businessinsider.com/aoc-democrats-wont-get-elected-without-student-debt-expanded-ctc-2021-12.

21. Gabriel T. Rubin, "Government Losses on Student Debt Climb above $100 Billion amid Pause on Payments," *Wall Street Journal*, January 13, 2022, https://www.wsj.com/articles/government-losses-on-student-debt-climb-above-100-billion-amid-pause-on-payments-11642029455.

22. Andre M. Perry et al., "Student Loans, the Racial Wealth Divide, and Why We Need Full Student Debt Cancellation," Brookings, March 9, 2022, https://www.brookings.edu/research/student-loans-the-racial-wealth-divide-and-why-we-need-full-student-debt-cancellation/.

23. Tim Murphy, "Are We Rome Yet?" *Mother Jones*, October 6, 2020, https://www.motherjones.com/media/2020/10/are-we-rome-yet/.

24. Sarah F. Brosnan and Frans B. De Waal, "Monkeys Reject Unequal Pay," *Nature* 425, no. 6955 (2003): 297–299, https://doi.org/10.1038/nature01963.

25. Barbara J. King, "Feeling Down? Watching This Will Help," NPR, February 27, 2014, https://www.npr.org/sections/13.7/2014/02/27/283348422/that-s-unfair-you-say-this-monkey-can-relate.

26. Thomas Piketty and Emmanuel Saez, "Income Inequality in the United States, 1913–1998 (Series Updated to 2000 Available)," *National Bureau of Economic Research, Working Paper 8467,* September 2001, https://doi.org/10.3386/w8467.

27. Facundo Alvaredo et al., "Global Inequality Dynamics: New Findings from Wid.world," *National Bureau of Economic Research, Working Paper 23119,* February 2017, revised April 2017, https://doi.org/10.3386/w23119.

28. Bjorn Lous and Johan Graafland, "Who Becomes Unhappy When Income Inequality Increases?" *Applied Research in Quality of Life* 17, no. 1 (2021): 299–316, https://doi.org/10.1007/s11482-020-09906-2.

29. Shigehiro Oishi et al., "Income Inequality and Happiness," *Psychological Science* 22, no. 9 (2011): 1095–1100, http://www.jstor.org/stable/41319994.

30. Oishi et al., "Income Inequality and Happiness," 1097.

31. Oishi et al., "Income Inequality and Happiness," 1099.

32. Thomas Piketty and Arthur Goldhammer, *Capital in the Twenty-First Century.* The Belknap Press of Harvard University Press, 2014.

33. Kurt Vonnegut, *Harrison Bergeron* (Mercury Press, 1961)

34. Craig Hlavaty, "When Boris Yeltsin Went Grocery Shopping in Clear Lake," *Houston Chronicle,* January 31, 2018, https://www.chron.com/neighborhood/bayarea/news/article/When-Boris-Yeltsin-went-grocery-shopping-in-Clear-5759129.php.

35. Steve Exeter, *Severus: The Black Caesar* (independently published, 2019).

36. Molefi Kete Asante and Shaza Ismail, "Rediscovering the 'Lost' Roman Caesar: Septimius Severus the African and Eurocentric Historiography," *Journal of Black Studies* 40, no. 4 (2010): 606–618, http://www.jstor.org/stable/40648530.

37. Joshua Getzler and Mike Macnair, "Septimius Severus: African Roman Emperor, Legislator and Judge," St Hugh's College, Oxford, October 7, 2021, https://www.st-hughs.ox.ac.uk/black-history-month-profile-2/.

38. "Severus: The Black Caesar," IMDb.com, https://www.imdb.com/title/tt5090084/.

39. Franco C., "Septimus Severus," History Cooperative, July 17, 2020, https://historycooperative.org/septimus-severus-roman-emperor/.

40. "Hannibal Barca of Carthage, North Africa," *Black History Heroes,* http://www.blackhistoryheroes.com/2012/07/hannibal-barca-of-carthage-north-africa.html.

41. Ricky Riley, "History Channel Portrays Hannibal as Black, White People Cry Foul over 'Historical Revisionism,'" *Atlanta Black Star*, June 7, 2016, https://atlantablackstar.com/2016/06/07/history-channel-portrays-hannibal-as-black-white-people-cry-foul-over-historical-revisionism/.

42. Sidney Halpern, "Hannibal of Carthage Was No More Black than King David," *New York Times*, July 20, 1991, https://www.nytimes.com/1991/07/20/opinion/l-hannibal-of-carthage-was-no-more-black-than-king-david-337391.html.

43. Spencer McDaniel, "Was Septimius Severus a Black Roman Emperor?" *Tales of Times Forgotten*, September 7, 2019, https://talesoftimesforgotten.com/2019/09/07/was-septimius-severus-a-black-roman-emperor/.

44. DontWantToSeeYourCat, "Professor Severus Snape Is Indeed Descended from a Line of Roman Emperors," *Reddit*, September 2, 2013, https://www.reddit.com/r/FanTheories/comments/1lmiga/harry_potter_professor_severus_snape_is_indeed/.

45. Jake Wright, "In Defense of the Progressive Stack," *Teaching Philosophy* 41, no. 4 (2018): 407–428, https://doi.org/10.5840/teachphil2018112198.

46. Jesse O'Neill, "Congresswoman Criticized for Using Term 'Birthing People,'" *New York Post*, May 8, 2021, https://nypost.com/2021/05/08/missouri-congresswoman-under-fire-for-calling-women-birthing-people/.

47. Benjamin Fearnow, "Biden Admin Replaces 'Mothers' with 'Birthing People' in Maternal Health Guidance," *Newsweek*, June 12, 2021, https://www.newsweek.com/biden-admin-replaces-mothers-birthing-people-maternal-health-guidance-1598343.

48. Joseph Guzman, "Experts Warn Gender-Neutral Language like 'Pregnant People' May Put Mothers at Risk," *The Hill*, February 2, 2022, https://thehill.com/changing-america/respect/diversity-inclusion/592335-experts-warn-gender-neutral-language-like.

49. Michael J. Mooney, "The Boogaloo Bois Prepare for Civil War," *The Atlantic*, January 15, 2021, https://www.theatlantic.com/politics/archive/2021/01/boogaloo-prepare-civil-war/617683/.

50. Sarah Moon and Steve Almasy, "Man Allegedly Linked to the Boogaloo Movement Pleads Guilty to 2020 Fatal Shooting of Federal Guard," *CNN*, February 12, 2022, https://www.cnn.com/2022/02/11/us/steven-carrillo-california-federal-officer-killing-plea/index.html.

51. Ben Collins et al., "Whitmer Conspiracy Allegations Tied to 'Boogaloo' Movement," *NBCNews.com*, October 9, 2020, https://www.nbcnews.com/tech/tech-news/whitmer-conspiracy-allegations-tied-boogaloo-movement-n1242670.

52. Lois Beckett, "'Boogaloo Boi' Charged in Fire of Minneapolis Police Precinct during George Floyd Protest," *The Guardian*, October 23, 2020,

https://www.theguardian.com/world/2020/oct/23/texas-boogaloo-boi-minneapolis-police-building-george-floyd.

CHAPTER EIGHT: THE NEED TO FORGIVE

1. Christopher Caldwell, "This Poll Shows Just How Much Trouble Democrats Are In," *New York Times*, January 25, 2022, https://www.nytimes.com/2022/01/25/opinion/gallup-poll-democrats.html.
2. Jeffrey M. Jones, "U.S. Political Party Preferences Shifted Greatly during 2021," Gallup, January 24, 2022, https://news.gallup.com/poll/388781/political-party-preferences-shifted-greatly-during-2021.aspx.
3. Cristina Marcos and Mike Lillis. "Democrats Hit 30-Year High for House Retirements," *The Hill*, February 19, 2022, https://thehill.com/homenews/house/594797-democrats-hit-30-year-high-for-house-retirements.
4. Caldwell, "This Poll Shows."
5. Sean Illing, "'Wokeness Is a Problem and We All Know It,'" *Vox*, April 27, 2021, https://www.vox.com/22338417/james-carville-democratic-party-biden-100-days.
6. Jeffrey S. Solochek, "Florida House Approves CRT, 'Don't Say Gay' Bills," *Tampa Bay Times*, February 24, 2022, https://www.tampabay.com/news/florida-politics/2022/02/24/florida-house-approves-crt-dont-say-gay-bills/.
7. CS/HB7, "An Act Relating to Individual Freedom," https://www.flsenate.gov/Session/Bill/2022/7/BillText/e2/PDF.
8. CS/CS/HB 1557, "An Act Relating to Parental Rights in Education," https://www.flsenate.gov/Session/Bill/2022/1557/BillText/e1/PDF.
9. Conor Friedersdorf, "Talking about Race with the KKK," *The Atlantic*, June 22, 2021, https://www.theatlantic.com/politics/archive/2015/03/the-audacity-of-talking-about-race-with-the-klu-klux-klan/388733/.
10. Rebecca Savastio, "KKK Member Walks up to Black Musician in Bar—but It's Not a Joke, and What Happens Next Will Astound You," *Guardian Liberty Voice*, November 21, 2013, https://guardianlv.com/2013/11/kkk-member-walks-up-to-black-musician-in-bar-but-its-not-a-joke-and-what-happens-next-will-astound-you/.
11. Friedersdorf, "Talking about Race with the KKK."
12. Nicholas Kristof, "'How Can You Hate Me When You Don't Even Know Me?'" *New York Times*, June 26, 2021, https://www.nytimes.com/2021/06/26/opinion/racism-politics-daryl-davis.html.
13. Friedersdorf, "Talking about Race with the KKK."
14. Friedersdorf, "Talking about Race with the KKK."
15. "Scott Shepherd Reformed Racist Free at Last!" *Scott Shepherd Reformed Racist Free At Last!*, http://racistnomore1.blogspot.com/.
16. Kristof, "'How Can You Hate Me?'"

17. Friedersdorf, "Talking about Race with the KKK."

18. United States Supreme Court, *Jacobellis v. Ohio*, June 22, 1964, *Legal Information Institute*, Cornell Law School, https://www.law.cornell.edu/supremecourt/text/378/184.

19. Murray, *The Madness of Crowds*, 176–177.

20. Murray, *The Madness of Crowds*, 176–177.

CHAPTER NINE: A THEORY OF DUTY

1. John Rawls, *A Theory of Justice: Revised Edition* (Belknap Press, 1999), 266.

2. Rawls, *A Theory of Justice*.

3. There are a number of depressing videos documenting the shopping experience at Soviet supermarkets; for instance, this one: Rick Suddeth, "USSR: Grocery Store Uncut," YouTube, February 9, 2015, https://www.youtube.com/watch?v=t8LtQhIQ2AE.

4. Bill Clinton, "Remarks by the President at Presentation of the National Medal of the Arts and the National Humanities Medal," National Archives and Records Administration, September 29, 1999, https://clintonwhitehouse4.archives.gov/WH/New/html/19990929.html.

5. Adrian Wooldridge, *The Aristocracy of Talent*, Kindle ebook (Skyhorse, 2021), 291.

6. Robert Nozick, *Anarchy, State, and Utopia* (Basic Books, 1974), 160–161.

7. Gary M. Pomerantz, "A Giant Shadow: Did Wilt Chamberlain Have a Son?" *Sports Illustrated*, March 3, 2015, https://www.si.com/nba/2015/03/03/wilt-chamberlain-aaron-levi-a-giant-shadow-son-secret.

8. Wooldridge, *The Aristocracy of Talent*, 59.

9. Wooldridge, *The Aristocracy of Talent*, 194.

10. Wooldridge, *The Aristocracy of Talent*, 62.

11. Virginia L. Ma and Kevin A. Simauchi, "Harvard's Endowment Soars to $53.2 Billion, Reports 33.6% Returns," *Harvard Crimson*, October 15, 2021, https://www.thecrimson.com/article/2021/10/15/endowment-returns-soar-2021/.

12. Emmie Martin and Yoni Blumberg, "Harvard's Freshman Class Is More Than One-Third Legacy—Here's Why That's a Problem," CNBC, April 11, 2019, https://www.cnbc.com/2019/04/07/harvards-freshman-class-is-more-than-one-third-legacy.html.

13. Wooldridge, *The Aristocracy of Talent*, 194.

14. Ma and Simauchi, "Harvard's Endowment Soars."

15. Wooldridge, *The Aristocracy of Talent*, 67.

16. Machiavelli, *Discourses on Livy*, book I, chap. 10.

17. *Gladiator*, directed by Ridley Scott, Universal Pictures, 2000.
18. Wooldridge, *The Aristocracy of Talent*, p. 70.
19. Simon Kuper, "This Economist Has a Radical Plan to Solve Wealth Inequality," *Wired UK*, April 14, 2020, https://www.wired.co.uk/article/thomas-piketty-capital-ideology.
20. "Tax on Extreme Wealth," BernieSanders.com, https://berniesanders.com/issues/tax-extreme-wealth/.
21. Lydia Saad and Jeffrey M. Jones, "What Percentage of Americans Owns Stock?" Gallup, November 20, 2021, https://news.gallup.com/poll/266807/percentage-americans-owns-stock.aspx.
22. Lauren Feiner, "Bill Gates: Taxing the Rich Is Fine, but 'Extreme' Politicians like Alexandria Ocasio-Cortez Are Missing the Point by Focusing on Income," CNBC, February 12, 2019, https://www.cnbc.com/2019/02/12/bill-gates-supports-wealth-tax-like-aoc-but-income-is-a-misfocus.html.
23. Thomas Piketty and Emmanuel Saez, "A Theory of Optimal Inheritance Taxation," *Econometrica* 81, no. 5 (2013): 1851–1886, at 1851.
24. Piketty and Saez, "A Theory of Optimal Inheritance Taxation," 1858.
25. Ramaswamy, *Woke, Inc.*, chap. 2.
26. Piketty and Saez, "A Theory of Optimal Inheritance Taxation," 1874.
27. *Woke, Inc.*, chap. 11.
28. Dio Cassius, *Roman History*, 73.1.2, Loeb edition, translated by E. Cary.
29. *The Meritocracy Trap*, p. 12.
30. Wooldridge, *The Aristocracy of Talent*, 375.
31. Wooldridge, *The Aristocracy of Talent*, 375.
32. Wooldridge, *The Aristocracy of Talent*, 377.
33. Wooldridge, *The Aristocracy of Talent*, 377.
34. Wooldridge, *The Aristocracy of Talent*, 377.

CONCLUSION: REINCARNATE

1. "Denial, Anger, Acceptance," *The Sopranos*, created by David Chase, season 1, episode 3, HBO Entertainment, 1999.
2. Wooldridge, *The Aristocracy of Talent*, p. 182.
3. Louis B. Wright, "Thomas Jefferson and the Classics," *Proceedings of the American Philosophical Society* 87, no. 3 (1943): 223–233, http://www.jstor.org/stable/984869.

ABOUT THE AUTHOR

VIVEK RAMASWAMY is a *New York Times* bestselling author and entrepreneur who has founded multiple successful enterprises. A first-generation American, he founded Roivant Sciences in 2014 and led the largest biotech IPOs of 2015 and 2016, eventually culminating in successful clinical trials in multiple disease areas that led to FDA-approved products. He has founded other successful healthcare and technology companies, and in 2022, he launched Strive Asset Management, a new firm focused on restoring the voices of everyday citizens in the American economy by leading companies to focus on excellence over politics.

Ramaswamy was born and raised in southwest Ohio. He graduated summa cum laude in biology from Harvard in 2007 and began his career as a biotech investor at a prominent hedge fund. Ramaswamy continued to work as an investor while earning his law degree at Yale, where he was a recipient of the Paul and Daisy Soros Fellowship for New Americans. In 2020, he emerged as a prominent national commentator on stakeholder capitalism, free speech, and identity politics. He has authored numerous articles and op-eds which have appeared in the *Wall Street Journal*, the *New York Times*, *Harvard Business Review*, and *Newsweek*. He is the author of the bestselling Center Street book *Woke, Inc.*